RAG RAG MEIN MUMBAI

LIFE & TIMES IN THE CITY THAT NEVER SLEEPS

SAMEER PIKALE

I would like to this book to my wifey Kashmira my soulmate, pillar of strength and my anchor during turbulent times. She has always stood by me egging me on to accept life's challenges and face them head on. Sometimes cheering me sometime castigating me for my short temper , but always loving me . You make me complete.

To my daughters Netra and Bhakti my angels and my reason to live.

To Microverse Automation and the Mehendale family for giving me a purpose in life to take Indian Technology beyond the seven seas and make it recognized as a Global Leader in Automation and Digital Transformation.

To my Rotary Club Ponda New Generation for providing me with an opportunity to give back to our society in any which way I can. By creating hope in the world with a simple mantra of Service above Self.

Contents

Contents

Contents

Preface

Hi, this is me Sameer Pikale, an Engineer by profession. A hobby artist by nature, dabbling in water color paintings in between busy work schedules and a writer by heart , living his dreams penning passionate blogs and technology related articles..

Professionally I have always been passionate about Digital Technologies, IOT, Analytics, Big Data, Cloud, SaaS & PaaS Technology solutions.

25 years of extensive experience in Industrial Automation (DCS & PLC), Manufacturing & Infrastructure IT Solutions Sales, Business Development, Advance Analytics and Asset Performance Management Solution Sales.

Well versed with Consultative high-value Business outcome selling to C-Level Executives.

Expertise is in Driving New Business growth in the Process Industry (O&G, Chemical, Power, Metal) with a PAN India exposure handling Direct Sales & Channel Partners.

Proven Track record in achieving and exceeding Order & Sales Plan along with Contribution Margin responsibilities.

Proficiency is in Industrial Internet of Things (IIoT), Manufacturing Operation Management, Advance Analytics, Asset Performance Management, SCADA, and Control System solutions.

Expertise is in organizing Techno-commercial Resources to carry out business operations and have a clear understanding of developing new businesses in Indian & Middle East.

Hands-on experience is in exploring new markets, identifying the right customer's and partner to accelerate business growth in India & Middle East Market.

Exhibited the ability to lead the teams of Solution Architect, Proposal/Estimation, and Engineering professionals.

In-depth knowledge of operations in various Process Industries like Power, Chemical, Metal, Cement, O&G & Life Science.

Competent Communicator and Negotiator having strong analytical, problem solving & organizational abilities.

Travelled for business across the length and breadth of India and also to Dubai and America

Prologue

About the book

"Rag Rag Mein .. Life & Times in the city that never sleeps ". This book is a sequel to **"Mumbai Meri Jaan – Life Travel Food & Some Childhood Memories"** . Its from a collection of blogs written by me over a 4 year period , chronicling my experiences on life travel and food in my Janma Bhoomi , Mumbai. I have also included some of my childhood memories while growing up in Mumbai which my readers can correlate. As an avid traveler I have included my experiences in different places i have visited while out on work or on vacation. Hope you enjoy reading this book and experience the same joys that i have tried to put in words.

Happy Reading.....

Rag Rag Me Mumbai ....City that never sleeps

After walking around the by lanes of Matunga for a year now, I decided why not extend my walks to the neighbouring places to bring out the flavour, the nuances and the little tit bits which define their character. Each neighbourhood having its own culture and specialties. Also to make it a little more interesting I will not only talk about the places in the neighbourhood but about the various places across India, which I visit due to the extensive travelling I do as part of my Sales profession. Sharing some personal experiences and thoughts.

The other day I turned on the FM and heard **Shukhvinder** crooning .... **"Rag Rag Me Mumbai City Rag Rag Me"** ...Thought how true. Once a person is born and brought up in Mumbai or has stayed for a large part of his life in this City it tends to grows on him/ her and literally runs through the blood...

So decided let me bring out the various facets of my Janma bhoomi , Mumbai. The city I was born and grew up in , the maxim city of Mumbai. The financial capital of India, the jewel in the crown of India, a city that never sleeps. A cosmopolitan city , a cultural cauldron of various religions ,faiths , castes and creeds. A city with heart of gold but its soul tied to the ever-ticking clock of life.

So here goes a beginning of a new innings ....

On a lazy Sunday evening, I decided to walk around **Shivaji Park** which is a little further from where I live that is Matunga. This place is steeped in its **Marathi culture** and represents the vibrant lifestyle more in synch with the buzzing nature of Mumbai. The minute you ask anyone of Shivaji Park the first thing that comes to mind is the **Shivaji Park Gymkhana and the Maidan.** And also, the Chowpatty which I will elaborate in my next blogs. The Shivaji Park Gymkhana and Sports club is **synonymous with the Cricket.** The park maidan has been host to such celebrities like the **"God of Cricket" Sachin Tendulkar his buddy Vinod Kambli, Little Master Sunil Gavaskar and Colonel Dilip Vengsarkar.** One end of the ground (maidan) is reserved for the nets of Cricket coaches who train the budding and talented youngsters in the age group of 6-16 years. The most well-known coach who had nets here was **Achrekar Sir** coach to Sachin Tendulkar and Vinod Kambli. It is on these very grounds, Sachin practiced his perfect cover drives , the straight drives hooks and pulls thus starting his illustrious sporting career. The ground support staff here are the best in class and toil away at their manual rollers, water the ground and prepare the right pitch be it a bouncy wicket or a slow turner to give ample practice to the students. On any given day during summer camps, you can see at least a group of 30-40 boys training and practicing their game under the observant eye of their coaches. They stretch, they run , they dive around the ground with a hope in the heart and a dream in their eyes of becoming great cricketers and being selected in the Mumbai Ranji team or any of the IPL teams as stepping stone to being part of the Indian Cricket team.

After a strenuous work out you will find most the boys at the most famous enterprise right on the Shivaji Park ground close to the **Samarth Vyayamshala, home to gymnastics and traditional sport like malkhamb**. This stall has been churning out the yummiest batata bhajjis and hot batata wada's for ages. Whenever you visit the stall you will find the owners a courteous family of typical Marathi husband and wife manning the counter ably supported by their cook and the other staff. The bhajjis are perfect in taste and deep fried to make them real crisply. The sweet and sour tamarind chutney is the perfect dip accompanying the hot bhajjis before they are wolfed down by the eagerly waiting customers. You can have the wada or the bhajji's alone or can have them stuffed in the soft pav smeared with garlic chutney to give that extra zing. Orders fly thick and fast and the hot wada's and bhajjis get consumed real fast making the big Thali in which they are unloaded look empty in less than 15 minutes of their arrival.

Just next to this stall are couple of new stalls one serving the famous Mumbai Chowpatty bhel and Pani Puri to the foodies gathered around. The other serving Sandwiches , regular or toast depending on your liking. But neither can give a semblance of a fight to the tasty batata wada or the mouth watering & crispy bhajji.

Walk ahead and you come to the **Udyan Ganesh** a temple dedicated the **Vighnaharta Lord Ganesh**. A small temple some time back before it was restored and renovated to the current beautiful structure in White marble. The temple itself is very old and well known among the Ganesh devotees. Every evening you will find it brightly lit and can be seen shining from the entire Shivaji Park neighborhood . The light emanating giving a feeling of hope and security to the observer and the devotees alike. The temple itself is small with a small but serene Ganesh murti in its garbha griha or the **sanctum sanctorum**. All your stress and worries melt away the moment your close your eyes and stand with folded hand in front of HIM. You feel blessed and happy once you have visited this temple .

Another famous land mark here is **the Bengal Club and the Durga temple** on the precinct of Shivaji Park ground. Every year during Navaratri the nine nights days leading up to **Dassera or Vijayadashami** , the Begali community hold **the Durgotsav from the Shashti till Dussera**. A huge pandal is put up with the idol of **Goddess Durga striding on her Lion** installed at the center and the **scene of Mhaishasura mardan** (Mhaishasura the demon or Asura who had the blessing of Lord Brhama and who could change forms and who had oppressed the Gods. Finally slayed by Goddess Durga). People from all communities and not just the Bengali's throng the pandal during these 4 days to enjoy the atmosphere and specifically the food stalls right behind the pandal. Famous caterers of Bengal specially come all the way from Kolkata to sell their Bengali delicacies. I have been a regular at these stalls along with the Missus and the kids gorging on the **Kati Rolls** be it egg , chicken or mutton . The taste is exemplary a little spicy but finger licking. The kids love the misthan or the Bengali sweet , **Sandesh , Cham Cham , Misthi Doi (dahi) , Gulab Jamun and the Rosogulla.** Pick any sweet , it melts in your mouth the moment you eat it leaving a overdose of sugary taste in your mouth. Forget about the calories and do try the Misthaan at least once , you will surely come back for more. To burn the calories you could always walk around the other stall showcasing the Cotton **Malmal Sarees** , ethnic ware and handicrafts .

If you visit this place on Navmi its teeming with activities. A dance group from Kolkata would be performing on stage , another group would be entertaining the crowd with sweet **Robindro Sangeet** while the finale would be the staging of the Mhaishasura Mardan act. Walk away smiling at the dark night on Navmi which will make way for the bright day of Vijaya Dashmi or Dassera , the day on which **Lord Rama won the war against Ravana** symbolizing the **ultimate truth the victory of Good over Evil and giving hope to the entire humanity.**

Happy Dassera to all my readers

Happy Reading

CHAPTER TWO

Mumbai ....A City of Dreams

In my travels across India during my sales trips , I have had the good fortune of observing some of the major cities at close quarters. Each city has its own character, a way of life and attitude of its own. Be its cultural repertoire, its vibrant night life, safety for its inhabitants, the way it treats the outsiders who come for a living, its food quotient or the clean and secure environment it offers to citizens. You could say I am biased, but I still find Mumbai with highest scores in all these indices. Being born and brought up here I have lived and breathed this city and experienced much it has to offer. Needless to say, **true Mumbaikar** is the only living being even when he feels a lot of pride about his city, will not shy away from berating his city during a heated discussion on the lack of amenities and infrastructural bungles it faces. If in group someone says aloud that Mumbai has gone to the dogs and its infrastructure is collapsing due to administrative mismanagement, a true Mumbaikar will join the chorus and put out 10 more points on why Mumbai is losing the game as compared the other famous Global / International cities. As a tradition Mumbai has always been compared to cities like New York due to Manhattan skyline and similar space constraint or to London due to the red busses and for a matter of fact that it was directly ruled by the British for a long, long time than the regional rulers like the **Maratha's, Mughals or the Nizam's** of the south. It has always been influenced by the British or the Portuguese who rule before them. The Mumbaikar felt let down when its storm water drains failed and it got compared to Venice, as its streets were flooded during 26/11 or was scarred when its heart was ripped out during the 1992 serial bomb blast and the riots that followed during 1993. This was much before the world got its taste of terrorism during 9/11 in New York.

Still it is a fact that the soul of Mumbai is very resilient and every time it has been knocked down by bomb blasts or has faced the wrath of mother nature it has always stood up and taken the punches squarely on the chin , without complaining and making the whole Nation proud because of this resilient nature which is at its core. This unique nature has been ingrained in the DNA of every Mumbaikar.

Where else will you find a city which is Cosmopolitan in nature and allowing each and every one coming to this dream city and letting them be absorbed in its bosom and be treated at par. Be it the local neighbourhood **sabjiwallah** who has left his native **somewhere in Bihar or UP** and travelled all the way to this maxim city to earn a livelihood. Or the **Lambadi** families migrated **from Rajasthan** and earning a living working as manual labourers at construction sites Or the Northeastern girls and boys working in hotels or hospitality businesses Or the well-educated and hardworking Keralite women working as care givers in its many a Hospitals as nurses. This city has always given a safe and secure place to all those who want to make this city their **Karma Bhoomi** and make it big by living out their dreams.

Another aspect of Mumbai and which is the most taken for granted and often verbally abused is the travel infrastructure built over centuries. Starting from the **Railways which the British built** starting from VT (Victoria Terminus and now renamed as Chatrapati Shivaji terminus) to Thane or the highly unionized **Kaali Peeli's or Taxi's** and the Rickshaws which scurry around like rats ,moving through most traffic snarls and then there are the **BEST buses modelled on the Red Bus in London**. I still remember hurrying up the stairs of the big **Double Decker** bus and fight our way through the crowd to catch the seat right at the front on the upper deck . Looking out and enjoying the City view. Or during monsoon days taking the bus route winding down the Marine Drive enjoying the splashing of the waves of the big pontoons. You may curse the Taxi drivers or the Auto wallah but where else will you be able to hail a cab or that odd Auto in the middle of the night or at crack of dawn on a silent street or that creepy -eerie street with just a wave of your hand. You could thank your stars that you live in a city which never sleeps and never let you go hungry even if it's 4 o'clock in the morning and you want to grab a bite. You will always find some place open serving you a hot pav bhaji – Mumbai's very own all-time favourite fast food or that **garma garam Vada pav** with that spicy garlic chatni or even a yummy and lip-smacking **Unda Burji Pav** right across a busy railway station and fill your stomach with food and your heart with that special warmth.

Mumbai has a unique magnet –**The Bollywood** home of the arc lights and all that glamour and jazz that attracts people from far and wide to come here and try their luck at striking gold in the Film Industry as it is called. So you will find young boys and girls from Delhi, Himachal, Punjab trying to grab the attention of the event promoters , ad producers , photographer to get a toe hold in the film line with a wee bit roles or ad campaigns. You will find these young crowd hanging around the Café's in Juhu trying desperately to catch the attention of these connect people. Though most of them have a lot to struggle before they get a meaningful break , there are stories of a certain a lad from Bhuleshwar who turned into India's first Superstar – Rajesh Khanna or a certain Jaikishan Shroff a Gujju tall lanky boy staying in Teen Bati area striking gold when found by Subhash Ghai and turned into a overnight sensation of Jackie Shroff or in recent times a young kid from Delhi doing VJ jobs on Television becoming the new heartthrob "Ayushmann Khurana".

This city has also given wings to person of business acumen and turned petrol pump attendants to Multi Million Dollar Industrialists like the one and only Dhirubhai Ambani. Or even the lad from UP but a IIT –IIM graduate going by the name of Dheeraj Gupta turn a simple Vad Pav into a franchise chain business like the McDonalds – our very own Jumbo Vada Pav. This city has nurtured talents like Sachin Tendulkar's and now the current crop of cricketers like Abhishekh Nayar or the copy book batsmen like Ajinkya Rahane.

Though the city is congested and at times it feels claustrophobics moving around town , it still has a vibrant Arts and Cultural ethos. In South Mumbai you have the **Art District around Jahangir Art Gallery** and **National Gallery of Modern Art** just across the famous **Chatrapati Shivaji Sanghrahalay or the Cities Museum** which is host to a lot of historical artifacts. Every year during February there is the **Kala Ghoda festival** where there are lot of contemporary performances by musicians and artist coupled with lot of food stalls on the streets of Fort area from Jahangir Art gallery right upto The iconic Gateway of India. During the 10 days the city folks enjoy the experience of walking this art district and have fun.

This city also plays host to innumerable classical singing program like the **Pandit Waman Rao Sadolikar Sangeet Samelan** arranged and hosted by the famous Jaipur Atroli gharana singer and his daughter **Shruti Sadolikar Katkar.** This is open to music lovers and hosted at the **Shanmukhanand Hall in Matunga –King Circle.** This hall has been a hub of activities to promote musical and especially the classical singing talent. Many a stalwarts like **Pandit Jasraj , Late Pandit Bhimsen Joshi , Pt. Shivkumar Sharma (Santoor maestro) , Pt. Amjad Ali Khan (Sarod Maestro) and Pt. Hari Prasad Chaurasia (Flute maestro)** have performed and keep performing here to mesmerize the listener's and take them on a musical journey which out of this world.

So next you are calling names to our Mumbai city and are cribbing about issues step back for a while and think how great this city has been how it has evolved over time .And why did I choose this topic , I want all my readers to exercise their franchise on Tuesday Feb 21st of voting for the Municipal Council election , which may seem very trivial but remember to vote for those who have delivered on the promises and made this city a little better place to live .....Do take part in electing the right candidates , those that can carry on the development , take care of the special ethos or the character of the city and maintain the cultural diversity. **Let this city of Mumbai always be the city of dream fulfilment, a city with never say die attitude and a city that never sleeps....**

Proud to be a Mumbaikar......

CHAPTER THREE

New Foodie Joints on the Block

Every few years the local landscape changes more so in Matunga than any other place. You can see new shops popping up , new line of business take shape , new food joints mushrooming enticing the customers to try something new. Over the years I have seen whole lot of changes in our area right from the Kirana shops giving way to clothing business, hotels changing management or cuisine all together to appeal to the changing customer taste.

I still remember a Hotel going by the name of **Coffee House in Matunga market** just opposite the Matunga Railay station. This was the newest joint during my growing up years that was different from the typical Udpi joints crowding the space. At this restaurant you could experience a fine dine atmosphere with proper seating, glass cutlery, table napkins, set of forks spoons & knives neatly arranged on the table. The menu was exhaustive with starters, soups, salads, main course and desserts. Even the snacks like Sandwiches, Burgers, Frankie were more appealing to upwardly mobile crowd and not the typical idli and dosa's. My dad would take us to this fancy restaurant to celebrate some special occasion like success in our exams or a special milestone birthday like 10th or a 13th birthday. We would sit at the decked-up table and order for a Tomato soup. The soup would be served piping hot in proper soup bowls with dollop of butter on top and breadcrumbs sprinkled on top. The crunchy and tangy taste would sooth your throat and fill your stomach. Next, we would order for some starters followed by main course. The dinner would end with a scoop of ice cream with chocolate sauce. We would walk back home with great memories of a wonderful family time.

As I said in Matunga the food landscape changes every few years. I noticed a new joint near King Circle with an interesting name and an even interesting décor. **"Café 2.0"** signifying a version 2 of café, but I don't remember a first version of this food joint. Anyways this one's located near Gomathy Moorthy Idli –Dosa Atta Centre. It used to be a garage which would be leased out to fruit sellers during Mango season to store crates / boxes of mangoes. Now it has turned into this hip open air food joint patronized by the college crowd from Ruia, Poddar, Khalsa and VJTI. The interior walls are painted with **"Joker" that famous super villain from Batman** with **punch line "Why So Serious"**. And that goes for the food that is served here. It's mostly snack items like **French fries served in a Cone**, then there the **Pizza fries or the Chipotle Fries** (fries served with Chipotle & cheese) , Or try their Chilly Cheese fries or Cheese Mayo fries which tastes great .For the spicy taste buds you have the Schezwan Cheese fries or Salsa Cheese fries. You can also try the same flavours in Wedges which a little thicker in size and softer than the fries. For a little filling snack try their wraps like **Smile Wrap** (crispy happy potatoes tomatoes, onion, lettuce, mayo & chilly sauce) ,

Popper Wrap (with Cheese poppers) or the little fancy Cheese Corn Nugget wrap. They also serve the regular burgers, Nachos and nuggets / poppers. One interesting dish which their specialty is the **Twisted Potato**, it's a large potato made into a crispy screwlike shape and fried to perfection. Can be eaten with Salsa or Schezwan sauce. All this can be downed by the thick milkshakes that they serve. Try the Belgian Chocolate shake, chocolaty and sinful. The other favourite are the Oreo milkshake, Caramel milkshake and the chocolate milkshake. Enjoy the food in this funky looking fast-food spot with their funky interior designs and blue neon lights that has opened up in Matunga just a few months back and has quickly grabbed the attention of everybody.

The just nearby you can grab a bite at the **Rahul's Food Court** serving fast food snacks from the erstwhile Aarey Milk booth, those white and blue wooden box like booths which distributed milk bottles and pouches early in the morning. With times changing the owners of these booths were given liberty to start additional business to add to their income. One such milk booth has now turned into Rahul's Food Court. They serve little heavier snacks and not just fries, wedges and shakes. Here you can get variety of option from dosa to sandwiches, Maggi to pasta, panini sandwiches to pizzas. Some of their best creations are the **Paninni's** those subway type sandwiches with multigrain breads, stuffed with veggies, lettuce to give a crunch and a volume and loaded with cheese to give it taste. In pizza besides the regular Cheese, Onion and fresh Veggie you could try some new ones like the **Italian Pizza with Maggi & pasta topping** or the Pizza Mongolian with Capsicum, Tomato and Paneer with some pungent sauce. Also a hit with the young crowd is the Square pizza with broccoli, red

, yellow and green bell peppers and loaded with Mozzarella Cheese. They also serve pasta – **Alfredo in white sauce or Arabitta in red sauce**. Also to cater to the Jain community all the items are available in Jain variants. The popularity of his joint can be gauged by the mingling college crowd during the day and family crowd at night on the open seating that is made available to them.

Both these small eateries have adopted new age technology to maximize their reach in the locality by tying up with food delivery specialist **"Swiggy"** . You can now sit back relax in your homes and order from these fast food joints and you are sure to get your Chipotle Fries in the Cone or a Panini Sandwich still hot in its container when the Swiggy guy rings your door bell.

Another craze that has erupted in Matunga is the **Belgian Waffle Co** – A specialist in those sweet, yummy, crisp pieces of heavenly dessert called the waffle. For the unacquainted a **waffle** is a dish made from leavened batter or dough that is cooked between two plates that are patterned to give a characteristic size, shape and surface impression. There are many variations based on the type of waffle iron and recipe used. Waffles are eaten throughout the world, particularly in **Belgium**, which has over a dozen regional varieties. Waffles may be made fresh or simply heated after having been commercially precooked and frozen

At the **Belgian Waffle Co** you get close to a dozen variety to satisfy your sweet tooth. If you are chocoholic you can order for their Choco Overload stuffed with creamy dark chocolate or the Dark & White Choco Fantasy with the milk chocolate filling. Bite into the crisp waffle and savour the gooey chocolate and smack your lips after each bite. For the regular eaters like you can order the Honey

Butter or the Maple butter – waffles covered with Honey or the Maple syrup. Giving a sweet –salty taste. For the fruit lovers there the **Blueberry Cream cheese, Strawberry Cream cheese** or the **Banana Salted Caramel.** And for the Nutella fans they have the **Naked Nutella Waffle** stuffed with that crazy and addictive hazelnut cocoa spread . Little high on calories but delicious and heavenly to the last bite.

Take your pick of these new age food joint at Matunga, as they say on an airline announcement – Sit back relax and enjoy your foodie journey........

Happy Hogging....

CHAPTER FOUR

Aathawda Bazaar ... The mesmerizing world of Weekly Bazaar.

It's well know that India is an Agrarian society and 80% of its population still lives in its villages. Its heart lies in these culturally diverse but all-encompassing small in-habitation known in local languages as **Gaon or Gaav.** Much has been written and said about the village life. Even today most of the villages don't have proper shops or all in one malls that we in the cities take for granted. The simple folks of these villages sell or buy their produce at the local markets called the **Aathwada bazaar or the weekly markets.** The local administration usually the Gram Panchayat earmarks a vacant plot of land where shops are allowed to be put up by the villagers to sell what they produce or procure from neighbouring towns. A fixed day of the week is designated for this weekly market hence the name Aathwada bazaar as it falls on a specific day of the week. Easy to remember and shopping for the entire week for all the folks. Usually its in the middle of the week "Wednesday" or on the weekends "Fridays" , when the market is set up. Most of the shop owners are the farmers or fruit vendors or grocers . Sometimes if the Bazaar is well known then people from neighbouring villages also set up their shops to get a larger audience.

The best experience of these Aathwada Bazaar can be had in villages in Konkan especially in Ratnagiri area. SATURDAY morning, 7 o'clock or thereabouts, a certain madness sets into Ratnagiri as housewives and men of the house get up early and make a dash for the 'Aathwada' bazaar near the old ST bus-stand there. And this is a weekly bazaar that has been going on here for the past ten years or so. There's nothing official about it, of course, but the Aathwada bazaar is encouraged by the local Municipality. The municipality comes in on Sunday to clean up the place and return the area to its somewhat less than pristine glory of before the Aathwada bazaar. The bazaar is held, like a flea market on a Goan beach, once a week on Saturday. This is a good day for a bazaar because most people shop for the entire next week here. And they get an opportunity to bump into old friends and gossip. It is not as if Ratnagiri does not have its regular markets. Most housing colonies have a small bhaji Wala outside that caters to the residents. And on prominent streets in the city, on a smaller scale than the Aathwada bazaar, fruit and vegetable vendors run a small market on Tuesdays.

Besides which, at the Aathwada bazaar venue on week days, Ratnagiri's 'Maamis' in their half-Navaris (nine-yard sarees) sit on the footpaths and sell veggies and fruit grown locally. Whatever is in season, and whatever quantity they have, is put up for sale. It could be anything from firewood to jackfruit. These Maamis don't do business by weights but deal in portions. They don't understand kilos and litres. Everything is a "Wata" measure here. The Aathwada bazaar goes on all day. The vendors come with fruits and vegetables and other consumer items from all the small villages in and around Ratnagiri. Some come from as far as Sangli and Miraj in trucks, driving overnight for five or six hours, so as to be early at the Aathwada bazaar with their produce.

The Maamis don't come on out Saturday. This day is meant for serious, big-time shopping. When everything is sold by weight. When people come for "imported, exotic" vegetables and not the local greens grown in the backyard of the Maamis' homes. And where the bhajiwalas have fixed spots and fixed customers who enjoy their weekly bargain with them. Everything is garden fresh. And the variety is vast and complete. Not like the small Tuesday market on the local streets. Vegetables and fruit are the big draw at the Aathwada bazaar. And spices. The bazaar has any number of vendors with their spices in big sacks and in small watas.

One small section is segregated, perhaps because of the smell, for the dry-fish sellers. These are all generally women. And though Ratnagiri is a coastal city and has a jetty where fresh fish be bought daily, there are several takers for the dry fish here. This too is sold by the Wata, not the kilo, and the fish vendor has measures made of brass and wood to sell the dry fish.

By evenings, the fruit, vegetable and dry-fish vendors leave, and the Aathwada bazaar is taken over by sellers of household items. Everything from buckets and pans to aluminium scrubs and junk jewellery. The last sales are done under lights thrown by lamps.

A recent phenomenon of the same type experience in our very own city of Mumbai is the **"Farmer's Market"** at various location. Once such farmers market happens very near to where we stay at King Circle at the grounds of

Indian Gymkhana. Here **on a Tuesday's** farmers co-operatives from as far as Nashik, Kolhapur, Sangli and Satara come with their farm fresh produce in small tempos. You can wander around their stalls and be awestruck at the size and freshness of the vegetables they bring. The veggies are green and mostly organically produced with no chemical fertilizers. You can get the largest Cauliflowers and cabbages . The potatoes and onion are also of best quality, which do not get in your local neighborhood markets. Even the exotics veggies like **Broccoli, Zucchini –Green& Yellow, Bell peppers – Red & Yellow , Celery and Iceberg Lettuce are the freshest and mouth-watering.**

There are fruit vendors bringing fresh and juiciest fruits from across Maharashtra. Grape growers association bring the best ever grapes. They are cherubic, large and sweet to the core. Not like the piddly ones we get at the local fruit seller. The **Strawberries from Mahabaleshwar & Panchgani** are ruby red and mix of sweet & sour taste. Even the Ber or the Bor fruit which arrive just before Makar Sankranti are of good variety. Large, golden and very sweet. The green ones are the size of small apples. The pineapples are bright orange and sweet to the core. Even the watermelons from Ponvel or Aliabug are bright red on the inside and real sweet. Make a glass of juice or have just like that for a healthy life.

At other stalls you even get fresh grains like rice, wheat, bajara & jowar. Pulses like Channa, rajma, chawli also of good quality. The puffed rice or Poha are soft, fresh and white. And you expect the best Poha dish when you make the traditional Maharashtrian Kande or batate pohe. Some stalls keep the fresh ground masalas like red chilly powder, turmeric power and special mixture like garam masala or the Kolhapuri masala used in non-veg dishes. Expect the taste to be spicy and hot when put in dishes like Missals or in Chicken and Mutton gravies.

All these farm fresh vegetables and fruits are at very economical rates as they are directly sold by the farmers themselves. There are no overheads of the APMC market or the middle men .

If you want to experience some fun and chaos and shop for some sundry item head to the **Budhwar Bazaar** or the **Wednesday Market near St. Micheal's Church at Mahim.** Vendors put up their shops on the footpath leading to church. Here you can have a wonderful time picking up accessories like hair clips, hair band, wrist band, oxidized anklets etc for the girls and women. Some sell handbags, sling bags, clutch bags and purses sourced from whole sellers in and around Mumbai city. Some bring hosiery tops, frocks and dresses from manufacturing units in Vasai or Bhiwandi. These are soft and cute. You can also get lot of regular use stationary items like erasers in different shapes and sizes, colour crayons, sketch pens , glitter pens and foot long ball pens. Some sell house hold items made of recycled plastics like boxes , containers , buckets , washing brushes , scrubs at bargain prices. Some sell cotton bed sheets and cushion cover in good colours and designs.

So next time you want to shop for fresh veggies, fruits or even some sundry item do head to these Aathwada bazaar's and experience the thrill amidst the chaos ..

Have fun and enjoy the shopping...

CHAPTER FIVE

Brindavan ki Holi Aur Goa's Shimgotsav--- Asli Holi

Just the other day I was watching a rerun of the epic Bollywood blockbuster **"Sholay"** for the 100th time , I guess. Some movies you can watch over and over again and it feels better every time you watch them. This cult movie was the only movie in the History of Bollywood to have cassettes of its dialogues flying of the shelf faster than a hot bajia from a food counter. All the characters right from **Soorma Bhopali, to theAngarezon Ke zamane ka Jailor , to Ramu Kaka , Thakur , to Jai –Veeru to the epitome of villainy or the Baap of all villains "Gabbar"** are all house hold names and have become immortal long after the film has taken down from the theaters.

Do you remember the scene in which Gabbar's henchmen come back defeated from a skirmish with Jai-Veeru and He scowls with a mean look and asks Sambha (the skinny guy who always sit on the Hill top) **Holi Kabh Hai ......Kabh Hai Holi.........**

Yes it will be Holi time next week and the festival of colors will hopefully bring real happiness in our lives than our beloved Prime Minister's promised Acche Din…Jokes apart Holi is truly a festive of joy and happiness. On the occasion of Holi a fire is lit in every big society compound as a token of burning away all the misery and sorrow and starting a new life , a life full of bright colors and happiness. The next day is celebrated as Dhuli vandan or festival of colors where young and old, men women and children enjoy the company of each other and have fun with Abhir-Gullal and other bright colors.

What we celebrate is just a fraction of the real festival. During my early days as a Sales Executive, I had been to the land of **Lord Krishna in Mathura –Brindavan**. I was accompanying my project engineer stationed at Mathura for our Software project at IOCL Mathura. We were put up at a Kothi a ground plus two storied house of an Class 4 employee Mr. Ramgopal Yadav of IOCL refinery. A tall lanky fellow working as an electric technician at the refinery. His family of 4 would reside on the ground floor which was a 3 BHK unit. The leasing of upper rooms of his house being his extra income. The upper story included a 2 BHK unit with a big balcony facing the wide street in Mathura. The bedrooms had huge coolers –those ancient devices pre-historic to the modern AC's. They were needed during the summers to cool the rooms so that you could sleep , else you would get fried in the heat .The weather outside would touch temperatures close to 45-48deg Celsius during daytime and around 35-38deg Celsius. The electricity to these items of luxury was tapped illegally using local **Katyiabaaz** who would tap the local electric pole with an ingenious metal hook.

During my stay I was fortunate to see the Holi celebration in this land of Krishna. Holi celebration in **Brij Bhoomi** starts a week before the actual day of the festival and continue for a few days after Holi. An enactment of beating up of men folk by the women folk symbolizing , beating of Krishna and his Gwala's by the Gopi's of Nandgaon is performed on the day Holi. With Holi songs playing in the background, women beat up these men with sticks as they try to protect themselves with improvised protective gear. This is the famous **"Lathmar Holi".** The Holi with Colors can be experienced at the **Bankey Bihari Temple in Brindavan**. The hub of Holi celebrations in Brindavan is the **Bankey Bihari temple.** The temple, built in the 19th century, has four gates (three for entry and one for exit) and is dedicated to Lord Krishna. The season for Holi in **Bankey Bihari** starts off with **Phoolan ki Holi** where Holi is played with flowers and ends with the main festival where color and Gullal are thrown. The entire temple complex is smeared in shades of pink even the air is filled with this Gullal thrown by the locals celebrating the festival. Remembering those scenes of fun and frolic with these simple folks enjoying the festival of colors brings a smile to my face even today.

Another place where Holi is celebrated in its traditional spirit is Goa. Though I personally have not experienced it , I have been itching to go there hearing of the celebrations from my brother –in –law Jagdish Katkar. The Holi is this sun kissed region is known as **Shimgo or Shigmo.** The festival is celebrated mostly by the masses following all religious traditions. As expected from the Goans, the festival is accompanied with fanfare. Performance on drumbeats and epic enactment of mythology are religiously followed. Vivid and vibrant colours of gulal and neel are abundantly used. **Shigmotav** is highlighted with performances of troupes in the form of parades and cultural dramas. At dusk, huge effigies are taken in processions and prizes given away.

The 14-day celebrations of Shigmo coincide with Holi celebrations all over the country. For a good part of March, the streets of Goa transform into a cultural center full of dance and drama. The Shigmo festival is significant in many ways. It commemorates the homecoming of the warriors who had left at the end of Dussera to fight the invaders. It is also the spring festival of Goa where farmers celebrate the harvest season. There are two forms of Shigmo celebrations in Goa. Dhakto Shigmo and Vhadlo Shigmo. While Dhakto Shigmo is generally celebrated by farmers and the rural population, Vhadlo Shigmo has a broader appeal and is celebrated by everyone together. Dhakto Shigmo is more about singing, dancing and procession on the streets while Vhadlo is to do with celebrations inside temples. The processions carried out during Shigmotav are characterized by colorful umbrellas or dindis, modern floats depicting ancient Hindu mythological episodes, and folk dancers in traditional costumes. One of the dances performed is the **Ghode morni** or the horse dance and the **Phugdi** dance.

Shigmo and Holi make Goa extremely happening and convivial during March. Not only do you get a slice of Goan culture, you also get to interact with locals, play the festival of colors with them and participate in various Holi events all across Goa

So next time you want to try a different experience during the festival of colors do try visiting these special places be it Mathura-Brindavan or Goa during Holi or Shimgo.....And have a time of your life....

Wishing all my readers a Happy and a Safe Holi

PS: Did you know there are other places in the World where similar celebrations with either bright colors or water or even a vegetable like Tomatoes is carried out.

Water Fight in Thailand - As Thai New Year arrives, it is welcomed with the world's biggest water fight. Thai people and tourists indulge in water fights, approaching each other with water balloons. This festival, held between April 13 and April 15, envisages the concept of cleansing with water to purify and renew.

Colour Music Festival in Texas - Color Jam, a colorful music festival was held in Texas in 2015. The festival featured live music concert, color throws and color fights.

The Color Run in London - One can get a taste of Holi in London, where 'The Color Run' festival takes place. Participants run in a five-kilometers street, wearing a white shirt and as the colors are sprayed at them they, get covered from head to toe with every kilometer of the course. The event takes place in the cities of London, Manchester , Glasgow and Birmingham.

Life In Color in Florida - One of the biggest color festivals, 'Life In Color' started out as a college festival in Florida in 2011, later progressing into a worldwide color party.

Color Festival in Kiev , Ukraine -The most colorful event, which is eagerly expected by a lot of Kiev residents and tourists - Holi colors festival. Yes, the main feature of the festival will be paint. All the participants will be able to shower each other with bright colors, thus giving a smile, a laugh and a loud outburst of emotion around and the feeling that there is no monotony of everyday life and everything is bright and wonderful.

And finally **La Tomatina in Spain** --- is a festival that is held in the Valencian town of Bunol a town located in the East of Spain, in which participants throw tomatoes and get involved in this tomato fight purely for entertainment purposes.

CHAPTER SIX

Chivda Gully ..... Spice of Life

It's a custom in most Marathi household to offer some snacks along with the afternoon tea if any visitor drops in. Even otherwise we normally have some biscuits or light snack while drinking tea. The fastest and best dry snack to offer is the **"Chivda"** made of lightly fried or roasted poha or puffed rice. Each region in Maharashtra has its special recipe, be it the **Laxmi Narayan Chivda of Pune or Kondaji Chivda of Nashik or Namdev Chivda of Solapur.** Each with its unique taste and a special recipe handed down through the generations.

A trending household name since 1935, **Laxminarayan Chivda** is famous among Punekars for producing savories such as peanuts, rice flakes and authentic spices. Mr. Laxminarayan Datta, the founder of Laxminarayan Chivda started his journey towards establishing a business by using a handcart selling snacks. But it was his sole creation of making Chivda using a blend of rich ingredients. Fried Poha Chivda spiced with Indian spices and condiments, laced with a rich dose of dry fruits make this Chivda special. These fresh crispy Chivda are a perfect accompaniment to piping hot tea. Now Laxminarayan Chiwdas are not limited to Pune city, you can get it anywhere in India.

The specialty of **Kondaji Chivda** is its unique taste of fried / caramelized onions mixed with the usual garlic, nuts and poha along with the right amount of spices which creates a mouthwatering flavor and tantalizes your taste buds. You can enjoy its hot and sweet taste for every occasion.

Another famous Chivda is Namdev Chivda of Solapur which has a history of 140 years. Made from the finest spices and poha, its taste lingers on in your mouth even after the tea you have used to wash it down.

All these talk of Chivda makes me go down the memory lane of **visiting Lalbaug market** to pick up dried red chilies and some garam masala at the legendary spice stores of **Khamkar's.** There are 3 **stores P.B Khamkar, G W Khamkar and Ashok Khamkar** all belonging to the Khamkar family, legendary for their spices and sourcing of dried red chilies and rice from Konkan and beyond. On orders of my mom just before the onset of monsoon, I used to go to either of these 3 stores to pick up 2-3 kgs of Bedgi or Byadgi mirchi that special flavored dried red chilly from Karnataka. It is a famous variety of chilly mainly grown in the Indian state of Karnataka. It is named after the town of Byadgi which is in the Haveri district of Karnataka. The business involving Byadgi chillis has the second largest turnover among all chilli varieties of India. Did you know an oil, oleoresin extracted from these chilies is used in the preparation of nail polish and lipsticks. That's why the women who use the red nail polish and deep red lipsticks look so hot and spicy I guess.

Byadgi chilly is also known for its deep red color and is less spicy and is used in many food preparations of South India. Byadgi chilly has also been accorded Geographical

Indication (GI) in February 2011

Another option was to pick up the Sankeshwari Chilies. This spicy chilly is what gives a lot of regional cuisine, including Konkani food, its unique flavor, spicy zing and red color. Used in the powdered form in fish preparations, assorted gravies and sambhar, this chilly is popularly used by the Konkani community.

After picking up the chilies I used to tread the small by-lanes of Lalbaug just behind the shops.

The most conspicuous thing in the market are stacks and stacks of red chilies. Several varieties are on sale. There were women sitting behind the chilly sacks, sorting the chilies by size. Another popular item sold in this market is dried copra. Coconut trees are plentiful in the coastal areas of Maharashtra, so it is used in both fresh as well as dried forms. Copra is ground along with garlic and red chilies to make lasun chutney, a local favorite.

For those who wish to make their own masalas, the stalls offer a range of spices. From Kala Jira (nigella), methi (fenugreek), dhania (coriander), jeera (cumin), rai of two types (mustard), saunf (fennel), Safed til (white sesame), and ajwain (carom),(Anas phal) star anise, two more jeera boxes (cumin), jaiphal (nutmeg), kalimiri (pepper), lavang (clove), dalchini (cinnamon), tirphal (Sichuan pepper) and dagadphool (stone-flower, a lichen) and tamaalpatra (bay leaf). While most of the spices above are familiar to all Indians, tirphal (Sichuan pepper) is not. It is something you see only in Konkani cooking especially in Fish curry. As Tirphal grows in and around Goa.

The people who shop in this area are typically Marathi-speaking communities (erstwhile mill-worker families). Although most of the mills are no more, the area continues to remain home to the workers, who have now moved to other occupations. There are also Gujarati-speaking women, but fewer in number.

Once you buy the spices, you can bring them to the grinding mill if you want your own customized spices

In Chivda Galli, there are several shops selling different types of Chivda and farsan. You can also see the workshops where the farsan is made and packed.

Here you will be engulfed by the wafts of spicy , tangy and sweet smells of the numerous shops selling Chivda's. The shops started decades ago to cater to the hunger pangs of the mill workers living in the area. Slowly, similar shops selling variety of Chivda mushroomed all over the lane and before long the lane started to be called the 'Chivda Gally' also known as Chivda Galli. The shop owners prefer to make the traditional Chivda and farsan in large quantity. Today, there are over 12 Chivda shops in the lane selling the snack. According to the shop owners, the Maharashtrian population living in Lalbaug and nearby areas like Cotton Green, Currey Road, Parel prefer to buy traditional Chivda rather than the several new varieties. Over 7 tons of Chivda and farsan is sold by most of the shops every month.

Earlier this area was where most of the mill workers lived. Chivda was the kind of evening snack they preferred after their working hours. Even while celebrating a festival or during any kind of family function, the mill workers preferred distributing Chivda and farsan in their neighborhood since it was light on the pockets. Looking at the trend, many shops selling Chivda started sprouting on this lane which became popular as Chivda Galli.

The oldest Chivda shop in the lane is tasty Chivda which opened in the year 1965.

The poha Chivda made of rice flakes, farsan, batata Chivda made of potato, Makka Chivda made of corn flakes and potato chips were the items relished by the mill workers. Festival season like Diwali, Gudi Padwa and Holi are the peak season for sale. People come to buy the snack in large quantities. Over 300 kg of Chivda and farsan is made every day during this time. People usually get freshly made products since they are made in the shops themselves. Workers start making the items from early morning."

As the choices of the shoppers began changing, the shop owners began stocking more items. Looking at the demand of buyers and the preference of children they have started selling products like Schezwan chakli, soya chakli, tomato chaklis, Kadak Ladoo. This helps them to keep their business stable and the customers happy. Only the residents living nearby the area prefer to buy the traditional Chivda. These days people rarely distribute Chivda during family functions, which is very sad. A tradition is lost and the demand for the Chivda is dwindling down.

So next time you are having a cuppa of piping tea or coffee and want to have a light snack open that packet of Chivda pour it in a plate ,,add some diced onions, sprinkle some lemon juice on top and pick up a handful and eat it with a flick of your palms that's the real way of eating it not the civilized way using spoons.

Isme Maja hi Kuch aur Hai...

Enjoy the sweet and spicy concoction as they say spice is the essence of life.

Happy Reading....

CHAPTER SEVEN

R.D.Burman ....Pancham the musical genius.

We in India have the habit of celebrating birth and death anniversaries of Historical figures, a day to remember their life and teachings. So we have Oct 31 the birth anniversary of Sardar Patel as Shakti Divas. September 5th the birth anniversary of our ex-President Sarvapalli Radhakrishnan as Teacher's Day , November 14th the birth anniversary of our first Prime Minister Pt. Jawaharlal Nehru as Children's day which falls exactly 9 months from February 14th the Valentines Day...Is it sheer coincidence or nature way of have some fun...... Jokes apart but we celebrate so many days in India for more trivial reasons that its hard to even count and remember. But what with the world accepting June 21st as International Yoga Day, influenced by our current Prime Minister Narendra Modi's efforts and recognized by the United Nations. I feel we should have a Music Appreciation Day or a Bollywood Music Day in recognition of Indian Film Industries contribution to Indian music. We as a civilization have always revered the sound of "OM" and believe all universe was born out of this ethereal sound. Even the images and stories our gods have influenced our leanings towards music , be it Lord Krishna mesmerizing Brindavan with his flute or Goddess Saraswati the god of Vidya (Knowledge) playing her Veena. We have always been appreciative of Music in our lives.

So in this last week of June specifically on June 27th a legend was born to create such melodious music that till date we hum his songs and enjoy his compositions whenever they are played of the radio and these ever green tunes have been mixed and re-mixed by little know composers and DJ's, and provided them with livelihood. I am talking about none other than the maverick music composer **R.D.Burman known to every one as Pancham Da or simply Pancham...**

Story so goes that R.D.Burman father Sachin Dev Burman or S.D Burman a legend himself used to tell his wife that their son RD when an infant would cry and that sound was similar to the musical 5th note of "Pa" as in Pancham. So he decided to call his son by the nick name of "Pancham"....

R.D.Burman started his musical journey as early as 9 years when the music composed by him like **"Aye meri Topi Palat Ke aa"** was use by his father in the Hindi film **Funtoosh.** Even the famous song **"Sar Jo tera Chakraye ..Ya Dil Duba jaye"** was included in the soundtrack of Guru Dutt's famous film "Pyaasa"..As he grew up he took formal Indian Classical training under the tutelage of **Ustad Ali Akbar Khan (Sarod Maestro) and Pt. Samta Prasad (Tabla)** to hone his skills in music. Later he even assisted his father **S D Burman and Salil Chowdhary** on lot of compositions for a slew of hit movies.

R.D Burman's **first released film as an independent music director was Chhote Nawab.** When the noted Bollywood **comedian Mehmood** decided to produce Chhote Nawab, he first approached Burman's father Sachin

Dev Burman for the music. However, S. D. Burman declined the offer, advising him he was unavailable. At this meeting, Mehmood noticed Rahul playing Tabla, and signed him as the music director for Chhote Nawab for a Shagun of Ekyavan Rupaiya (Rs.51/-) . The story has it R.D Burman didn't take any money beyond the Shagun from Mehmood since he had given him his first big break. R.D Burman later developed a close association with Mehmood, who he regarded as Bade Bhaiya and **made a cameo in Mehmood's Bhoot Bangla again for free.**

R.D.Burman first hit film as a film music director was **Teesri Manzil**. He gave credit to lyricist Majrooh Sultanpuri for recommending him to Nasir Hussain, the producer and writer of the film. Vijay Anand also said that he had arranged a music session for R.D Burman before Nasir Hussain.Teesri Manzil had six songs, all of which were written by Majrooh Sultanpuri, and sung by Mohammed Rafi. Four of these were duets with Asha Bhosle, whom RD Burman later married. Nasir Hussain went on to sign Pancham Da and lyricist Majrooh Sultanpuri for six of his films including **Baharon Ke Sapne, Pyaar Ka Mausam and Yaadon Ki Baaraat. R.D.Burman score for Padosan** was well received. Meanwhile, he continued to work as his father's assistant for films including Jewel Thief and Prem Pujari

The hit Kishore Kumar song **"Mere Sapnon ki Raani"** from Aradhana, though credited to his father, is rumored to have been Burman's composition. Kora Kagaz tha Yeh Man Mera from the same film was also his tune It is believed that when S. D. Burman fell ill during the recording of the film's music, Burman took over and completed the music. He was credited as an associate composer for the film.

All these are well documented facts , but there are little known facts which the legendary Composer himself confessed to in certain television interviews. But ver few people knew that R.D.Burman composed Latin American music with equal ease.

R.D. Burman was mostly known for his film music, but among his non-film work was the little-heard album *Pantera* (not to be confused with the American heavy metal band), which combined Latin American music with elements of rock, jazz, and funk. It was recorded in the United States in '83-84 but released only in '87. Comprising contributions from established Latin American musicians of the time, it was produced by Pete Gavankar, who was based in the US and had good contacts with local musicians. In India it released to a very lukewarm response. Pancham Da was very upset that Indian listeners didn't connect with it. He managed to gain some closure a few years later, when he used the main theme of one of the songs from *Pantera*as the *mukhda*to **'Rang Rangeeli Raat' from Priyadarshan's** ***Gardish.*** The album hadn't worked, but the song did, and it made him very happy that Indian listeners had accepted at least one of his Latin American tunes.

And did you know that he wrote lyrics for an English song for an important scene in the Amitabh starer "Deewar". There's a scene in Deewar where Amitabh meets Parveen Babi at a bar. A soft English song plays in the background **"I am falling in Love"** , the lyrics to this were penned by Pancham Da himself.

Pancham Da was known for the distinctive growl, a husky and a full throated voice which he lent to his vocals when singing in songs such as **'Mehbooba Mehbooba' from Ramesh Sippy's** *Sholay* **or the other favorite "Yama Yama" from Shaan**, this was inspired by the stylings of

American jazz legend Louis Armstrong. He was fascinated by Louis Armstrong and didn't want to be stereotyped as a conventional playback singer. He used to say: *'Meri awaaz ki koi pehchaan honi chaahiye* (my voice should have its own identity)

Most of us know that Pancham Da could make music from all most anything. In the song **'Raat Gai Baat Gai'**, **from the Dev Anand-Zeenat Aman starrer** *Darling Darling* , at one point, a beat is heard which doesn't sound like a conventional percussion instrument. In the song's picturization, it is Aman who is creating the beat by tapping various parts of her own body (as well as a few extras). In the studio, that beat was played by Burman, literally, on the back of one of his trusted percussionists, Amrutrao Katkar. During the recording, he asked Amrutrao to remove his shirt. Naturally, he [the percussionist] was embarrassed and bewildered by this. Then, **he proceeded to play a Latin American beat on his back, with a microphone recording everything.** It was okayed in one take and used in the movie.

R.D.Burman had a penchant for using natural, folcy-inspired techniques or unusual instruments to create interesting sounds and rhythms in his songs, which would be depicted on screen similarly. In **'Chura Liya Hai Tumne'**, from *Yaadon Ki Baaraat*, **the spoon-on-glass sound heard in the beginning is an actual recording of a glass being struck by a spoon. In 'Dheere Dheere Zara Zara'** from *Agar Tum Na Hote*, the rhythm created by actress Rekha on screen, where she's shown tapping a piece of jewelry around her waist, **was the sound of a bunch of keys that was used in lieu of the traditional hi-hat.** Only Pancham Da could do such orchestration and create magic which is remembered till date by his fans.

Like many Bollywood composers, R.D Burman's tunes were often 'lifted', either directly or partially, from Western compositions. However, he was always honest about the sources, unlike many music directors, and didn't quite consider it 'stealing'. He would say, 'I am trained in Indian classical, not Western or jazz, so I can't just create something I don't know out of thin air. But what I'm doing is not stealing: I'm merely taking the essence of the tune and making something unique with it.'"

Many are aware of numbers like **'Mehbooba Mehbooba'** (inspired by Demis Roussos' version of the traditional Cyprus tune 'Say You Love Me') and **'Mil Gaya Humko Saathi'** (whose *mukhda* resembles the guitar intro to ABBA's 'Mamma Mia'), which were done at the behest of the film's producers, taking advantage of the unlikelihood of legal action at the time, when Bollywood was a self-contained industry.

But the genius as he was Pancham Da would succeed in changing a song beyond recognition, citing the example of 'Chura Liya Hai Tumne', whose opening chords resemble those of **Bojoura's 'If It's Tuesday, This Must Be Belgium'.** "The opening bars are similar, but then he took the song and added so many arrangements and layers to it, He made it his own. That's why he was such a genius.

This blog is my tribute to that genius of a composer who created lilting melodies and foot tapping dance numbers with equal aplomb.

So next time you hear R.D.Burman hit song stop a while listen carefully and enjoy the unique composition which has his trademark style written all over it.. Like the song O Hansini

O hansini meri hansini, kahan ud chali
Mere armaanon ke pankh lagaake kahan ud chali)

Aaja meri saanson mein mahek raha re tera gajra
Aaja meri raaton mein lahek raha re tera kajra
Ho, aaja meri saanson mein mahek raha re tera gajra
Ho, aaja meri raaton mein lahek raha re tera kajra
(O hansini meri hansini, kahan ud chali
Mere armaanon ke pankh lagaake kahan ud chali)

If you listen carefully you will hear a violin playing out the melody as Kishore Kumar sings the Mukhda and when he opens each Antara. There is an Interplay between Trumpet and Accordion which dominates the rhythmic component. A melodic riff played out on a hammered dulcimaer which sounded like a Santoor , followed by a turnaround phrase played out on the strings to bring in the tail end of the interlude.

The 2nd interlude revisits the prelude which begins with Hammered Dulcimer and acoustic guitar, while shakers provide the required consistent percussion. A fading wafting flute -toned riff is tossed into the mix. The accordion plays out a short melodic riff, which is notable for introducing the triton. A special improvisation unique to Pancham Da....

You are sure to get lost in the ethereal music of this timeless classic....Hats off to this great music composer ...simply called Pancham....

Click the below link to enjoy the song " O Hansini"
https://www.youtube.com/watch?v=R4Vj_XsfHTM

CHAPTER EIGHT

Pandharpur Chi Wari
......Road to Salvation

A few years back I , sometime in June I was going for a Terms & Conditions negotiation meeting at Thermax in Pune. A meeting which had more to do with legal clauses like Limitation of Liability, Intellectual Property Rights, Export Control, Payment Terms etc, than the usual Sales discussion. A rather nerve wrecking and dull affair, which required me to be a legal expert than a Salesperson. Anyways as usual in those days, I took the early morning Shivneri -the blue coloured Volvo run very efficiently by Maharashtra State Road Transport Corporation or MSRTC or simply know as ST. Some of the best things of the bus is its comfortable seating and on time departure unlike the unprofessional attitude of the private bus operators. As usual took an aisle seat quite towards the back and snoozed into a light slumber. By the time we reached the Lonavala -Khandala the scene outside had dramatically changed with the clouds literally coming down over the hill side accompanied by a consistent shower of rain. The greenery all around made it pleasing to the eye and the atmosphere was more romantic than dull prospect of the meeting I had embarked upon.

As the bus neared the town of **Dehu road** on the old Mumbai-Pune Highway, I could hear sounds of Taal and dhol beating in rhythmic sequence followed by chants of **Shree Hari Vitthal -Jai Hari Vitthal**. I hopped on to the now vacant window seat peered through glass. I could make out a crowd of nearly a thousand people chanting, singing and walking in a disciplined manner at the side of the road. The serpentine que secured by ropes on either side. People of all ages were walking along. You could see men in their white Kurta and dhoti with mala of Tulsi beads in their neck and a white tikka on their forehead singing abhangs or chanting Shree Hari Vitthal Jai Hari Vitthal and Gyanba Tukaram followed by women in traditional Navaris (nine yard) saree with their heads covered or with small pots of tulsi balanced over their heads . You could even see tiny tots on the hips of these women or if little older walking along with their families in half shirts and worn – faded half pants shouting the chants at the top of their voices or swaying – dancing enthusiastically.

The scene was vibrant with hordes of people walking with single minded focus of reaching the land of the **Lord Vitthal at Pandharpur**. These people were from Warkari Sect. They embark upon this annual long march – Wari every year which starts around 21 days before the holy day of Ashadi Ekadashi and culminates a day before Ekadashi at Pandharpur the abode of Lord Vitthal. in the Indian state of Maharashtra, in honour of the deity. palkhi (palanquin processions) carrying the paduka (footprints) of various saints - most notably Dnyaneshwar and Tukaram - from the Warkari (Warkari, "one who performs the Wari") sect (which venerates Vithoba), are taken from their respective shrines to Pandharpur. The tradition is more than 700 to 800 years old. Dnyaneshwar's palkhi leaves from Alandi, while Tukaram's begins at Dehu; both in Pune district of Maharashtra. This March on foot from various locations in Maharashtra to Vithoba temple, Pandharpur, attracts a total of over a million pilgrims. The journey takes 21 days. Numerous palkhi join the main Tukaram and Dnyaneshwar palkhi that starts from Dehu and Alandi respectively.

Pune city and the industrial town of Pimpri-Chinchwad are caught in a Warkari wave with lakhs embarking on the three-week pilgrimage that will continue till Ashadi Ekadashi. As has been the tradition the annual **palkhi processions of Sant Dnyaneshwar and Saint Tukaram** are welcomed in Pimpri-Chinchwad and Pune city, amid chants of bhajan and sounds of traditional music instruments.

Both processions enter Pune through separate routes and by evening, streets in Shivajinagar and Peth areas were filled with lakhs of warkaris. They descended on temple town Dehu and Alandi from various parts of Maharashtra and a few other states.

Divided into several **"dindis" (groups)**, some carried idols of **Dnyaneshwar and Tukaram** on their heads, while a few others carried "Tulsi" pots. Several Warkari swayed holding saffron flags. The old, the infirm, men and women walked hand in hand to honour their commitment to the tradition of "wari."

The Warkari halt in Pune for 36 hours and proceed towards Pandharpur. Making Pune the hub of spiritual ceremonies during this period and making this place the best place to be if you want to soak in this mesmerizing atmosphere.

Along the highways, activists, families and members of social and voluntary organisations wait to provide food, biscuits, fruits and water to Warkari

On their way, the pilgrims not only play musical instruments like veenas, mridangams, dholkis and chiplis. The pilgrims especially the women also play the traditional folk dance "fugdi" with their infectious enthusiasm and energy. With the saffron coloured triangular 'paatakas' (flags) in hands and Tulsi leaves on their heads the pilgrims present a perfect picture of the Bhakti tradition of Maharashtra.

The wari culminates at the Vithoba temple on Ashadi Ekadashi. Devotees from Maharashtra and nearby areas set out for Pandharpur, wearing holy basil beads and singing the glories of Vithoba and songs like "Gyanba Tukaram", commemorating the saints. Upon reaching Pandharpur on Ashadi Ekadashi, these devotees take a holy dip in the sacred Chandrabhaga River before proceeding to take Darshan (see) Vithoba central icon in the main temple. These devout pilgrims got the reward for their long journey when they witnessed the "Maha puja" of Lord Vitthala and his concert Rukhmini in Pandharpur on the Ashadi Ekadashi day

Participation in Ashadi Dindi helps an individual in many ways by bringing good health, peace & prosperity in his life. Chanting the continuous glory of the God in the Ashadi Dindi procession and Seva Dindi purifies an individual, there is an inner cleansing that takes place in Mind, Body and Spirit and the participants tend to lose their individual identities and experience bliss. It develops all aspects of human personality and helps us understand the true purpose of Life.

This culminates the long and arduous journey on the road to Salvation.

Dev Maza Vithu Savala , Mal Tyachi Maziya Gala
Vithu Rahe Pandharpuri ,Vaikunthch He Bhuvari

Bhimechya Kathi Dule Bhakticha Mala
Sajire Rup Sunder ,Kati Zhakle Pitambar
Kanthat Tulsi che Haar , Kasturi Tila
Bhajanat Vithu Dolato Kirtanat Vithu Nachato
Ragun Jayi Bhaktancha Lala

CHAPTER NINE

The Door Bell keeps ringing....

Living in Matunga all these years first in an old building, ground + 3 with no security guard and now in a high rise with security guard and inter-com (mostly non-working). I have seen all types of vendors, salesmen and seller of unique items coming in and going out of our building. Much habituated by constant ringing of the main doorbell and having to get up to open the door every time it rings. Often getting annoyed at the thought of leaving the work at hand and rushing towards the door to check who has come. But sometimes looking at the familiar faces across the door just melts away your irritation.

I still remember the vegetable vendor we used to call him **"Vasaiwale"** since he used to come all the way from Vasai the far-off suburb of Mumbai. He used to come every week either on a Tuesday or a Thursday when most house hold in our neighborhood used to buy and make vegetables. Typical was his avatar – a dark coloured checkered full shirt but kept unbuttoned and a dark brown or Khaki half pant literally measuring up to his knees. He must have been the first person who had started the trend of what is now called Bermuda Shorts or Khaki's. And which we were with aplomb at home on the weekends.

He used to bring the freshest veggies of the season in his **Kawad**. A unique contraption of two large cane baskets hanging from a long wooden pole held over his shoulders when he moved around the neighborhood. During monsoons he would bring green vegetables like fresh **jadi methi** or the spiky **Shepu.** Sometimes he would bring **Kel-Phul of the Banana blossom** and my Aai would make a sweet sour sabji of it which we ate with Tandlachi Bhakri. At other times his Kawad would be brimming with fresh green leafy vegetables like Chavli , Lal Math or exotic by Indian standards and which you will never get in the local vegetable market , Aamchuka or the sweet sour green leafy vegetable made into a gravy based curry or the Shevgyachya Pala (leaves of the Shevgyachya shenga) which were made into a tikki type pattice by mom , served with garlic chutney or your regular tomato ketchup it tastes divine.

In the monsoons, they would bring fresh **garlic chives, White onions, the freshest organic cilantro**, kantol or teasel gourd. In winter they carried held beans, **ghevda** – a cultivar of sweet beans, Toor beans etc. They would also have those big light green lady's finger, which Aai selected by breaking the tips to check if they were fibrous and mature. He would admonish her for doing it as she left behind the fibrous ones. These light green bhindi delighted me as a kid as they were exclusively meant for stuffing with a delightful onion and coconut masala to make **bharleli bhindi.** The spiky brinjals were another opportunity to stuffing the masala to make **bharleli Wangi.**

Vasai's famous sweet, yellow-skinned bananas were always picked for naivedya and shikaran – a cardamom spiced milk and banana dish that Maharashtrian children love. At times, we would order dried bananas too, a signature variety of Vasai. Dried bananas are eaten as a power-packed snack just like other dried fruits.

Old Mumbaikars like me miss them grossly. These vegetable sellers guided buyers about selecting the right **Aalu (Colocasia) leaves** for **Alu wadi** those crispy disc shaped typical Maharashtrian starters and how the rotund bottle gourds were prized for making **dudhi halwa** as they had more delicate and fleshy centre than the elongated bottle gourds that dominate the market now. Most buyers like us had special relations with these vendors as they satisfied their needs of exotic yet local vegctables. They were thus addressed as Vasaiwale mamas. Memories come flying back as I see him vend his wares in our neighbourhood still at the ripe old age of 60.

Other vendors who rung our door bell were the **Nankhtai Wala** who came bi-weekly with his enormous steel trunk. The trunk was laden with his Khazana. The trunk would open to reveal all the wonderful goodies neatly arranged in different compartments - square, oval and round shaped biscuits topped with almonds or cashews or pistachios or tutti-frutti, begging to be picked up. His specialty were the of **Nankhtai those sweet round or rectangular biscuits topped with almonds or pista** and which melted in your mouth. Much before the cookics became famous these Nankhtai would be served to special guest when they arrived at tea time. He also used to bring in those fluffy & crispy Khari biscuits which were best companion for the afternoon tea. Then again he had choice of golden brown rusk or toast as we call them, in baby variety or the large ones in the size of a bread slice.

Another person most looked forward to by all our Gujarati neighbours and of whom we also got habituated was a fellow who travelled all the from the distant suburban part of Dombivli carrying his bag filled with what else but **"Khakhras"** . Khakhras are those crispy and raosted chapatti type discs you can eat at any time to fill those in between lunch/ dinner hunger pangs. Since they are of the roasted type are much healthier option than snacking on wafers of the oil fried munchies. Ask him the options and he will roll out a menu of flavours that would spin your head. He had the **Schezwan Khakhra (little spicy), Tangy Tomato Khakhra, Chatpata Pani Puri flavoured Khakhra , the Punjabi Masala** for the spicy tongued person , or the Crisp Methi ones or Jeera flavoured Ghee Wala Khara which were melt-in the mouth. This was apart from the standard plain slated Khakhra. The sizes also varied as per each families requirement coming in large or minis. Most families would buy at least 3 varieties as per their taste . We stick to one flavour either Methi or Punjabi Masala though and by the time these Khakhras get over , the Khakhra Wala is back at the door for his bi-weekly sales call.

One more person who did the round of our building and the neighborhood much before this area turned into a Kutchi-Gujarati dominated region were the **fishermen and fisher woman** from the Wadala fish market. Now most of them don't frequent the building in Matunga as they don't find enough customers. But they do move about in Dadar Parsi Colony which is a stones throw away from our housing society. You will find typically the UP Bhaiyya with their tin tubs laden with different varieties of fish going from house to house of their loyal clients. The lady of the house usually place their orders well in advance with the techno-savy fish sellers on their Mobile phones and they in turn arrive with the freshest catch at the doorstep. A little bargaining and the deal is done and the fish seller get down to business of cleaning and cutting of the freshest **Pomfret** or the **Rawas or King Fish (Surmai) or the Macrel (Bangda)**. Even the prawns are de-shelled and cleaned and handed over ready to be fired or curried. Making the buyer smile with content of the impending fish curry lunch......

So though I hate getting up and opening the door literally a hundred times on an off day , for these special vendors who make a living by visiting home to home I would gladly open the door and interact with some real people than spend time on FB interacting with virtual people...

Salute to these natural sales people.....

CHAPTER TEN

The Screamers down the society compound

Has your sweet siesta on a Holiday been broken by the screaming sound of someone down below in your society compound trying to attract your attention by shouting out something like **Juna PuranaSaaman or Junaabo** . You peer out of your French window or from your balcony and what do your see , but a man pushing his hand cart converted into a small carriage by nailing a few sheets of aluminum on three sides so as to make space for carrying the old and unwanted items he collects from different falt owners . In exchange he offer some paltry sum , but you are glad because it has reduced the clutter in your otherwise spic and span home. He has an art of bargaining with you and eyes of a hawk finding the finest cracks and chips to your wooden or ceramic / glass item bringing the price to few Rupees instead of a Hundred and give you an assurance that you got a good deal. He picks these odd item and carts them away . You will find him at the odd Wednesday or a Friday Bazaar selling those very things like a side table an old ceiling fan a couple of chairs or even a few ceramic showpieces all refurbished and ready to be picked up by those who love old and archaic items.

During my childhood days there used to be a **lady who used to frequent our society carrying a cane basket filled with gleaming steel utensils. These she offered in exchange of old clothes** from every house hold. She should carefully sift through the pile of old clothes strewn in front of her making up her mind as what she can offer in exchange. If the clothes had a god Saree cotton or a nylon she would offer a Steel Katori else you would have to satisfy yourself with a steel lid . If the pile had some good children's clothes like a good frilly frock or an decent party ware shirt and pant she would magnanimously offer a copper plated small katori or an kadhai. And you would gladly part with your old clothes for a great deal. Just like the old wares merchant she would then take these old clothes and sell it for a princely sum to labourers and daily wage earners at the same weekly bazaars in working class areas of Lalbaug , Parel or even in old Fort area in Colaba.

Some street screamers had nothing to sell but rather offer there services for some money like that old man in a pure white dhoti and kurta topped up with a khadi jacket and head covered by a white topi. He would arrive on his cycle the typical one which a Milkman uses like a Hero or a Hercules and shout out **"Kalaiyaaa--Kalaiyaa"**. He was the tin man who took your big Pital (Brass) utensils which would have turned green on the inside due to oxidation **for a process known as "tinning"** to make them shining again. He had his loyal customers like my Aai who would trust him with her 3 big Tope's or big cauldron handed down the ages from one lady of the house to the other in the family. The tin man would make a note of the utensils in his small dairy and take them away only to come back the following week with same utensils , now gleaming and polished ones which looked as if they were as new as on the day they were bought. Bringing a warm smile on both his and my mother face.

Then there were the usual **Raddiwala or the Phool wala** , both coming mostly in the morning time one to collect you old papers and cart them away on his cycle . The other who brought small sapling of colourful flowers like hibiscus – red ,pink and white or marigold (gonda / genda phool) or the sweet smelling mogra or parijaat . Some standard plants like Tulsi or exotic like water lilies or some time on demand from particular customers saplings of jasmine , or boganvile . Some would ask him to bring medicinal plant like aloe vera or citronella or some romantic one would request for roses in red , white pink and and yellow. He would bring them neatly packed in his plastic crate held aloft his head or sometimes on some ones borrowed cycle. Just before the monsoons he would also bring special packets of soil med with cow dung to be put in pots for boosting the growth of the plants in his customers collection. The chant of "Phooloa" breaking th morning routine , making the people with green thumbs peer out of their windows to check if any new plants were part of the Phoolwala's collection.

Some odd ball vendors which have vanished due the consumer philosophy of use and throw were like the bucket repairing guys. There used to be a person who would come late in the afternoon with his hot coal sigdi and varied sizes of screw drivers shouting **"Baldiaa" to attract his customers**. If your plastic bucket started leaking due to a crack at the bottom or the side , he would examine the bucket under his magnifying glass or a watch repairs monocle and tell you where all he would have to put a patch to stop the leak. He would then get down to business, first he would light the small sigdi to heat the coals then he would keep his screw drives heating in them and start by cutting small plastic pieces of same colour as the bucket from his collection and then press them agains the crack in the bucket to fuse this piece with the main bucket to close out the leak. Once done he would ask for some water to test whether the leak was stopped. Smiling he would hand over the buket to the owner and demand his fees which would be as low as One rupee to maximum of Rs.10 if there were multiple leaks.

One of the bygone street vendors who still call on their loyal customers going from building to building are the knife and scissor sharpeners of the **Dharwala's** . With their big grinding wheel fixed to their bicycle. They mount the bicycle on the stand and start the business by shouting out **" Dharwala Dharwala --- Chaku Churyaan Tej karalo...."** Come and get your knives sharpened. People who need their services send their maids down with all the knives that need sharpening and get them ground and sharpened on the big grinding wheel. For the next few days you need to be extremely careful as the sharp knives could cut your fingers unknowingly as you tend to forget its renewed sharpness. These guys still do brisk business but they too have fallen back to technology as most of the machine sharpened steel knives you get today cannot be sharpened as the old iron ones used to be .

So next when you hear a call from below you windows or the gallery and see a little commotion don't get alarmed , it just might be one of these small time vendors trying to attract your attention with their trademark calls be it **" Juna do ....Kaliayaaa ...Dharwalaa"**...and trying to etch out an honest living using their god gifted skills .....

Kuch Meetha Ho Jaaye......

With the just concluded Raksha Bandhan one of the very first festivals in the festive month of Shravan or Sawan and many more lined up throughout this month , we get eat a lot of sweets / mithai as part of traditional way to sweeten our mouth or as we say Muh Meetha To Karlo. In Western part of India there have been traditional sweets ear marked for such special festivals . Like the Maharashtrian Narli Vadi – made of coconut , sugar and fortified with Kesar and crushed Pista. This delicacy is best bought from typical Maharashtrian Sweet Meat Shops like Panshkar's of Mumbai or Chitale of Pune. This yellow square barfi type mithai is yummy and melts in your mouth with every bite. At Panshikar's in Girgaon or Dadar , people queue from early morning to pick this wadi and going by the demand the line stretches nearly for 100 -200 mts in the bylane next to the Panshikar's at Dadar in the heart of Mumbai. Panshikar's have been in this sweets business from a century with the 4th generation holding the fort now at their various shops across mostly the Marathi dominated areas of Mumbai , Thane and Kalyan.

Another sweet that is similarly associated with Raksha Bandhan od Teej festival as celebrated in the Northern parts of India is the Gewar from Rajasthan. The sweet itself is unique in its looks , a spindly disc shaped mithal with perforated layers and a hole in the centre all coming together to give your that mouth watering taste. It can be eaten in its regular form or served with chilled Rabdi making it more rich and heavenly.

One thing I have been doing over the last 13 years of my marriage is that whenever I go outstation on my Sales trips I bring back the local sweet / mithai from that city or state so as to enjoy the sweet taste of Indi with my family. And the idea was given to me by my sweet heart Wifey Kashmira. Even if the schedule is tight during such Sales visit I make it a point to ask the locals be it the Hotel Front desk person or the driver of the car hired for local use to point me in the direction of the best sweet shop in town to pick their local sweet. So when I am in Bangalore , I will make it a point to visit the nearest Nandini Sweet shop to pick the Mysore Pak . History has it Mysore pak was first prepared in the kitchens of the Mysore Palace during the regime of Krishna Raja Wadiyar IV, by a palace cook named Kakasura Madappa. Madappa made a concoction of gram flour, ghee and sugar. When asked its name, Madappa had nothing in mind, simply called it the 'Mysuru pak'. Pak (or paka, more precisely) in Kannada means sweet. It is traditionally served in weddings and other festivals of southern India, and is very popular in baby showers as well. *Paaka shastra* (short *paka*) in Kannada means 'cooking procedure' or 'cooking techniques'. Also *paka* in Kannada refers to sticky sugar syrup obtained by simmering sugar with equal amount of water; specifically for Mysore Pak, the simple syrup is heated to the soft ball stage. The syrup is flavored with various spice essences like cardamom, rose, honey etc. *Paka* syrup preparation is a skilled art mastered by few cooks, some of whom keep their methods secret.

Same is the case when I am in Chennai. If it's a day trip and I don't find time to shop for any sweets I will surely pick up the Ghee wala Mysore Pak at Sri Krishna Sweets at the Chennai Airport. It's not unusual for passengers on flights out of Chennai to make a short stop at the airport counter of **Sri Krishna Sweets**

This store's 'Maysurpak' has developed a loyal legion of fans including me & my family and all those well beyond the Vindhyas. Most 'dessertarians' or sweet lovers find the melt-in-your-mouth texture of this sweet quite irresistible.

The texture of the traditional 'porous' Mysore Pak is meant to be slightly hard on the outside and yet 'crumbly' when you bite into it. A contrast from the soft and 'melty' texture that has been made popular by **Shri Krishna Sweets**. Another popular sweet shop in Chennai - **Grand Sweets**, veers towards the traditional Mysore Pak. These two styles have virtually split the Mysore Pak fans into two camps. It's not just the texture, some of Chennai's sweet shops have crafted their own versions from a Horlicks Mysore Pak to a Cashew Mysore Pak that traditionalists in Mysore might frown upon.

I have even picked up the best ever pedhas, those brown coloured sweet round balls made of pure mava during my rail journeys to reach clients like IOCL refinery in the holy place of from Mathura. They say if you are in Mathura and you have not visited **Krishna Janma bhoomi** and tasted the Mathura's famous pedha "To Mathura mein aake kya kiya".

There are numerous sweet shops across **Mathura** who sell these Pede but the most famous ones are from **Brijwasi Sweets and Radhika Sweets** . the recipe of this sweet is really simple as its basic ingredients is cows or buffaloes milk heated with sugar for several hour to make it thick . In this process ghee is added frequently so that the milk does not burn and turns into khoya or mawa. The khoya is then fried by frequently adding ghee .Frying khoya makes these peda's it last long.

Mathura peda is so famous in India that the term is often used in local saying like *"Mathura ka peda aur Chhattisgarh ka kheda* **means** "(famous are) the peda sweet of **Mathura and hemlet in Chhattisgarh. Mathura acts as a brand name for peda sweet.**

Another famous sweet quite close to my heart for its wonderful texture and taste is the **Agra ka Petha.** This sweet is a translucent soft candy from specifically from Agra in North India. Usually rectangular or cylindrical, it is made from the measly white gourd or the safed dhoodhi or ash gourd vegetable (also known as winter melon or white pumpkin, or simply **petha** in Hindi and Urdu). The Petha is said to have originated in the kitchens of Mughal Emperor Shah Jahan.Petha manufactured in Agra is covered by a Geographical Indication label to certify their origin. The best petha is found at Panchi Petha Store in Sadar Bazaar. The real house of the original petha , I had asked a local auto rickshaw driver on one such visit on which is the original one and he obliged me by saying " Bhai agar alsi petha khana hai to Panchi Petha khana par Sardar Bazaar wala Panchi petha se hi lene , baki sab naki hai.." I asked him how do I know all other shops which are going by the same name of Panchi Petha are nakli . He wisphered to me in a conspiratory tone and said please check the sign boards of these other panchi Petha there will always be some addition , I looked to one which was right in friont of me it had the name Panch Petha written in Bold letter alright but just besides was written " Pure" in thin black letters" same was the case with some other shops down the lane. I asked this autowala to takle me to Sadar bazaar. Again I checked the sign board it said **" Panchi Petha"** no prefix no suffix , home of the asli wala Petha.

The moment I entered the shop , I could understand the appeal petha hold for people. Rows and rows of inviting syrupy , perfectly arranged colorful chunks of the soft translucent sweet greeted me. A giant board inside proclaimed the nearl;y 20 varieties of this sweet. The counter staff offered me several variety from Angoori to Kesar to Rose flavoured. I was totally confused the understanding staff recommended I buy the traditional white and dry petha and the cylindrical Keshar one and for its mouth watering flacour the small round angoori ones. I was satisfied. When asked about its history the staff person pointed to the picture frame behind the cash counter of **Late Seth Pancham Lal Goyal** fondly called Panchhi. He started with one store and now this 100 year old business has around 7 branches in Agra alone. It has now started branches in Delhi , Ghaziabad and Lucknow. Keeping up with the changing demands and tastes of consumers **,Panchhi Petha** aims to create newer types of pethas to keep the interest alive. Recently they have introduce a sugar free variety that allows even the diabetics to enjoy it too.

Most of us eat sweets as Prasad or an after dinner dessert but Kolkata must be the only place in India no no I guess the whole wide world , where you will find people scurrying across to the nearest sweet shop at any time of the day to eat sweet just like that. Be it in the morning as breakfast or after a heavy lunch or dinner as dessert. So when in Kolkata head to K C Das on Esplanade East

.founded by Nobin Chandra Das . It was a humble beginning in a tiny obscure corner in Bagbazaar set up as a sweet shop in 1866. But he did not want to be known as any other Halwai or Mithai wala. The passion to create something new soothing unique was overpowering. He wanted to create a very original sweet which will be lovedf by the Bengali palate.An ultimate delicacy.After months of hardwork he came up with small balls of cottage cheese and boiled them in hot sugar syrup. The result was succulent , spongy, juicy sweet with a unique & distinct taste. Nobin Das christened them the "Rossogolla" and a legend was born. Eat it as syrupy sweet or squeeze the syrup out and bite into this melt in your mouth Rossogolla.But the story doesn't end at Rossogolla ,enter their shop and your will be lost in the sweets they produce, be it the classic Bengali Sandesh or the Cham Cham or the peda like soft Khirkadam or the Malai Sandwich like Rossomadhuri Channar Toast or the Khirmohan. Even the aam dahi has been transformed by the Bengali into the heavenly Misthi Doi chilled and served in small kulhads. Eat away standing there at the shop or at the well placed chairs in the corner of the shop. Try each one and smack your lips and lick your fingers.

So every time I come back from one of my business trips , my kids eagerly await those mithai boxes filled with the heavenly sweets and we all enjoy tasting them after a good family dinner. And I would like to thank my wifey for this great habit she has instilled into me of picking up the best of sweets from every part of India.

So to end on a sweet note ,I would say lets discover India from its sweets and forget the bitterness in our otherwise mundane life.

To Kuch Mitha Ho Jaye......

Wafers..... Those salted crunchy crispy's.

Is it just me or do you feel addicted to those crispy salty potato wafers once you bit into one . The next thing you know is you would have finished the bowl full and craving for more.And if you are directly eating from the plastic packet you will not know when its over as most often than not since your eyes would be glued to the television watching some movie or an interesting cricket or a soccer match. Your fingers will be fishing for even the small scraps of these salted wafers from the bottom of the pack. These potato wafers are hit with people of all ages be it kids or teens or us who are middle aged but young at heart.

I still remember the time we went to our best buddies birthday parties which would be organized at home unlike today's generation don't think twice before throwing a lavish party at the latest trending restaurant leaving you high and dry while paying the bill. At those small get togethers where we friends would gather at the birthday boy's home the menu was set it would be either be a Samosa or a bata wada with a sweet and minty Chutney sandwich along with those crispy potato wafers. If the party was a little grand you would have a bread roll or a pav bhaji and of course there would be a big piece of the birthday Cake –chocolaty and sweet. Every one would be happy just talking and enjoying some music on the in house music system or even a tape recorder. Some gossip , some discussion on the school portion , talks about the latest movies or the last cricket match watched. What a fun.

But till today the potato wafer remains the all-time favourite accompaniment for any snack plate you offer to your visitors during any function be it small or big .And do you know where these crunchie's and best bought it is at some small shops across Mumbai.

Inside the cottage-lined by-lanes of Khotachi Wadi in Girgaon, sits Venkatesh Subbiah's **Ideal Wafers.** Ask passersby for directions and they'll walk you right up to it. Or you can simply follow your nose.

It is 11AM, and the pocket-sized cooking area at the back of the shop is already overrun with drums of freshly fried potato wafers. In still more vats filled with water are spud slices, waiting to be lowered into the giant frying pan. Every four minutes, a new batch fried in 60 litres of vanaspati is whisked out and added to the drum. In about an hour, the batch is cooled, packed, and placed on the shelves outside. At one corner of the shop his staff supervised by his wife, Vaidehi, busily packs bagful of the salted wafers for the customers.

Looking at him going about his business a thought strikes my mind "How does he manages to stand for so long in front of the pan, and that too for so many hours, every single day." After Subbiah has finally exited the kitchen, mopping his brow, he agrees that the wafer business can be rather demanding. "In fact, if someone asks for my advice,

I'd tell them to not get into this business," he says laughingly. Ideal Wafers, is one of Mumbai's oldest family-run wafer businesses. The salted potato wafers and peppery banana chips have been drawing buyers from across the city for over five decades now. They are so light and tasty you would easily eat away the half kg pack all by yourself in one sitting.

Until about two decades ago, other family-run establishments like Gala Wafers, Coronation Wafers and Golden Wafers flourished in Mumbai. Today, real estate prices, labour shortage and bigger brands have forced many to down shutters. Ideal is among a handful of its kind still going strong, along with **Janta in Malad, A1 Wafers in Dadar (E) and Grant Road, and Welcome Wafers in Mahim**

The last two were set up by entrepreneurs, both inspired by wafer veteran, **Coronation**. While **A1's customers include retailers, movie theatres, cafeterias and restaurants, Welcome Wafers has made inroads in Punjab and Gujarat too**. It has come a long way from the 1970s, when founder Velji Gada made wafers by hand and sold them in the neighbourhood on bicycle. Today, the range has expanded to include varieties like tomato, cheese, banana chips, a newly launched "tangy" flavour called **Golden Bites, and namkeen like chivda and masala salli.** "Never say never," says Sameer Gada, Welcome's second-generation owner. According to him "You need to keep experimenting. The tomato flavour, took over a 100 tries before we got the perfect combination."

Inputs from regular customers and retailers are key. The Gujarati community often prefers a less spicy variety, while masala-packed wafers are popular up north, Gada adds. Supply also follows festival and school schedules. At Ideal

Wafers, the production of plain potato wafers is cranked up during Shravan, while Gada's retailers ask for tangier, kiddie-favourite flavours when school holidays begin.

This namkeen manufacturing is mostly unregulated, and family-run businesses face competition from both international brands as well as the unbranded, sasta wafers. Welcome Wafers countered this with corporate branding and good old-fashioned business smarts. They also have to watch out for new flavours from these international brands as the customer then look out for a particular taster or flavour in these local wafers too. The idea is to look at the bigger brands not as competition, but straight up opportunity. Formulae are closely guarded, and it is not unheard of for rivals to send a spy to copy the secret recipes.

But what can't be replicated, is the staff with decades of skill. Old-timers can slice a potato in half and know the starch content just by the crunch it makes, rater than the litmus test carried out by quality control persons.

We all know Lonavala is famous for its chikkis those sweet slabs of jiggery mixed with peanuts , cashew or til. But you also get the best variety of Potato wafers at **Rupam Chikki.** Their wafers and really thin , crispy and literally melts in your mouth when eat them. Fresh wafers are made every day and sold . such is the demand that the stock last fro few hours each morning and evening when they put on sale. Do try and pick a packet next time you in Lonavala to enjoy it cool and pleasant climate.

Yes you may put on some extra calories eating these addictive salted snacks but then what life without such small sinful namkeen's...

CHAPTER THIRTEEN

Off Dips, Sauces, Podi's and Chutneys ...

If you have kids in the house I am sure you would have tried Italian or Mexican food multiple times. Or the other favoured cuisine Chinese you would have observed that the waiter brings a lot of salad dressing or sauces on your table much before your starter or main course order. If its Chinese you will find the typical 3 bowls of dark soya sauce , Chilly or Schezwan sauce and Chilly in Vinegar, these to be used in small proportion with your Fried rice to enhance the taste a little more . If you love the steamed dumplings or Momo's as they are called you will be served a side dish **called kimchi** This puréed mixture of kimchi seasoning is a simple combination of red pepper flakes, garlic, ginger, sugar, lime juice, water, salt, and fish sauce. It's punchy and sharp, tangy, and incredibly invigorating.

Another dipping which is typically served is the **Black Bean-Peanut Butter Dipping Sauce** With Maple Syrup Chinese fermented black soy beans are eye-bulgingly salty and all kinds of funky. And the jarred sauce, which is usually spiked with some additional seasonings, isn't exactly the kind of thing you'd want to eat with a spoon. But some unlikely additions anchor that powerful saltiness and let the black beans' more subtle flavors shine. Maple syrup coaxes out a distinctive layer of sweetness, while creamy peanut butter softens the blow of that sharp, fermented tang. Chili oil ties it all together with some warm heat, and a splash of water thins it out just enough. The result is thick and rich, but still very much dipping-friendly.

In Italian and Mexican cuisine dips and dipping sauces are fundamental to most of the dishes / recipes. A **dip** or **dipping sauce** is a common condiment for many types of food. Dips are used to add flavor or texture to a food, such as pita bread, dumplings, crackers, cut-up raw vegetables, fruits, seafood, cubed pieces of meat and cheese, potato chips, tortilla chips, and falafel. Unlike other sauces, instead of applying the sauce to the food, the food is typically put, dipped, or added into the dipping sauce (hence the name).

Dips are commonly used for finger foods, appetizers, and other easily held foods. Thick dips based on sour cream, crème fraîche, milk, yogurt, mayonnaise, soft cheese, or beans are a staple of American hors d'oeuvres and are thinner than spreads which can be thinned to make dips. Alton Brown suggests that a dip is defined based on its ability to "maintain contact with its transport mechanism over three feet of white carpet"

Dips in various forms are eaten all over the world and people have been using sauces for dipping for thousands of years.

More so in our Indian way of life. Growing up in a house hold where most of the food was home made we always had stock of typical side dishes like the dry chutneys which would be eaten during heavy rains when even the standard vegetables become scarce. You could then eat a bhakri with a simple onion and a dry chutney mixed with a little oil. Another Maharashtrian traditional dry chutney is the **Methkut,** a mixture of rice ,wheat, udad dal , chana dal ,moong dal in equal quantitities alongwith small quantinties of coriander (dhania)seeds , cumin(jeera) seeds , methi (fenugreek) and pinch of khada masala like hing , dalchini , jai fal all finely powdered in the grinder to give a dry chutney. This is best had with soft a spoonful ghee ans pinch of salt. A filling but soothing dish for the hungry tummy.

These dry chutneys are also called Podi's in South of India. Dry chutney powders are a kind of chutney which are in dry powdered form. In every South Indian house, it is very common to find at least one or two podi varieties at all times. The Telugu people and Tamil Brahmans mostly like to start off their meal with a little podi rice. A little podi is mixed with steamed rice and some ghee is drizzled on top. After having this, rice is had with other curries and sides. Even in traditional restaurants podi is surely served.

Usually wet chutneys cannot be stored for more than a couple of days. These dry chutney powders can be stored for 3-6 months in air tight jars. It can be served with rice or other food items like idli, dosa, uthappam, paniyaaram etc. It is typically mixed with some ghee or sesame seed (gingelly) oil and consumed. The best thing about having these podi's on hand is that they make busy mornings and evenings on a working day very easier. Instead of making a curry, rice or idli or dosa can be instantly served with some podi. Its not only satisfying but very tasty too. These podis come handy during long road trips or train journeys. Rice or Idlis with some podi stays good for more than a day in room temperature. Podi varieties are a good companion to hostelers. College students who are away from home can still enjoy some homemade podi with rice.

There are many varieties of podis made depending on the region. There is the **idli podi** from Tamil Nadu, kandi (red lentil) podi from Andhra Pradesh, poondu (garlic) podi, chammandhi podi (with roasted coconut) from Kerala, peanut podi, curry leaf (karuvepilai) podi etc. There are also podis made with vegetables which are dry roasted. The shelf life of these may not be very long. There is also podi made with dried fish (karuvaatu podi) and with dried prawns (chemmen chammandhi).

Most widely eaten podi is the Milagi Podi made famous by the numerous Udipi Restaurants serving the hot piping idli's and dosai's. There are people like me who love to have this as an accompaniment even if there is sambar, chutney or other curry as a side for idli or dosa. It is so tasty, you have to try it to believe it.

Then again the taste of fresh wet chutney is all to gether different. Mostly in coconut base there atleast 50 varieties in India to make you smack your lips.

The most widely accepted and eaten wet chutney are those served in Udpi restaurants along with Dosa's and Idli. There is the white chutney with a hint of asafetida (hing) and spiked with a tadka of mustard seed and red chilly most likely the southern variety of Bedgi . Then there is the red chutney with a spicy touch best eaten with crispy Rava Sada or smeared on the Mysore Sada. If you order the need dosa that soft velvety dosa made of rice flour and which melts in your mouth while eating , you will be served with 2 more varieties of chutneys the green one made with coriander and a hint of lemon to give it a tangy taste and a simple sweet chutney made from jaggery and desiccated fresh coconut

If you are in Hyderabad , formerly in Andhra Pradesh and now part of the new state of Telangana ou will be fascinated with their rich culture of chutney's . Each made of unheard of ingredients and excotic to the person north of the Vindhyas. They have the Carrot Chutney made of sweet carrots which goes well with the Dal wada or the Pessaratu Dosa, then there is the thick an delicious Penut Capsicum chutney which is served even with thier rice preparations. Or some unusal one like the **Dondakaya Pachadi** or the **Tindora chutney as** known in Hindi. Another unique chutney is made from **Gongura or the sour leaves known as Ambadi** in Marathi and Pitwaa in Hindi. A blackish semi dry chutney served with Southern Paratha .

But if you are a fan of the samosa or kachori do head to D.Damodar's at Dadar TT circle and ask for their kajur (dates) and imli chutney a sweet sour combination which goes well with the hot farsan snack. If you buy fresh fafda a typical Gujarati farsan snack you can ask for the special yellow chutney , a sweet and salty combination with crunchy taste mostly served at Tea time in morning. Fafda made from Gram Flour and Chutney combination of Gram Flour with Curd, Green Chilies.

Another typical regional delight is the sweet curd-based chutney served with Maharashtrian fasting snack of Sabu dana wada. A mixture of coconut , peanuts and curd and lightly sweetened to give a unique taste. If you a are the spicy type do try the Kolhapuri thecha a pure fiery chutney made of what else but chilies. Eaten with Bhakri this is sure to put your mouth on fire and smoke through your ears .But you will love the taste so much you will surely ask for more with your teary eyes.

So try these mouthwatering accompaniments with your dished .

Try them one by one and enjoy your meal with Dips, Sauces , Podi's and Chutneys ...

CHAPTER FOURTEEN

Band Baaja .... Visarjan

Last Tuesday was **Anant Chaturdashi , Bappa's immersion day** . The end of the 10 day festivity when the much loved and adored God Ganapti Bappa the rotund Lambodar comes down from his abode in the heavens to stay with his devotees . Bhakts across communities in huge pandals or in tiny homes. A mini vacation for the kids to revel in festivities , fun and sweets. Gobbling up the modak pedas like the god himself. A day of the final journey back to his abode in the sky. With a wish of every lips **" Ganpati Bappa Morya .....Pudhchya Varshi Lavkar Yaa"**

Each year right from my childhood in this magical place of Matunga , this day of Anant Chaturdashi is celebrated with grand fervor on the roads of Matunga. With huge idols of the Ganesha from various Ganesh Mandals of not just Matunga but its neighbourhood's like Sion –Dharavi-Koliwada (GTB Nagar) and even from as far as Chembur –Panjarpole- and Vashi naka ,being taken on Trucks and trailers to be immersed in the sea front at Girgaon or Dadar Chowpatty . We as a family make it a point to go down to the main raod of B.A. Ambedkar Road enjoying the sights and sound. Yes the immense sound of the Visarjan procession, each mandal trying to out do the other in terms of the song and dance routine played out on the streets. The noise pollution activist would be at their wits end about all this cacophony. But in the midst of all this cacophony there are certain gems.

Head to Ruia Naka for the now famous well-choreographed and well-co-ordinated procession. Organized by the College students of Ruia and Poddar this Ganesh Mandal boasts of nearly 20 year history of the **"Vidyartghaynch Raja"** among all the other Raja's from Fort Cha Icchapurti Raja to the Chincjpokli Cha Raja to Parel Cha Raja to Andheri Cha Raja and the all famous Lalbaug Cha Raja. This Vidyarthyancha Raja is dedicated to the students and celebrated as the Vidya Daivat the Lord of Education. Hosted for 10 days at the Ruia Naka which otherwise is famous for Student gatherings and Gossip mongering or the acts of naïve romance and wooing. A Panda is hoisted at the corner or the road half on the footpath half on the road but not much disturbing the usual traffic. Each year the theme is about some current topic from Sportswomen getting us medals at Rio Olympics to this years 125 years of Sarvajaniik Ganesh Festival Celebration promoted by Bal Gangadhar Tilak or the Lokmanya.

On the immersion day their procession is not to be missed for the real traditional fan fare. The show strats with special mandals brought from as far as Nashik , Pune and even Kolhapur. This year it was the turn of **"Nyana Prabhodhini Mandal"** to mesmerize the crowds with their traditional acts. The procession was lead by a group of nearly 20 -30 young men with wooden sticks called the **Tiprya.** Dancing to the rhythmic beats of the **Nashik Dhol and Tashaa.** Starting with simple moves of beating the sticks to give a loud and steady click , to manoeuvring themselves into a short dance much like the Gujarati

Dandiya, but looking more masculine and filled with Veer Rasa as compared to Dandiya which more feminine filled with Shringar Rasa. These dancers were followed by again a groups of boys / young men palying out a dance simply by clapping their hands and moving in rhythm to the beats of the Dhol. Again much similar to the Gujrati Garba but minus the huge circle in which it is played. The more different we think our communities are the more examples of similar traditions immerge in such art forms.

But the loudest cheer ad roar went out to the group of men carrying enourmous drums the "Dhol" requiring real strength not just to carry them but also to beat them in rhythmic action giving out sounds of **"Dhum – Dhum"** , **drowning out all other sounds** . If you listen closely you can hear the all-pervading sound of the Omkar in its beats . The eternal sound from which this universe itself was created . Well supported by the strong sounds emanating from the flat drums known as Tashaa. The combined sound of Dhol and Tashaa reverberating in the sky and making the atmosphere magical. The procession winding down the by-lane and finally concluding as they reached the main road

This procession is always followed by a small mandal with its pristine Ganesh moorthi decked up on a small tempo truck. The uniqueness being the music being played out by the local boys in true Mumbaiyaa style – **The Banjo Party**. The Banjo or the Bulbul Tarang literally meaning "waves of nightingale". The Banjo or the Bulbul Tarang is an instrument which employs two sets of strings, one set for drone, and one for melody. The strings run over a plate or fretboard, while above are keys resembling typewriter keys, which when depressed fret or shorten the strings to raise their pitch.The sound coming out a unique mix and when played by experts sounding ethereal . The current version used is the electric one with an amplifier plugged in and more sounding like a Rockstars Guitar. And the songs selected are typically loud but enjoyable by the masses .

A sharp contrast is the procession of the richest **Ganpati Mandal the GSB Mandal of Wadala** where the Ganesh idol is bedecked with gold and diamond jewelry worth Crores. All part of the royal procession for the Visarjan. The Sevaks and the priests bring out the reagal moorthi amidst holy chants and brass bells rung and metallic gongs being struck. The idol is then placed on the Truck with all its majesty , decorated with freshest flowers and more jewellery fit for the King of Gods. The truck is followed by musical band performing on traditional south Indian drums called the Mridangam to be played sideways and Kanjira the more robust drum palyed with wooden sticks and held verial and hung from the players neck just like the Dhol. These are accompanied by the long wind instrument of Nadaswaram. Belting out traditional Carnatic music and devotional songs. The procession winding down from the landmark temple of Ram at Wadala to the road connecting the Khodadad Circle od the Dadar TT circle. Led by the musicians followed by GSB sevaks dressed in traditional orange dhoti and white angavastram some chanting some playing the Thaalam – brass cymbals. Followed by the women folk in rich Silk sarees in a well disciplined line trowing petals and flowers in reverence to **the Lord Ganesha lord of 14 Vidyas and 64 Kala's , Ekdanta, Vakratunda and the destroyer ot obstruction – The Vighnaharta....**

The night of revelry coming to an end with the sounds getting milder milder till they disappear into the dark sky, only the faint chants reverberate the air as we bid good bye to the most loved God our Bappa with final cheers of

Ganpati Bappa Moryaa...Pudchya Varshi Lavkar Yaa...

CHAPTER FIFTEEN

Bandra Fair.....

When you say Fair or Jatra what comes to your mind..the huge crowds , floodlight paths leading upto the sanctum sanctorum of a holy place, giggling kids , protective parents hold their children, the.. Ferries Wheels (Giant Wheels) , the food stalls , all the nick-knacks and the hearts filled with joy. Last Sunday we as in me and the missus decided to relive our childhood days through our kids Netra and Bhakti.We decided to visit the famous Bandr Fair..

The **Bandra Fair** is celebrated in the pious vicinity of the **Mount Mary Church in Bandra** . It starts on the Sunday following September 8th , the birth day of Mother Mary , mother of Jesus the Son of God.The Bandra Fair is commemoration of the Nativity of Mary or the Birth of the Virgin Mary and celebrated at the **Basilica of Our Lady of the Mount or locally called as the Mount Mary Church** a Roman Catholic Church located at Bandra . According to historical records, the statue of 'Our Lady of Navigators' was in the chapel at the mount from 1700 to 1760. It is said that in 1760 Arab pirates attacked Bandra and they chopped one of the arm of the statue. The statue was later reinstalled in 1761. Over the years the Virgin of the Mount came to be known in different names in colloquial **Marathi, 'Matha Mavli', 'Mothi Mavli' and now 'Mot Mavli'** The 9 days before the Bandra Fair, from 1 September, 2017 to 9 September, 2017, Mount Mary Basilica performs "*Novena*" (prayer) for the Blessed Virgin Mary

The actual fair starts on the 10th day .It is estimated that the Bandra Fair is around 300 years old. The fair started when a statue of Mother Mary was found floating in the Arabian Sea between 1700 and 1760, which, according to a legend, a Koli fisherman had dreamt about a few years earlier.

During the Bandra Fair, the entire area is decorated with festoons and buntings. Besides the religious experience, Bandra Fair also includes the social experience of relaxing, camaraderie, alms-giving and enjoyment. There is an atmosphere of fun as we go through the various stalls that constitute the Fair. During Mumbai's Bandra Fair, 430 temporary stalls selling religious artifacts, food, toys, clothes, handicraft items, etc, are set up at Mount Mary Church, Kane Road, Mt Mary Road, Eastern steps of Mount Mary Church, St John Baptist Road and Rebello Road. Most of these stalls are allocated to local residents.

We took a rickshaw from Sion to reach this place. In hindsight it was the best decision as we could avoid getting trapped in the traffic jams along the road as the rickshaw wallah deftly maneuverer the rick going extreme left or zig zag through the bumper to bumper traffic from Bandra Reclamation towards Mount Mary Roads. We alighted at Kaner road and decided to walk the rest of the away to experience the thrill of the Fair. Our first stop was obviously the Giant Wheel for the kids , though little Bhakti was a little terrified still she enjoyed and had fun holding her elder sister Netra for dear life.

Next stop was the multi coloured merry go round in shape of gleaming cars and all lighted up. This Bhakti enjoyed with full vigour. Once done we started to walk further looking at all the stalls lining the streets. We picked a couple of Tiara's for the kids with white flowers , wearing them they looked like cute Flower girls from a Christian weddings. We moved along , a stall selling bright pink Cotton Candy Floss caught my eye as also of my mischievous little princess. Bought the soft candy floss and enjoyed its sweet flavour. As we walked further we noticed many more stalls.

There were stalls , which sold roasted grams, sweet items, religious objects like wax figures of the Virgin Mary, along with an assortment of candles shaped like hands, feet and various other parts of the body. The sick and suffering choose one that corresponds to their ailment and light it in Church, with the pious hope that Mother Mary will consider their appeals for help.

As we reached the Church we could see the preparation of the late mass in the small ground adjoining the Church. We then entered the Church to a spellbinding view. The Statue of Virgin Mary with the child Jesus was decorated with fresh flower arches and satin ribbons. Looking at her face you could feel the energy radiating in the holy precinct. We folded our hand in reverence and prayed . It does not matter of which religion you belong as long as you have faith in the Higher power in the sky. We saw many non catholics who had come from far sub-urbs with families in tow offering candles and offering a silent prayer. I enjoyed looking at the frescos on the walls of the Church depicting the birth of Christ , the The 3 wise men and their journey to find the baby Jesus on the dark and silent night of Christmas eve.The rising star and the smiling baby Jesus born in the barn. The experience was exhilarating .We then moved out to see the spectacular and pristine white Arches brightly lit with the statue of Mother Mary . The monument looking beautiful with the dark sky in back drop.

We decided to walk back to the base. Lining the church steps were stalls selling sweets and food delicacies such as Mawa Pedha, Home-made Cakes (wine, Plum, walnut, dates), Guava cheese, Fuggias, Kadio Bodia (Goan dish made of sugar and flour), Sorpotel, Vindaloo, Dodol (Goan sweet), etc. Bought some Goan authentic Khaja those sweet sticks and later some toys from the neighbouring stalls. There were stalls selling the famous Aam poli and Fanas poli and some selling salted namkeens brought from Kerala.

We descended the steps and reached the street below . Ready to leave I Looked back one last time at the Church , it was glowing in the lights or was it the rays of hope emanating from the Mother herself , spreading a halo of reassurance among all those who visited her in this earthly abode.....

CHAPTER SIXTEEN

Matunga Special... Agarbatti , Coffee and more

I have been writing about a lot of things , about my experiences while travelling through the lengths and breadths of India , its cultural diversity , natural landscapes and of course the gastronomical delights . But how can I forget my sweet old Matunga , that quaint little place some where between Dadar and Sion whose boundaries though not well defined but filled with unique & mesmerizing shades of emotions like a flamboyant painting with the sky as the Canvas made by the Creator Himself.

Figure this where do you remember having qued up the last time around. May be at Siddhivinayak Temple for the Darshan of Lord Gajanana , or at the movie theater if you have not booked your tickets on BookmyShow , or outside some government office for getting some important documents or if your are the old school outside the Telephone or Electric Company office to pay your bill. But have at any time come across an shop selling Agarbattis so famous that people que to get them.

Its here in Matunga in on of its by-lanes you will fiind **Acharya Products** largest traders of agarbattis or incense sticks since 1956 that you will find literally people queing up on occasion like Gudi Padwa or Pongal or the upcoming Dushera . The serpentine que starting at the shop on Laxmi Narayan Lane right upto the Kabutarkhana in Matunga market a good 100-150 meters. Acharya Products was founded by K Y Acharya in 1928 as a incense trading house and later started manufacturing some of the brands themselves. Currently managed by the 2nd generation and head of the family Raghu Achrya. They are sole distributors for nearly 32 manufactures and 500 fragant varieties of incense sticks beside another 10-12 manufactures of Dhoop sticks and brands.The first thing that hits you when you enter the shop is the heady mix of fragrances of all the incense sticks. Theres the strong smell of Kevda or a Mogra , mild scent of Champa or the sweet smell of Chandan . The shop is strewn with row upon row of neatly stacked packets of incense sticks in various sizes from small 10 stick pack to 100 stick packs to the packet on weights of 100 gms to 500 gms. They stock the usual variety of Gulab , Jasmine , Chandan & Lavender and even exotics fragrances like Musk , Akashphool, Amber and Marie Gold . Even some trending scents like Citronella and Fruit Blast.You will not only find individuals buying these incense sticks in small lots but also small retailers coming from across the city to buy in bulk quantities. As habit they keep small smples of the latests fragrances to be included in these large orders as a way of Marketing their stock.

If you ask Raghu Acharya who sometimes sits at the cash counter , what is their specialty , he proudly says , their expertise lies in accessing and assisting their customer's requirements in regard to quality of incense , fragrance and packaging. They have earned their reputation for maintaining strict delivery schedules and by offering competitive prices. They have huge stock of all leading brands and even have an listed Export company to ship these products to 58 countries like US , UK , Eupore , UAE and even some African countries where there is a large population of Inidans. They pride themselves on their products not containing any restricted forest produce or any species of wild fauna and flora and which are listed in the Appendices of the Convention on International Trade. A notice to this effect prominently displayed in the shop.They have been awarded the Top Exporter in Handicraft category for 3 successive years between 2002-2204 and the only company in this category to get this Hat trick of a award.To cater to the Western world they have now expanded into Natural oil based Soaps and Toiletries and even Aroma oils for Aroma Therapy at leading Spa's .So next time you are in Matunga and need some incense stick or dhoop sticks trust your sense of smell and walk in the dirction your nose tells you in this by lane and you will find yourself standing in front of Archarya Product written in bold Red on a Turmeric Yellow backdrop and with an interesting tag line "Bhakti Me Laye Shakti"...

If you trust your sense of smell walk just opposite to a small hole in the wall kind of shop just next to Hotel Ram Ashraya called **Quality Tea & Coffee.** If you are a lover and a Coffee / Tea addict this is the shop for you. They have been serving their loyal clientele since 1958 . This too started as a trading shop selling tea and coffee from tea estates especially from the south in Coorg and from up east in Darjeeling. They have now started manufacturing their own blends of both tea an coffee under the Quality

Tea & Coffee brand. Here you will get the finest variety of coffee which can be custom blended in 60:40 or 70:30 ratio of Coffee Arabica & Chicory. Or you could pick the pre-blended French coffee a strong brew to release your day long stress . They also sell coffee beans – Peaberry beans , Plantation beans in raw or roasted form which can be hand crushed or crushed using coffee machines to brew you own drink.

For tea lovers like me they have a wide selection from the standard CTC to Hiltop dust which is extra strong. Some other blended variety like A1 Premium , Mast ,Rasrang and Radical CTC .Where CTC referes to the tea processing term of Cut Toasted and Curled .They even keep newer Falvoured teas like Jasmine tea, Peach tea Orange Pekos , Premium Green Peko and Green Tea .Other flavours suited to the hard core teaf buff are **Lemon Grass (Gavti Chaha) , Cardamom (Elaichi), Cinnamon (Dalchini) , Tulsi , Ginger and even Rose flavored** .Brew these in milk as per tradition or drink it black to savoir its flavor .

Ek chuski chai ki ek pyaali sehath ki......

As I said Matunga is a place I am still discovering even after staying here for 40 years there are still secrets that lay hidden in its by-lanes like layers of a rose petals that need to be peeled one by one to reveal its beauty and fragrance...

CHAPTER SEVENTEEN

Desi Fizz....

Growing up as kids the best attraction during birthday parties was the cold glass of fizzy drinks like Goldspot or Thums Up. Till date we are habituated to drinking these carbonated drinks during dinners or at home for the fizz and most often than not to relieve us of the bloated feeling we get after a heavy meal. But sometimes you can try some offbeat drinks which not only give the end result but are great in taste too.

What do think when you hear the word 'GOA"....Beach , Beer , Babes ..Fun ..Frolic but did you notices those small shack like shops dotting the beaches or the pathway toward the famous temples like Mangueshi or Shanta Durga Temple. On any given scorching day you will find some cold drink –beverage shop for the average teetotaller like selling those cool cool drink made from the odd looking green bottles. If you keen observe these bottles they are deep bottle green with a contorted neck capped with a you guessed it right a marble or a Goti in local Konkani / Marathi language. Ask the fellow selling them to make you a drink and like an expert bartender , he will mix a little sugar solution from his earthen matka / steel drum ,with some jaljira masala , squeeze a juicy lemon into the glass and then finally top it up with the bubbly soda from the green bottle.

The marble will be depressed using a mini wooden mallet and the soda flowing out with the gas holding the marble to the bottle mouth with a squeaking sound....chooooiiiii. This is expertly mixed in the glass and served with ice. Drink it to quench your thirst and feel releaved from the heat and humidity of Goa. This local fizzy drink is local to Konkan and some parts of Norther India where it is known as "Banta"

Banta also known as **Fotash Jawl** in Bengali, **Goli Soda** (Goli = spherical object in Hindi) or **Goti Soda** (Goti = marble in Hindi) is a colloquial term for a carbonated lemon or orange-flavoured soft drink popular in India. Though the origin of its name is from Punjabi word for marble (banta), Banta has been sold since the late 19th century,long before popular carbonated drinks arrived. The drink is often sold mixed with lemon juice, crushed ice, chaat masala and kala namak (black salt) as a carbonated variant of popular lemonades shikanjvi or jal-jeera.It is available at street-sellers known as bantawallahs.

And if you are in and around Vadodara you can always go to the local Soda Shop . You can identify the small shop which is always surrounded by a crowd of about 30 people.It consists of two soda dispensers and several employees. On the counter will be a wooden box sectioned into a few dozen compartments, each with a plastic cup of soda - sort of an assembly line, allowing the staff to handle many orders at once. Several plastic bottles sit on one end of the counter. fashioned into squeeze bottles, some will be filled with fresh lemon juice and plain or flavored syrups. There will be canisters with spices and rock salt. A couple of employees fill the cups with soda water and placed them in the compartments for a third employee — the flavor man — to finish with syrups and spices. You will be amazed at how quickly and gracefully they move, like dancers, effortlessly squeezing fresh lemon juice, squirting in syrups and mixing in condiments, handing the finished sodas to customers. I remember the first time I tried a nimbusoda. The first sip flooded my mouth with fresh lemon and spices that I'd never expected in a cup of soda: chili pepper, cumin, ginger, black salt. Sweet, salty, Savory and a bit funky all at once. This was not just soda. This was masala soda, the single most flavourful sip of my entire trip, and I needed more.

The flavor I tried was the aerated cousin of nimbupani, a sweet and salty lemonade or limeade that many Indians drink to stay hydrated during hot summers. But there's a myriad other Flavors. The masala could contain as little as white salt, black salt and cumin, or an endless list of spices including amchoor(dried, powdered sour mango), black pepper, ginger, chili pepper (dried or fresh), turmeric, asafoetida, mint, even *anar dana* (dried pomegranate seed powder). A popular flavour in Mumbai and the state of Gujarat is *jal jeera,* a spice mix with roasted cumin that's otherwise used for another traditional summer drink of the same name — jaljeeraliterally translates to cumin water. The other most important ingredient of this masala is the *kala namak*, or black salt.

It's a rock salt containing sulphur, which lends a pungent, almost eggy smell to the drink. Carbonated water gives the drink effervescence, which can be further enhanced with a simple syrup and nimbu(meaning lemon or lime) juice or a fruit flavoured drink called sherbet. Sometimes its even served with commercial sodas, like Thumbs Up (an Indian cola) or Sprite. But the best combination is when had with pure soda .A drink with a punch and bubbly but with out the side effect effects of an alcoholic drink...

When down south in Chennai, a mysterious drink with a hint of dark fruityness flourishes in refrigerators all over the Tamil Land. Its placebo effect in case of an upset stomach is legendary. Locals will tell you that it is the one thing you should drink after a kari dosa or other fiery eats from the Chennai's streets. So when crates of Kalimark's Bovonto are unloaded from the local old cycletrailer at small tea stalls , there is a happy clamour. "Bovonto is timeless," says owner of Zam Zam Tea Shop, receiving three crates of south India's oldest homegrown soft drink. Forty-seven-year-old Mani, one of over two dozen Kalimark distributors in town, supplies to 60 shops every morning before popping open a bottle of grapey goodness for himself. I don't think Bovonto

will ever go out of business. For a generation of Tamils, soft drink is "colour" and colour is the neon orange pop of Torino or the caramel tint of Bovonto. A true-blue Indian soda pop that refused to cede the battleground to multinational colas, Bovonto is a formulation of the century-old Kali Aerated Water Works. Worth over Rs 100 crore, it continues to expand its footprint in south India.

Every year, the cola wars pit blue against red, Pepsi against Coke, 7Up against Dew as the multinationals stake out their territories across India. But, like the last outpost of Gaul defiance against the Romans, homegrown sodas survive in many parts of India — their fabled histories reminders of older times, their quirky flavours a part of many memories. In 1977, as Coca-Cola was beating a retreat from India under the provisions of the Foreign Exchange Regulation Act, Torino, an orange soda with a prodigious use of sugar, entered the market in south India. In no time, they had captured 90 per cent of Karnataka's orange soda market, says Pankaj Lakhani, the second-generation owner and MD of Bangalore Soft Drinks runs the business now. Torino has since been re-launched in PET

For homegrown soft drinks, trouble began to bubble over with the consolidation in the Indian carbonated beverage industry in 1993. Coca-Cola staged a comeback, acquiring Parle's classic Indian sodas — Thums Up, Limca, Citra and Gold Spot — and small local brands began a slide to obsolescene. PepsiCo picked up Duke's stable of masala sodas and Campa-Cola, a relic of socialist India, fizzled out.

A few unlikely survivors of the cola wars are now riding a wave of nostalgia and slaking the thirst of middle India. Torino, Bovonto, Sosyo and other sodas today cater largely to a niche outside the big cities that has tended to slip through the cracks of multinational brands. Even if they haven't been as fortunate, other brands continue to be a part of the lore of the cities they sprung up in. Like Delhi's banta. A lemon soda packed in quaint Codd bottles, and spiked with a kick of kala namak,

they are sold in carts across the city. Pandit Ved Prakash Lemon Wale, a shop in Chandni Chowk, has been selling the lemony drink for "at least 150 years" now. But local suppliers say the drink has lost its edge to bigger brands.

Of the triumvirate of raspberry sodas —Duke's, Roger's and Pallonji — of the Parsi community in Mumbai for over a century, only one remains. PV Solanki has been bottling Pallonji, a drink with a 149-year-old legacy, since 1979. He can not take on big brands, and if they flexed their muscles, there is no way he would be able to survive. So Pallonji's decided to make their own market, as Solanki. Instead of servicing Mumbai, Pallonji is distributed within a 100-km radius of its only bottling plant in the suburb of Mankhurd. Within city limits, you can find it at Irani stores and select petrol pumps if you are lucky. With a turnover of Rs 1.45 crore, Pallonji employs all of 40 people and Solanki says the business continues to be profitable

A trip to Surat in Gujarat is incomplete without a glug of Sosyo, a local pre- Independence-era soft drink that was an offshoot of the Swadeshi movement. Launched in 1923 by Hajoori & Sons in Zampabazaar, Sosyo's theme was **"Apna desh apna drink"** and its **USP an alcohol-like flavour**. The manufacturers recently repackaged and re-launched the product to survive competition, but there was a time when Sosyo was the only drink Surtis ever needed. It combined the flavours of apple and grape to position itself as an alternative to wine in a dry state, an after dinner digestive and a refreshing aerated beverage.

Indians love their masala sodas so much, that even global and regional companies are now bottling them. In 2012, Coca Cola relaunched a bottled masala cola called **RimZim that they bought in 1994, and PepsiCo India released 7up Nimbooz Masala Soda.**

But these commercial sodas lack customization and the atmosphere of a soda shop, which is a big part of the masala soda experience. As I learned in Vadodara, these Shops are also social hubs, especially in dry states like Gujarat that lack bars. It's a meeting place where people gather to sip masala soda and talk with their friends.

I tasted one my favourite masala soda from one such street vendor in Mumbai. It was made from kokum (an Indian mangosteen), which is not available commercially. For 20 rupees , I sipped my sweet, sour and mildly savory soda as I watched small groups of friends come and go, drinking their sodas and chatting. The taste and memory have lingered on till date.

And to let you into a family secret. A standing joke in our extended family is that whenever we go out for a family dinner, the bill is never requested till my wifey Kashmira asks for a Fresh Lime Soda – sweet and salted. That is the sign that the family dinner has come to a close much like a closing ceremony of a super special event. After a lot of leg pulling and laughing at her expense ,everyone on the dinner table has a sip of that cool drink .Finally with a large burp of satisfaction over the food we ate , there is a smile on our lips and fond memories of time well spent....

So Enjoy these Desi Fizzy drinks till they are still around fighting the large MNC's . More power to these real foot soldiers of the Make In India campaign....

CHAPTER EIGHTEEN

Interval ka mazaa.......Samose ke Saath.

If you are an avid movie buff and like to watch Bollywood / Hollywood movies on 70 mm in a single screen theater with the regular Aam junta like me .Enjoying the roller-coaster ride of action emotion, comedy and drama ... thoda rona –dhona ...thodi hasi aur bahut sara family fun and when the cinema screen flashes the sign of Intermission rush out to the snack counter with only one mission get that hot packets of , yes you guessed it right Samosaaaa...

Did you you know that more than 80% of the single screens across Mumbai serve that special crispy triangulated deep fried snack known as Samosa made by only one vendor and is famously known as A1 Samosa.They are among the most famous samosa makers in Mumbai. They make about 15000-18000 samosas a day and supply more 30 movie halls in the city.

Those crunchy, spicy, potato-filled triangles of happiness can make a bad movie tolerable and a good movie awesome! But to get an A-1 samosa, you don't have to go to the cinema, where they're priced quite high. At their main shop in Sion, near my house, it's 12 rupees a samosa.

The shop's nothing fancy, and it's often hidden from view behind a row of parked vehicles. But it's always bustling with customers. The Punjabi samosa is their classic offering – it's the potato-filled one you get in all the theatres. Their other favourites are the Cheese-Corn Samosa and the Chinese Samosa. The Chinese ones are stuffed with bright red, schezwan-flavoured noodles – but they're really not as strange as they sound. They also have a sweet variety in the Sweet Mawa Samosas but I have never tried it myself,. Do let me know how it tastes if any of you ever get top eat one. A recent addition is the Palak Paneer Samosa They are filled with paalak and paneer (spinach and cottage cheese). Bu t if you ask name which would I pick with doubt it will be their classic Punjabi Samosa.

A-1 was established more than 40 years ago by Kishanchand Nevendram, a Sindhi who came to Mumbai from Karachi, after the Partition. He is said to have left everything he had behind in Karachi. His grandson now owns the business.

There are two locations where the samosas are made: the first is at Champaklal Estate, Sion East. Here, the masala / stuffing is made, and the samosas are rolled into their typical triangular shape. From Champaklal, it is taken to the A-1 outlet in Sion West, where the samosas are first 'half-fried' and kept ready. Then they are deep fried in batches and brought out front. From here, they're distributed to retail shops, cinemas, school and office canteens, caterers and party organisers. As each batch gets sold or distributed, new batches are deep fried.

The distribution process is interesting: there is an army of freelance entrepreneurs on cycles, who buy samosas from A-1 daily, and sell them to various buyers across the city. Typically they have a 1 rupee margin per samosa. Sales are made in lots of 150 or 250 samosas (there is a weighing machine, so the samosas are placed on trays and weighed, not counted). Each freelance entrepreneur has his own set of contacts/buyers across the city to whom he sells.

So if you go to A-1 at any time of the day, you can see hot samosas, coming right out of giant iron woks, being piled into trays, then loaded on cycles and being taken away. The large trays you see in this photo above can hold 250.So if you're ever walking around in Sion, don't forget to stop by at A-1 samosa.

If you ask me Samosa is to the North Indians what vada pav is to us Maharashtrians. An any time snack and served best with a hot piping cutting chai – adrak mar ke.

What's rather interesting is that while this Savory snack is popular across the country, each state pretty much has its own version. For instance, the Punjabi samosais dominated by potatoes and peas, with raisins and cashews added in to enhance the flavour. In Gujarat, the patti samosa is quite popular. And this one is stuffed with finely chopped potatoes that are allowed to cook in the oil as the samosa is fried. The patti is also made with wheat flour instead of maida(refined flour) because cabbage is often an important ingredient, and refined flour can't quite hold that ingredient together.

The Bengali samosa, which is referred to as the singara, uses potato's and peas, and cauliflower, and even peanuts for a little crunch. Even though it's hot thanks to the chillies used, it's much milder than other samosas when it comes to the spice factor. In Karnataka, onion samosasis a big hit, as is keema samosa, made popular by some of the local bakeries. In Delhi, apart from the potato samosa, the one with keema, khova, or even moong dal are quite popular. Now let's go on a samosatrail, looking for some of the best in different parts of the country.

If in Delhi head to the Manohar Dhaba in Chandni Chowk that serves what is known as the Japani Samosa and no one know why it's called so. However, it apparently has 60 layers of flour, and is filled with potatoes. It's served with chhole and a pickle. Another famous samosa specialist is **Munni Lal Halwai** at Gole Market , he is famous for the classic potato samosa. Served with mint chutney, this shop seems to have perfected the recipe. And At **Kumar Samose Wala** near Milan Cinema in Karampura has quite a surprising range of samosas – starting with ones filled with peas and paneer, sweet corn, moong dal, vegetarian keema paneer, and even chowmein!

The samosa or singara in Kolkata is practically woven in to the Bengali food culture. And it's often served with sweet jalebis. Across stores, you get different varieties of the samosa. While most serve the more commercially viable samosa, the true flavour of the singara remains in the hands of the local sweetshops; stuffed with peas and potatoes and peanut, and if the shop is slightly upmarket, you'll also find bits of cauliflower florets in it.

Most famous Samosa wala is Tewari Sweets in Bara Bazaar is still known to have some of the best samosas in town, perfecting the art of spicing the filling, and frying the pastry in ghee. **Deckers Lane** and **BBD Bag** are known for their street food and this is also where you'll find some of the best Bengali and North Indian samosas. **Mrityunjoy Ghosh & Sons** on Sarat Bose Road, a century-old rundown sweetshop, is also quite popular for their Bengali samosa, stuffed with cauliflower of course.

Chennai has a few samosa stores it can boast about. Located in Anna Nagar is **The Samosa Factory** that serves up some decent ones. The Chinese samosa seems to be quite popular – filled with cabbage, beans, carrots, and potatoes, and cooked in soy and chillies – and is, let's put it this way, interesting. Tucked away in Adayar is **Rajpal's Street Snacks** , which serves rather good samosas too. The pastry and the filling are cooked just right.

Bombay Lassi on Ellis Road, apart from its lassi, is rather popular for their samosas too, and you get to eat them with sweet brown, and a green tangy dip. The **Tirunelveli Halwa Stall** , located on Valluvar Kottam High Road, is yet another place to go for the samosa in Chennai. The make fresh batches twice a day, and that contributes to the popularity of the place. Or, you could just head over to **Sowcarpet** to treat yourself to lots of those deep-fried triangles in plenty of tiny stores that dot the area.

Think of samosas in Bengaluru and you're reminded of **Albert Bakery's** keema samosas. . They're as crunchy as it can get, and decadent. If you have a slightly posh palate, most of the five star hotel coffee shops serve the samosa. But the flavour truly is on the streets. From the onion variety that is served at tiny roadside tea stalls across the city, to some of the popular sweet shops, one can literally find all kinds of samosas in the city. **Banchharam**, with its three outlets (Koramangala, Marathahalli, and Ulsoor), probably serves the best Bengali singara in the city.

The ones at **Bhagatram Sweets** in Commercial Street are considered to be one of the best in town though.

So next you are in mood for a fried snack with your cuppa of chai just go for this puckka desi snack of Samosa . eat away at the crunchy outer cover and bite in to the masale wala alu stuffing , dip it in the mint chutney or that plate of hot chole mixed with sweet and spicy imli ki chutney.. Lip-smacking and to die for.

CHAPTER NINETEEN

Diwali Icon's

Its been raining for last couple of days. Every evening around 6 PM it gets dark with black clouds looming in the sky . And it starts to rain followed by loud bangs of Thunder and Lightning as if it's a Special Light and Sound Show from the God's above. Its October and its still raining in Mumbai , I say to the Missus " Looks like Diwali will be a Damp Squib like all other festivals this year. Will have to light the Fire Crackers in the morning s at this rate". She Laughs . I hear Netra mouthing some lines with animated expression , I ask her what it is she is saying. She loudly proclaims " **Utha Utha Sakal Zhali Moti Sabnachi Vel Zhali" And we all have hearty laugh.**

Yes its true those were the nostalgics days . I still remember in my childhood getting up on Narak Chaturdashi the 1st day of Diwali really early at 5.30/6 AM . Bleary eyed made to sit on a wooden pat and Aai aaplying Tel (Oil) .Then taking the **Abhyanga Snaan (Pahli Anghol)** . A hot bath with Kubal Utne (perfumed powder like substance) and Moti Soap. That large round soap in either Sandal or Rose fragrance. The ritual still carried out till date in not only our home but across most homes all across India.

To let you into the history of this Iconic Soap, **Moti** was quite popular during seventies. It is thick round shaped soap positioned as luxury soap.It was a brand of **Tata Oil Mills Company (TOMCO).** In 1993 after merger of TOMCO with HUL, it became the property of HUL. Moti soap was launched keeping in mind certain points to differentiate it from other competitors. Such as its shape and thickness which was different from rest of the competitors. Its name was taken from Hindi language whose meaning is Pearl. It was introduced in differentvariants such as Sandal, Rose and Khus. At the time,Sandal, Rose and Khus were perceived to be precious and devout in our Indian society. In Hindu mythology it has been found that queens used to take bath with exotic herbs and flowers such as Rose,Khas, Sandal etc.In this way soap was positioned as exotic soap. As it was promoted as luxurious soap, it was priced around 25/- per soap in eighties competing other brand such as Dettol, Lux etc. But at the same time as it was quite big in shape so it was long lasting. Packaging was simple with respective colour of variants such as orange for sandal and pink for rose.

It was promoted heavily and as name of product was "Moti", print advertisement was giving importance to pearls. One of the popular print advertisements for magazine shows a soap anchored in big seashell on a beach, just like pearl. It also gave stress on its ingredients. In the nineties Moti was positioned as special occasion soap by its latest TV commercial .TV commercial of Moti soap gave stress on spirituality and purity. In this advertisement an Indian lady was shown as lighting the lamps, making Rangoli and using Moti soap. Overall, the advertisement was all about celebration, purity and tradition. As soap's ingredients are traditional, consumer started to perceive it as special occasion soap such as using at the time of Diwali. After this advertising campaign, Moti has become a special occasion (such as Diwali) soap.

After merger with HUL in 1993 Moti soap lost its sheen and HUL did not focus on this brand much and Moti was lost in the ocean of HUL's other soap products like Lux , Liril Ayush etc.. The fallout was that competitors such as **Mysore sandal soap another Iconic Soap Brand** from down South -Karnataka, local handmade soap and Ayurvedic soaps, HUL's own products started over powering this brand. In addition to this lack of innovation and increasing customer expectation from soap lead to decrease in its sale. It became necessary over time to either reposition the product or to take a strategic decision on the future of the branch because till this time Moti had become a soap which was having seasonal demand than regular demand. HUL relaunched a campaign to get back its market share by airing a new commercial in 2013.This commercial gave stress to the old Indian Diwali Custom of taking bath early in the morning on the first day of Diwali. A chawl has been shown in the commercial where a small boy knocked on everyone's door early in the morning and ask them to take bath with Moti Soap, similar to the habit of an elderly man who carried out this activity in his younger days (bringing the viewer to recall the earlier advertisements of the 80s and 90s). This advertisement was able to create nostalgic feeling among consumers. It was also telecasted in Regional languages of Marathi and Hindi. Overall this advertisement got lot of appreciation from customers and critics. And the loyal customer came back to this Iconic Soap again.

Looking at overall journey of this brand it's a success sustenance for more than 40 years is not an easy task and that too in era of dynamically changing market. While it has a selected and small market, it still has its set of loyal customers. Using Moti soap on special occasion has become a tradition and is getting passed on to next generations as cultural heritage in most of the Indian middle-class family.

Another Icon is the **Kubal Utne or Uptan** available in bright yellow paper packets at small and big retails vendors during the week leading upto Diwali It's a fragrant powdery mixture made of sandal wood powder , multani matti (mud) , neem powder and turmeric. This is applied to the face and the body during the Abhyanga Snaan. The ingredients are such that it nourishes our skin and if used regularly during winters can help in getting its glow back from the winter dryness. A Natural cosmetic passed on from ages

One more icon that strikes you and is so common that we take it for granted is the Calender on the wall...It's the Kalnirnay the Calender cum Almanac designed by the famous Astrologer Jayant Salgaonkar. **Kalnirnay** an apt name as in Marathi it translates to timely decision. It is a calmanac (Calendar +Almanac) published in Mumbai. The almanac gives simplified information about the Panchang, auspicious days, festivals, holidays, sunrise and sunset. It has recipes, stories on health and education, monthly Bhavishya and articles on Hindu astrology.

Kalnirnaya was founded in 1973 by Jayantrao Salgaonkar. It initially started as a hand-printed almanac for Marathi subscribers. At a time when the trend was to give away calenders for free this compact Calmanac which served as a reference point for not just dates and festivals but also gave the common man the power of Panchang with its easy to use auspiscious dates and time all in standard hours and minutes unlike the traditional Ghatika in say a Datte Panchang. The first issue was sold to 10,000 subscribers. It gradually grew to become the largest selling publication in the world, with around 19 million copies being sold annually.

Kalnirnay is published annually, by Sumangal Publishing, as a calendar almanac for all Indian religions. It contains auspicious dates, festivals and celebrations of Hindus, Muslims, Christians, Sikhs, Jains, Buddhists, Parsis and Jews are mentioned in detail. It also provides useful information about Daily Panchang, Shubh Vivah Muhurat, Sankashti Chauturthi Chandroday Timing, Daily Sun Rise – Moon Rise Timings, Monthly Astrological Predictions for all Zodiac Signs, etc. It is published in nine languages -English, Marathi, Hindi, Gujarati, Tamil, Telugu , Kannada, Malyalam and Punjabi with Marathi accounting for the bulk of its readers. In addition to dates and times of religious and cultural relevance, each issue also contains articles on topics such as health, food and beauty

An anecdote as shared by Jayant salgaonkar himself in an interview gives its utility not just for regular dates and auspicious time but also helps meat vendors and butchers to manage the stock of meat looking at the fasting days as mentioned in Kalnirnay. That's called making life simple in its truest form.

In keeping with the times a website was launched in 1996, its desktop e-version (e-kalnirnay) was subsequently launched, and it is now available even as an Android and an iOS app. ... **"Bhinti Wari kalnirnay asave...**

And how can Diwali the festival of Lights be complete without the mention of Fire Crackers . The Fire Crackers from Sivakasi in Tamil Nadu. One more iconic symbol of Diwali is the fire crackers from **Standard Fireworks.**

Standard Fireworks was founded by Sri NRK Rajarathnam in 1942 in the town of Sivakasi. The company started by manufacturing match sticks but later expanded to firework. The pioneer and market leader of firecracker industry in India. Head quartered in Sivakasi (Tamil Nadu), Standard brand of fireworks is available across the country through their retailers and dealers across the length and breadth of India.Just before Diwali you will find small and big shops displaying prominent Standard Brand banners alluring the buyers to choose from their wide variety of products and the new launches. Even today you will find someone in the family may be a distant cousin picking up small stocks of fire crackers and selling to a closed group of known family members and making part time earnings.

The most frequently picked up crackers would be the Sparklers big and small or coloured , Fountains or Flower pots as they are called , those conical crackers that bust into a flare of lights , the Zameen Chakri or circular discs which spin at top speed and release multi colored flares. Or the small barrel bombs like Laxmi Bomb or a Double Barrel which burst twice when ignited. Then there were the small string bombs packed into red or purle paper not more that 3 inches in size but bursts with a loud bangs another most sought after cracker was the Lal Mahal or Red Fort with the label prominently displaying the National Heritage sight the Red Fort in Delhi. Then during our child hood when Anti Sound or Pollution Activism was not as much as it is today , we would be definite to be woken up to those long strings bombs of 100 , 500 ,1000 or even a 5000 laddi bursting a goo 10 minutes. Or if you really wanted a big bang for your money you could burst the green colored sutli (tread) bombs or the yellow box type bombs. And then those who were a little affluent would bring the Rockets (a costly proposition) for the sky show. Once they started to getting competitions from Chinese Fire Cracker players instead of fighting them off they decided to join forces. Today they have collaborated with Chinese fireworks to bring a newer range of even more mesmerizing crackers . They even have a manufacturing facility in China.Churning out eye popping fire crackers that would make you jaw drop.

Times have changed but as they say more the things change more it remains the same. So these Icons will hopefully last our lifetime and would be enjoyed by the generations to come....

Wishing all my readers a Happy Diwali and a Prosperous New Year. Have fabulous but safe Diwali...

CHAPTER TWENTY

Walking amongst the flowers ....

The festive season has just concluded and everyone is back to the usual grind. The same old traffic jams the same old rush in the trains same old routine job.Looking at all this chaos around a song comes to my mind , a lilting melody ....."Yeh Kahan Aaageye Hum Yuhi Saath Saath Chalte" from Silsila . A song playing in the background as the tall angry young man Amitabh Bacchan and the beauteous Rekha walking hand in hand amidst the most beautiful places on Earth , among the valley of flowers especially the bright pink and red Tulips. Totally awesome ...

You wont find the same serenity but you can take that walk , a walk among the flowers right here in the midst of all the chaos in this Maxim City of Mumbai , close to the one of the busiest Suburban Railway Station if not The Busiest . That's right here in Dadar.

Just next to the station on the south side of the FOB starts a small lane filled with small hole in the wall shops . Close to 20 stalls lined right till the end where the flyover bridge opposite the Dadar station ends. The business starts here at the ghostly hour of the early morning around 4 AM every day. Tons of flowers come here from all across India mostly by trains or in huge trucks. The bags upon bags of flowers are transported to this small bylane known locally as the Phool Gully or the Dadar Phool Market.

You can see the flower vendors some owners of small shops some traders or even some who pick up loose stock converge here to pick the best lot at that ghostly hour. Pitch black except for the street lights and lights on the stations these flower vendors get to work. Opening up huge jute filled bags of bright Orange and Yellow Marigolds . Spilling on the ground like small pom-poms. Or now during the winters its those bright yellow or lemon colored Shevanti or the maroon and orange tinged small Zinnia's . Now a days you can you can even spot some exotic flowers like the Tulips or Orchids or even the Carnations which go into making of lovely flower bouquets . Those you can give to your sweet heart.

Walking here early in the morning is like walking among a beehive of activity or something similar to a warzone. You will find the unloaders , unloading the flowers in bulk at the stalls . Small and retail vendors haggling away with the shop owners to pick up a few 10's of kilos of the best and freshest flower to be carried back as far as Kalyan & Dombivili in the Central Suburbs or Borivili and Dahisar on the Western side. Some are local flower sellers who take their stock and sit below the flyover bridge and start making garlands weaving these flowers into multicoloured "haars" or garlands ready to adorn the necks of the various deities across the city in temples and in our homes. You can see largely the women folk working fervently at these flowers and deftly weaving them using nothing but a string of thread and magically transforming the flowers into those lovely garlands. Even small girls as small as 5 year olds work along their mothers , their aunts or the old grand mothers and transform these flowers into "Vennis" or "Gajra" . Both of these flower adornments used by the women to tuck into their hair buns and look gorgeous. You will find families upon families thriving upon the measly income generated after selling these garlands and Venni's to the people entering and exiting the station.

While walking among these flowers you can literally surrounded by the wafts of fragrance . The sweet smell of those red roses and pink roses that come from the dry Rajasthan or Kutch. The distinct fragrance of the small white "chadi" used in the Haar or the over powering smell of "Mogra" which are the costliest but the best for making the Gajra's. Not long ago a middle class Marathi manoos would profess his love for his wife by buying a couple of these delicate Mogra gajra's while returning home from work. A modest romantic gift for his wife to see that special smile on her lips , a smile which would melt his own stress and agony of day. A few moments of bliss shared between the two.

Then there are the faint lingering smells of flowers like white sontakka , bright orange chaffa or the yellow bud like kavti chaffa sold in lose by the dozen. I have seen people buying those small garlands made up of these orange chaffa at the traffic junctions or at the Red light Signals and placing them on the small murti's inside their cars .The fragrance so sweet and overpowering you wont even need to use an air fresheners for the entire day. Try it next time , its better than the artificial fragrance in our otherwise artificial and routine life.

Walking here in this Phool Market, transports you to an entirely different world. A world amidst the chaos but still fragrant from the beauty of nature.

CHAPTER TWENTY-ONE

Green Thumbs

Search Google and the most trending topic of discussion in news in developed and developing economies is "Climate Change" , the effects of which are hotly debated on news channels , World economic forums and International associations like United Nations. Believe it or not the effects of Climate are very real and very visible. Take the case of the smog choking Delhi every year this time of the year or the case of the incessant rains in Mumbai right up to Diwali in mid October. And the extreme temperatures currently observed during the day making you sweat and the sudden drop in temperature during the nights making it a health hazard for not just kids but also adults alike. Giving most of us the sniffles or a clear case of runny noses accompanied by mild fever. Such is the weather sometimes it feels not to step out of the home.

To top it all the local administrations in most cities is not geared upto handle the deluge due excessive rains. Take the recent news case of floods in Chennai making the lives of the people residing in the city. Flooding caused the city to come to a standstill for 2-3 days and the same thing happening in Bangalore a week before. City after city is fighting the same chaos and in hilly places like Uttarakhand such climate change can be catastrophic by way of landslides and many lives being lost as also damage to property.

But all this can be attributed to mans greed, one reason being unrelenting cutting of trees to develop land for housing and commercial activities. Creating more Concrete forest, when the need of the hour is more green cover.

Living in Matunga where fortunately the green cover is still intact in the quite precincts of Hindu Colony and Dadar Parsi Colony. Even during high noon when the Sun is overpowering in the sky you can take a pleasant walk among the shade of the trees in these places. Enjoy the cool breeze in the evening or even a night walk enjoying a little chit chat with your spouse under the amazing night sky brightly lit with twinkling stars and yellow full moon.

Growing up I still remember I had a green thumb potting plants in our wide and airy Veranda. We always had a Tulsi , that light green plant with medicinal properties . According to Ayurveda Tulsi is one plant which is a natural air purifier . If planted in abundance it can filter the polluted air entering our homes. The leaves can be used to make home remedies to beat that toughest of cold and flu. A few leaves in your hot cup of tea can recharge you with energy and a clears your system of all the daily stress. Then there are flowering plants like the white lilies which would bloom in abundance come April and May every year. The delicate white flowers rising up from the mud in the pots like stars on drinking straws. A bouquet of white bloom among the deep green grassy leaves. A wonderful sight to behold.

Another rare plant we have is the Brahma Kamal a variant of the exotic Lotus flower. If you look at the plant it appears like a shrub in a arid dessert with flat green leaves rising from buds buried in the mud in the earthen kundi or planter. It is said that Brahma Kamal flowers once in 6 years but when it blooms it's a sight to behold. First a tiny bud sticks out from the sides of those flat green leaves. Over a period a few day the buds grow in speed with a proper stem and a large bulbous conical bud at the top .The colour being a fiery red. On the day of its bloom you cannot miss the faint but sweet fragrance emanating from the bud which spreads across your home. The red bulb starts opening up late in the evening to reveal the soft and pristine white flower with faint yellow spores in the centre. When fully bloomed it is a sight to watch with a large flower holding centre stage like a beautiful goddess and right fully so the favourite flower of goddess Laxmi itself. But the life of the flower is only for a night as it wilts away when you check on it the morning after. Making the saying "Best things comes in small packages" so true.

The other plants we always had were the Sadaphooli of the ever flowering literally daily making its presence felt every morning with its cutely symmetrical pink and purple flowers or pure white and yellow combination. The flowers were plucked and offered to the gods during morning prayers . All these plants sitting pretty in the wrought iron stand fixed to the verandah or now in the window grills. With open spaces coming at a premium , most of the flat owners today have flowering and medicinal plants in their window grills. Some going on to make space for kitchen gardens with veggies like cherry tomatoes , brinjals , green chillies and green leafy vegetables like Methi or even a Palak.

Such is the demand for potted plants you are sure find many plant nurseries in Mumbai. At the end of the Tilak Bridge connect Dadar East to Dadar West you can find a very old nursery made out the step like holders placed along the bridge wall. Here you can get plants in all sizes from the small saplings of Chinese Rose in deep pink or purple. The ever flowering Sadafuli in pink , purple or white. The fresh bright orange Marigold or its other variant in sunny yellow. You can even get the Shevanti the bright yellow coloured flowers most often offered in the form of a garland . Special variety of the Shevanti which is cute as a button and literally called button Shevanti. They also keep fragrant flowering plants like Mogra , Jai and Jui . Some shrubs which flower in the night and spread their fragrance all across like Rat Rani or a Parijat. Since the demand for exotic flowers is increasing they even keep plants for orchids and carnations. Sometimes you can even get Gladiola .

If you are looking to plant some real trees may be in your building compound or a the society garden you can head to Kalina. Just on the roadside on the way to Mumbai University you will find nurseries growing sapling for palm tree , Jasmine or even fruit trees saplings of mango , chickoo or a guava. Most of the Facility Management Companies who are into Office management or even Landscape Decorators for Corporate Spaces come here to pick up these greens. You can even get real grass in rolls or turf which can be laid ut on open plots. Making the landscape really green and soothing to the eye.

So next time you are feeling a little depressed and under the weather I suggest you go to your small garden in your window sill just sit there staring at the small patch of greenery and see your worries melt away just like magic. Try it its and sure cure for all your moody blues.

CHAPTER TWENTY-TWO

Pickle Nation....

Every time someone asks for my name, and I say its Sameer Pikale, I get an odd look from the requester. Yeah I know what he or she is thinking. What a funny last name Pikale. If its an Indian and especially a Maharashtrian they are curious and ask me is it Pickle as in Amba Pickle or Kes Pickle , Pikle in Marathi is Ripened . And I say with a wry smile, yes Ripened with age and experienced, I guess. On other occasion and most often than not people pronounce my last name as Pickle or a spicy side dish in Indian Cuisine and I say its not Pickle but Pikale but at least I add some spice to life .

To think of it Pickle is not just some side dish or condiment it's one of the go to dish if you are down with cold & fever and the tongue is tasteless. Adds a serious bit of spice and taste to your food which otherwise would taste bland. It's the best complement to the other famous Indian rice recipe of Kichdi that soft yellow mix of rice and lentils made into a mush but tastier and soothing to the stomach than any of the Chatpata dishes that you normally gobble. It also goes well with your Chicken / Mutton Biryani to enhance the spices and the flavours of the Biryani itself. Growing up in a home where something was cooking up all the time, I mean in the Kitchen. We used to have fresh pickles being made by Aai all the time. If it was Gudi Padva which comes in the months of March-April , it would be pickle made from raw mangoes cut into pieces , marinated in turmeric , chili powder and salt and them tempered with hot oil and mustard seeds. Kept away for a few days before the special day and eaten on Gudi Padva . To think of it I remember Aai making pickle from fresh vegetables like for example the fluffy Cauliflower, cut into pieces and mixed with the same spices , the pickle so made had a totally different texture giving it a great taste . Or take the case of the Carrot pickle made from the red carrots , a mix of little sweet and spicy taste and the crunchy texture makes me take a second helping evrytime I have it even today.

Another one of my favourites was the pickle made from fresh and **wet Turmeric roots , we call it the Oli Halad** . Its looks like Ginger but when cut is bright orange inside and has a little pungent taste. Mixed with this was the Ambe Haladi , this again is a distant cousin of the turmeric looks like ginger but is bright yellow from inside and has a distinctly tangy taste. If you bit into a small pice with your eyes closed you will confuse the taste with that of a raw mango , hence the name Ambe (Mango) Haldi. Made into a pickle and served with curd rice it tastes like heaven.

One more of my favourites and an acquired taste was the green chilly pickle my Sudha Aatya used to serve when I stayed at her place during vacations in my childhood days. We had named it the **"Nakaat janare lonche"** or the pickle that used to go to your nose as an after taste due to the ground mustard base. One small bite of the **green chilly** piece and you were sure to get the zing. But I loved it and it went best with my aatya's favorite rice recipe of **Teen Rangi Bhaat or the tri-coloured rice** with its exception flavour and the most visually appealing dish I ever had .

To think of it Pickles are second nature to all Indians. Even while using the same main ingredients, Indian pickles can vary widely in flavor due to differences in the preparation techniques and spices used. A mango pickle from South India may taste very different from one made in North India, and is generally a lot spicier than a pickle from North India. In the southern states, sesame oil is generally preferred, while mustard oil is generally preferred in the northern states for making pickles. The capital of India, New Delhi is home to many centuries-old pickle brands, one of them being **Harnarains**. It was originally started off in 1860s, and still continues to be one of the best in India. Single main ingredient varieties prepared with mango, chilli and lemon are ever popular, but the city is famous of **pachranga** (literally 'five colors', prepared with five vegetables) and **satranga** (literally 'seven colors', prepared with five vegetables) which are matured in mustard oil using main ingredients such as **raw mangoes, chick peas, lotus stem, karonda and amlas or limes, pickled with whole spices**. True to its Haryanvi and Punjabi origins, this pickle is large hearted with its range of ingredients and spice. Pachranga achar was first created by Murli Dhar Dhingra in Pakistan in 1930, his Dingra and Malik descendants brought it to India in 1943. Panipat produces over INR50 crore worth of achaar every year (2016 figures), supplied to local markets as well as exported to UK, USA, UK and middle east.

In Southern India, most vegetables are sun-dried with spices, taking advantage of immensely hot and sunny days throughout the year, thus making pickles an everyday staple. The sun-drying naturally preserves the vegetable, along with spices such as mustard, fenugreek seeds (methi), chilli powder, salt, asafetida (hing), and turmeric.

To speed up the preparation process, vegetables may be cooked first on slow heat.

The states of Telangana and Andhra Pradesh are famous for their spicy pickles. Unripe mango with garlic and ginger (**Aavakaaya in Telugu**), unripe **tamarind coupled sometimes with green chillies (Chintakaaya in Telugu)** and red chillies (**Korivikaram in Telugu**) are a staple in everyday meal. **Gooseberry (Usirikaaya in Telugu)** and Lemon (**Nimmakaaya in Telugu)** are also widely eaten pickles as well. All these are best eaten with the all time favourite Hyderabadi Biryani.

The state of Tamil Nadu makes a **mango pickle called maavadu,** which is usually made early in the summer season when mangoes are barely an inch long. The preservation process uses castor oil, giving the pickle its unique taste. Another pickle from Tamil Nadu is **narthangai** consisting of unripe **Citrons or EEd Limbu** as we know cut into spirals and stuffed with salt. Tamilians also use sun-dry chillies stuffed with salted yogurt, thus making a dry condiment called **Mor molagai** that is typically eaten with rice. We have a similar variant in Coastal regions like Konkan where these de-seeded **Dhabbu Mirch** as they are called are stuffed with salt and spices and dried. These and then fried in small quantity of oil and served with curry and rice.

In the state of Karnataka, the tender whole mango pickle is a traditional pickle recipe. This is preserved entirely by dehydrating tender whole mango known as **Appe Middi** a special variety of mango which is small in size and a little flat in structure. This is marinated with salt and spices and made into a very salty and sour pickle. A special type of this is appe midi pickle is has a refreshing aroma.

People residing in Coastal India have their own special recipe for pickle made from fish. Yes take the case of **Prawn Balcao from Goa** a pungent pickle made from tiny prawns or shrimps. In Tamil Nadu, karuvadu is made by salting and sun-drying various species of fish. **Nethili karuvadu**, made from anchovies, is among the more popular varieties of **karuvadu.** In Kerala, tuna and sardines are finely chopped and marinated in spices and later cooked on stovetop, resulting in **Meen achar.** Andhra Pradesh and Telangana also make fish and shrimp pickles but are more famous for their lamb and chicken pickles known for their spiciness and all around flavour.

The list can go on and on but one thing is for sure that Pickles add a spicy flavour to your thali or the food plate with the usual dal ,sabji , chapatti and rice. So next time you are feeling tasteless or simply want to enhance your food grab a spoonful of the pickle and enjoy your dinner.

Bonn Appetite....

CHAPTER TWENTY-THREE

Un Dino ki Baaten ....
Down Memory Lane

Currently my daughter and the Missus are hooked on to a serial being aired on **Sony TV ... Yeh Un Dino Ki Baaten**. I too have caught up some of the episodes , looks interesting . The story revolves around bunch of teen aged kids guys and girls in a school in Ahmadabad. The plot moves with their crushes, classroom rivalries some background stories all set in the the '90's period. A period of television boom , friends get together's ,watching movies on VCR , their emotional turmoil's . Depicted in the 90's setting perfectly.

Watching the episodes got me thinking of my own memories from an even before nostalgic times of the 80's. I still remember watching the episodes of the first India Soap Opera and the longest running serial on Indian Television – **"Hum Log"** on the only channel available **"Doordashan"** , the state owned television channel. Hum Log's story revolved around daily struggles and aspirations of a typical lower middle class family in Delhi with veteran character artist **Vinod Nagpal** as the head of the family **Basesar Ram** . A alcoholic who has lost his zeal for life. His **wife Bhagawanti played by Joyshree Arora** as the mother who holds the home together inspite of the struggles and depressing conditions all around. The four kids eldest one **Lallu (Rajesh Puri)** a loveable and affable character and little naïve and dumb evoking a much needed humour in the story line , **Bhadki (Seema Bhargav nee Pahwa ,** last seen in the movie Shubhmangal as the mother of actress Bhoomi Pednekar explaining the birds and bees with a hilarious analogy of Alibaba and 40 chor) the strong willed elder daughter willing to sacrifice her life and ambitions for the family , taking care of the younger two siblings the dashing **Nanhe (Abhinav Chaturvedi)** an aspiring Cricketer and fire brand **Chutki (Loveleen Mishra)** aspiring to be a doctor. The episodes were light hearted and sometimes serious a perfect mix of the every day life of a family in India which the viewers could relate to. The icing on the cake was a flawless synopsis at the end of each episode by the vertan **Dada Muni – Ashok Kumar** in his trade mark style of soft and slow talking and the punch line .. To **kal phir dekhen Aage kya hota hai"Hum Log"**

Those were the days of just a single channel of Doordashan entertaining the entire country .I still remember the black and white strips across the TV screen with a sharp screeching noise every time when the TV was put ON and the television programming was still broadcast. Then as if magic the revolving logo of Doordarshan moving across the screen and finally the pictures started streaming IN.

(Paste the link below in yur browser to enjoy the nostalgia)

https://www.youtube.com/watch?v=9-7JmGB9BRA

The programming was also very limited , it would start in the early morning around 6.30AM with prayers or bhajans followed by a capsule of News in Hindi followed by the same news repeated in English. This was followed by regional programming like in case of Maharashtra in Marathi. A few childrens programs and some in Hindi. Later in the evening you had special childrens programs like "Kilbil" a little drama , some songs , some puppetry all in Marathi and focused on children in the age group of 3-12.

Some Hindi dubbed programs for children also included the Japanese adventures of **"Johnny Sokko & his Flying Robot"** a Giant Robot controlled through a watch in the hands of special child agents Johnny Sokko alias U9 and his friend U7 giving orders to fly , fight with rockets from his finger tips , a flame thrower in his palm etc. Each episode they would battle some evil enemies who looked like aliens from another planet masterminded by the evil **Emperor Guillotine.**

Later in the day you would even have agriculture based program like **"Aamch Mati Amchi Mansa"** giving information on agriculture , crop science , fertilizers and animal husbandry. I used to watch them just for the fun of it also you get an idea how India's rural population lived and how they worked in the fields so that we urbanites could have a good square meal on out dinning tables in our cozy homes.

I still remember the regional programming in Marathi had such gem of a programs like **Hasra Gajra** a comic episodes with stalwarts like Dilip Prabhawalkar , Ashok Saraf and the king of slapstick Laxmikant Berde. Each episode was really humours and filled with true sarcasm making you laugh from the core of your belly. Much later when Color programming started the best ever stand up comedy was presented by none other than the prolific Marathi theater playwright , humorist presenting his deeply stroked and etched out characters from his famous book Vyakti Ani Valli . The humour with touch of tongue in cheek sarcasm could bowl you over and strung your heart. Laughing and crying with the humorist famously known and Pu La talking on stage with a standard speakers podium and a Tambya (waoter jug) for company.

There were special boolywood music programs **"Chitrahaar" and "Chayaageet"** much like the Top 10 songs on today's channels like 9XM , Zee Music or Masti . Each Wednesday and Friday these programs would beam out around 8PM and take you through the lilting melodies of Bollywood classics from composers like S D Burman , Hemant Kumar , Naushad, and sung by greats like Rafi , Kishore Kumar , Manna Dey , Lata Mangeshkar and Asha Bosale in Chaya Geet and latest 80's songs from movies of Govinda , Amir Khan , Rishi Kapoor in Chitrahaar. We used to look forward to listening these back to back songs in those programs.

During the nights you had Indian classical programs both Instrumental and Songs from stalwarts like Pt. Bhimsem Joshi , Pt. Jasraj , Prabha Atre , Kishori Amonkar and Parveen Sultana . Listening to their melodious voices would transport you to a differnt realm altogether . You would feel as if in a trance. Sometimes and mostly on weekend we used to watch Classic films from noted directors like Satyajit Ray or Adoor Gopalkrihnan , films in Bengali and Malyalam / Tamil with sub-titles. Films like Pather Panchali , The Appu Trilogy , Agantuk , Ghere Baire were content rich and made us aware of different cultures and traditions and of diversities in our country.All these have greatly impacted me and have made me aficionado of our Indian Classical Music and regional language movies.

Saturday evenings were reserved for watching Marathi movies in the evening be it black and white classics like Mohityanchi Manjula , Maratha Tituka Melavava and other movies depicting Maratha Valour. And some time the whole hearted comedy movies from Sachin Pilgoankar and Mahesh Kothari's stables with Ashok Saraf and Lakshmikant Berde in the leads . Movies like Gamat Jamat , Ashi Hi Banva Banvi , Dhadakebaaz , Dhoomdadaka made you roll in the aile with their funny stories and one liners hitting home spot on.

In late 80's you had foreign serials which gained popularity . I still remember laughing to the slap stick comedy of Didi's Comedy Show a German comedy television show created by and starring Dieter Hallervorden 'DiDi' dubbed in English . Didi was a bumbling detective who is struck by "brilliant" ideas which turn out disastrously; he eventually comes out on top, however.

The show is based partly on Didi's comedic antics, many of which would be impossible in real life. For example, he takes part in a hammer throwing competition at a police sports event, forgets to let go of the hammer, and is pulled by centrifugal force into the skies; he is saved by hanging on to an aeroplane. It was quite popular in India as a comedy show on the national television station Doordarshan.

Then there was the other German Crime thriller Old Fox much before the Crime Patrol's and CID's of today ruled the roost as crime / detective serials

The Old Fox (original German title *"Der Alte"*, lit. "The Old Man") was a German crime drama created by Helmut Ringelmann. The series was part of the Friday Crime Night of the network.

It depicted the crime solving activities of four police detectives, Chief Inspector Erwin Köster, played by Siegfried Lowitzuntil .Humble and unassuming in appearance, chief detective Köster is the "Old Fox". By understanding the psychological make-up of his suspect, the "Old Fox" craftily leads the criminal into his own trap, to the great surprise of his often perplexed staff. The "Old Fox" had his own way of working. Wearied by the negative elements he has witnessed so often in society, the "Old Fox" provided a unique insight into human nature. Armed with the wisdom of age and experience, the "Old Fox" hunted down criminals in Munich, assisted by his colleagues.

Much later in the early Nineties on Sunday mornings you had the lavishly mounted Mythlogical serials like Ramayan and Mahabharat giving insights into Hindu Philosophy with stories that mesmerized the viewers with the in camera special effects which were new and astonishing in those days. During the war between Lord Ram and Rakshasa King Ravan , arrows would be fired with special effects like a halo or sparkling effects or lighning bolts. All giving the story a magical effect. The costumes and sets in Mahabharata were lavish the dialog were in chaste Hindi – Do you remember the heavy words like Bhratrashri , Mamashri and Pitamah ..

Serials like Surabhi a weekly show on Indian culture and unique traditions crafts and episodes on artisans of India hooked you with their intellectual content. Or the weekly News show **The World This Week anchored by the Psephologist and senior journalist Pranoy Roy under whose tutelage the current lot of TV journalist like Arnab Goswami , Srinivasan Jain , Rajdeep Sardesai , Vikram Chandra and Barkha Dutt gained prime time experience in news presentation.**

Those were the days much before the television explosion of the mid to late Nineties when nearly 100 channels crowded the TV and made you spoilt for choices.

Those were the best days of our lives and It all seems just like yesterday....Truly **Un dino ke baton ka jawab nahi...Woh majaa hi kuch aur tha....**

Mehndi .... Indian Tatoo Culture..

Where ever I see the GenX of today believe in stamping their bodies with the green ink Tatoos in designs and sizes of varying sizes and on various body parts . Be it a gentle butterfly or a chain like design on the ankles to the massive Macho eagle or a Shiva tattoo on the biceps or delicate designs on the back of the neck. Some etching the names of their beloveds on their forearms in simple to Gothic fonts. Its supposed to be their expression of their inner voice. An act of rebellion against traditions , I guess.

But long before the West adopted this body etching art , we Indians have been known to use the art of tattooing in our daily lives . In tribal culture a women getting married or newly married would go to the village tattoo artist and who would prick the skin on their forehead with small pin sized dots or write the name of her husband across her forearm. The process was called Godhana literally meaning etching.

But since this left a lifetime of green mark on the skin it was difficult to think it as a decorative or beatifying process. That was left to the all time favourite custom of the women "The Mehndi". Even the western culture today acknowledges Mehndi as the best ever non-permanent tattooing process.

The art of henna (called mehndi in Hindi & Urdu) has been practiced for over 5000 years in Pakistan, India, Africa and the Middle East. There is some documentation that it is over 9000 years old. Because henna has natural cooling properties, people of the desert, for centuries, have been using henna to cool down their bodies. They make a paste of henna and soak their palms and soles of the feet in it to get an air conditioning affect. They feel its cooling sensation throughout the body for as long as the henna stain remains on their skin. Initially, as the stain faded away, it left patterns on the skin surface which led to ideas to make designs for decorative purposes.

In the ancient Egyptian times mummies wore henna designs and it is documented that Cleopatra herself used henna for decorative purposes. Henna was not only a popular adornment for the rich but the poor, who could not afford jewellery, used it to decorate their bodies as well.

Today people all over the world have adopted the ancient traditions of adorning their bodies with the beautiful natural artwork created from the henna plant. It became a very popular form of temporary body decoration in the 90's in the US and has become a growing trend ever since. Celebrities like Madonna, Gwen Stefani, Yasmine Bleeth, Liv Tyler, Xena, and many others proudly adorn their bodies with henna and show them off in public, movies, videos, etc. People throughout the west have adopted the eastern tradition in their lives by having their hands and feet painted for weddings, bellies painted while in pregnancy, heads adorned with henna while going through chemotherapy, scars camouflaged to make them unnoticeable, etc.

Henna (*Lawsonia inermis*, also known as hina, henna tree, mignonette tree, Egyptian privet)is a flowering plant that grows 12-15 feet high and comes from the sole species of the **Lawsonia** genus. The English name "henna" comes from the Arabic (ḥinnā). The name *henna* also refers to the dye prepared from the henna plant and the art of temporary tattooing based on those dyes. Henna has been used for centuries to dye skin, hair, and fingernails, as well as fabrics including silk, wool, and leather.

Henna henna was used for cosmetic purposes in the Roman Empire, Convivencia-period Iberia and Ancient Egypt, as well as other parts of North Africa, the Horn of Africa, the Arabian Peninsula, the Near East and South Asia. It can be found in other hot climates like Pakistan, India and Australia. The plant grows best in dry heat climatic regions and contains more dye at these temperatures. It also grows better in dry soil than damp soil. The leaves are small and in pairs .The flowers are fragrant, with four white petals. The fruit is a dry capsule, containing numerous seeds.

The henna plant contains lawsone which is a reddish-orange dye that binds to the keratin (a protein) in our skin and safely stains the skin. The stain can be from pale orange to nearly black depending on the quality of the henna and how well ones skin takes it. A good henna, fresh from hot & dry climates, will stain the darkest.

For body decorations, the leaves of the henna plant are dried, crushed into a fine powder, and made into a creamy paste using a variety of techniques. This paste is then applied to the skin, staining the top layer of skin only. In its natural state it will dye the skin an orange or brown colour. Although it looks dark green (or dark brown depending on the henna) when applied, this green paste will flake off revealing an orange stain. The stain becomes a reddish-brown colour after 1-3 days of application. The palms and the soles of the feet stain the darkest because the skin is the thickest in these areas & contain the most keratin. The farther away from hands and feet the henna is applied, the lesser the colour. The face area usually stains the lightest. The designs generally last from 1-4 weeks on the skin surface depending on the henna, care and skin type.

Henna works on all skin types and colours. It looks just as beautiful on dark skin as light skin but because some people skin may take the dye better than others, it can look more prominent on one and not as much on another (even lighter skin). But nevertheless, henna is a symbol of beauty, art, and happiness and is meant for EVERYONE!

Because henna acts as a sunblock, there is an added benefit to having henna designs in the summer. For those who love to get a tan It leaves tan lines! In order to benefit from this, it is best to get a henna design, let its natural colour stay on for 3-5 days and then go and get a tan. This way you can enjoy the natural henna colour on your body, the henna colour with the tan, and then tan lines in the shapes of the design (once the henna fades away)! The tan lines last as long as the actual tan!

With the Wedding Season just beginning the Mehndi ritual attains top priority . Indian marriages are known for their many rituals. In fact, the beauty of Indian weddings comes forth in the numerous traditions that are associated with the special celebration. Indian weddings are incomplete without dance, music and lots of laughter. Furthermore, Indian weddings are not a one day ceremony. Pre-wedding ceremonies begin before the wedding and can sometimes be a week long celebration.

Among the many traditions that are infused into Indian weddings, one of the most prominent is the mehndi ceremony. This is the day when mehndi is applied on the hands and feet of the bride and even the groom. While the bride has a very elaborate pattern done on her hands and feet, the groom usually has just a token design. Mehndi is a very important part of both Hindu and Muslim weddings in India. In fact, application of mehndi is a custom during any celebration in India, be it Karva Chaut, Teej, Diwali, Ramzan or any other festival.

It is a common belief that the darker the color the mehndi leaves on the hands on a bride, the more will she be loved by her husband and mother-in-law. However, the significance of applying mehndi during weddings is not restricted just to sentiments and beliefs. Although these beliefs make the application of mehndi a much anticipated and charming tradition, the actual reason is of much deeper significance, which is sometimes forgotten in the present day.

Besides lending colour to the hands, mehndi is a very powerful medicinal herb. Weddings are stressful, and often, the stress causes headaches and fevers. As the wedding day approaches, the excitement mixed with nervous anticipation can take its toll on the bride and groom. Application of mehndi can prevent too much stress because it cools the body and keeps the nerves from becoming tense. This is the reason why mehndi is applied on the hands and feet, which house nerve endings in the body. Also, being a highly antiseptic agent, mehndi can protect the couple from viral diseases. Such diseases are totally undesirable just before the wedding and this medicinal herb can lend a strong shield. Any small cuts, burns or scratches that the couple might sustain during the course of so many rituals and customs can be healed easily with the application of mehndi. It improves blood circulation in the body and enhances general health. The initial practice of applying mehndi in ancient times began in order to protect the couple and keep them healthy.

Mehndi that is applied during Indian weddings is not just a plain paste of mehndi powder and water. Eucalyptus oil, a bit of clove oil and a few drops of lemon are added. These oils not only help in darkening the colour of mehndi on the body, but also enhance the benefits of mehndi and make the paste highly medicinal. The best part is that the smell, the beautiful rich colour and the health benefits that mehndi lends act as a powerful aphrodisiac. Also, since the colour and smell remain for days, it boosts the romance in the initial days of wedding.

Over the centuries, mehndi has become so ingrained in Indian tradition that today the mehndi ceremony is one of the major celebrations before the wedding. A family member or mehndi expert applies mehndi on the palms and feet of the bride. Elaborate designs are applied on the hands with a cone filled with mehndi. While the mehndi is being applied, other members of the family play the traditional dhol and dance to its beats. Every female member of family gets mehndi done on her hands and feet. The entire mood of a mehndi ceremony is extremely festive.

The mehndi ceremony takes place at the bride's place and usually, it is held a couple of days prior to the wedding. It is a night ceremony which is accompanied with relatives, music, laughter, food and a lot of fun.

The mehndi ceremony for the groom takes place separately at his home. The bride and groom do not usually get decked up very elaborately at the time of the mehndi application, and their ensembles are very simple. Once the mehndi for the bride is done, the female relatives of the bride, especially her sisters, visit the groom's ceremony. It is great fun as the would-be sister-in-laws play pranks on their future brother-in-law and try to get some money from him as a tradition! It is a very happy occasion for both the families. Traditional songs and music characterize the ceremony from the beginning to the end.

Although times have changed and a lot of new inclusions have been made in Indian weddings, the significance of the mehndi ceremony has grown in stature. Many families bring in DJs to play songs and celebrations that go on until late in the night. If something has changed about the ceremony, it is the designs and patterns. While only intricate Indian designs were traditionally applied in the past, brides today are experimenting with Arabic designs and Indo-Arabic designs and mixing shimmer pastes along with the traditional mehndi paste. Semi precious stones are also embedded in the design. It is traditional to write the name of the groom on the bride's palm. In some regions, this is also a small ritual after the wedding. The groom is made to search for his name, which is usually smartly written so as not be readily visible.

The mehndi ceremony is a reflection of the rich Indian culture, bringing together the knowledge of medicinal herbs with many lovely sentiments and beliefs. The result is a ceremony filled with fun and joy and the perfect precursor to the auspicious wedding day.

So this wedding season enjoy India's greatest gift to cosmetics and indulge in some mesmerizing designs and feel free to express yourselves through this ancient and beautiful natural art of body decoration.

CHAPTER TWENTY-FIVE

Mahim Cha Urs...

I have been staying in Matunga for now almost 40 years . Growing up soaking its traditions, cultures and all its vibrant atmosphere. Knowing most of its nuances like the back of by hand and some I am still discovering. Likewise the missus has grown up in the neighbouring and equally famous locality of Mahim . With its cross cultural ethos and cauldron of people's mixture right from traditional Maharashtrians , to Goan Christians to Saraswat Brahmins to native Kolis and Muslims . Each with their own unique life style contributing to the vibrant and effervescent environment.

One highlight that truly defines Mahim and sets it apart from the rest of Mumbai is the local patron saint **Makdoom Ali Mahimi and his Dargah** . A place of faith and reverence among all religions . A pillar of strength to the downtrodden , the poor and the real Aam Aadmi . The ones who believe in truth and hard work and go about their routine with a sense of responsibility and duty towards their families. Believing in the spiritual saying "**Karmanye Vadhikaraste, Ma phaleshou kada chana, Ma Karma Phala Hetur Bhurmatey Sangostva Akarmani**" ....., where Arjuna was not willing to fight the Epic war of Mahabharat and Krishna explains to him to perform his duties. , **You**

have a right to perform your prescribed duty, but you are not entitled to the fruits of action. Never consider yourself to be the cause of the results of your activities, and never be attached to not doing your duty

Going back into **History of Makdoom Ali Mahimi , was Sufi Saint, who is said to have lived between 1372 to 1431 AD,** had followers from all faiths. He is one of the first saints to have written a commentary on Quran. Mahimi was the first Indian scholar to write an exegesis on the Quran, which gained critical acclimation from numerous Islamic scholars including Shah Waliullah Dehlavi. Authoring more than 100 books but we only know name of 21 books from which only 10 books are available in different libraries in India, he was given the moniker Qutub-e -Kokan (Kokan's Pole Star). He was the first commentator of the Holy Quran in India . His commentary is known throughout the World and is called "Tafsirur Rahman." It is Unique among all the commentary of QURAN known to Scholars. Mahimi is revered by both the Muslims and Hindus, all Muslim sects hold him in high esteem. After his death in 1431, he was buried in Mahim. The site later became a Dargah (shrine) for devotees.

Every year there is the **annual ten-day Urs festival** celebrated on the 13th day of Shawwal as per the Muslim calendar, millions of devotees visit his dargah. Changing times haven't affected the enthusiasm with which the ten day-long Mahim fair is being held every year. Held in the honour of the Sufi saint, **Makhdoom Ali Mahimi (1372-1431)** the Mahim fair at the dusty Mahim beach is full of people on giant wheels, toy trains and enjoying gravity-defying stunts in the *'Maut Ka Kuan'*.

The **qawwali** tradition is being celebrated by the locals, too. "Hindi songs are not sung because they can get boisterous. Each singer comes and gives their **nazariayana (respect)** to the God and Baba. They all speak about how different religion say the same thing. Listening to them is like paying your respects to Baba. You remember him and his teachings.

The cops go easy even if the qawwalis go on till late into the night. The Mahim Fair is the only time when the police participate in an official capacity apart from providing security cover. It is a policeman who has the honour of applying sandalwood paste on the saint's grave, and offering it a chadar. There are three different versions of the story behind the involvement of the police. It is said a sepoy served water to the saint while he was dying. That is why the police have been putting the first sandal and the chadar on him.

According to another version, Baba was very close to the investigative arm of the police. He helped them crack a case and, out of respect, an assistant sub inspector offers the first sandalwood and chadar. Some others say in 1891-92, the city of Mumbai witnessed a brutal riot. So, the then police commissioner began offering the first sandal as a call for communal harmony.

It takes seven hours for the sandal to reach the police station from the Dargah in the midst of the police band and other bands. People also arrange for community eating. Mouth watering rice mutton curry free to whoever comes, to the Dargah nearly 600 people are fed daily.

During the Urs the street leading to the Dargah is full of festivity. There are street vendors selling toys for the kids accompanying their parent to this holy place of worship.

This year we too ventured out to soak in the festivity. While walking from the lane starting near Mahim's famous **Falooda maker Baba Falooda** , you are awestruck with the beehive of activities and the sparkling lights which light this lane. We picked up some toys for little Bhakti and then walked along the lane checking out the wares sold by the street sellers. You have the bagand purse wallah selling ladies clutches , hobos and shoulder bags in different sizes and colors tempting with their economical prices. Some stalls sell the anodized earrings and brightly coloured braclets . But the stalls that catch your eye are the numerous food stalls lined up on both sides of this lane. The cooks bent over the hot stove churning out delicacies of **Tandoori Chicken , Murg Pahadi Kebabs , Sheekh Kebabs ,Mutton Korma** to be devoured with the soft and fluffy Roomali rotis. Then there is the mouth watering and spicy Dum Biryani's cooked to perfection in huge Handi's and served with the deft scoop of the hand with the right mix of masala , rice and the succulent meat. The food from the stalls giving you a completely different gastronomical experience.

If you are the one with the sweet tooth head to the numerous sweetmeat stalls . Here you will see huge and deep kadhai's boiling over with oil in which the biggest ever puri is deep fried to the perfect golden brown, and what is it served with the special Ghee laden orange colored Sheera sprinkled with badam , pista Cashew and rasins giving it an exceptional taste. The famous stalls for sweets are from Sulieman Usman selling sweet Jalebi's , various halwa's and their famous Aflatoon and caloric heavy brown colored halwa. Then there is the Son Halwa from Joshi Budda Kaka Mithawala with a legacy of nearly 100 years.

After having savoured the festivities we walked up to the brightly lit Dargah . As we entered the inner sanctum sanctorum of the Shah Baba Makdoom's tomb we were engulfed in the serenity and peace . Crowds moved in orderly and disciplined manner offering a silent prayer to the Sufi Saint and asking for his blessings. Once we took the darshan and came out , we were struck by the ethereal beauty of the lighting and flower decked arched gate of the Dargah. Looking up I could see the moon in the dark sky shining so bright and spreading its light of assurance much like the light shining from the Shah Baba Makdoom's Dargah standing tall and firm amongst all the chaos in this city of dreams.

We bid farewell to one of the patron saint of this city with a qawwali which is so apt running through my mind.....

Tere darbaar mein dil thaam ke who aata hai ...Jisko tu chaahe , hey Nabi tu bulata hai

Tere dar pe sar jhukaane main bhi aaya hoon .. Jiski bigdi haaye Nabi chaahe tu banata hai

Bhar do jholi meri ya Muhammad .. Laut kar main na jaunga khali

Band deedon mein bhar dale aansu.. Sil diye maine dard ko dil mein

Jab talak tu bana de na tu bigdi .. Dar se tere na jaaye sawaali.

Bhar do jholi meri ya Muhammad .. Laut kar main na jaunga khali... Khali

CHAPTER TWENTY-SIX

SWAG Se Kar Lo Naye Saal Ka Swagat.....

We are in the last week of the year 2017 and yet again curtains will be drawn on this year. Looking back its been a tumultuous year with severe ups and downs. The Year started off with a surprise electoral win for **Donald Trump** ..the Maverick , Billionaire Businessman and presidential candidate of the Grand old Party (GOP) of USA The Republican's . A surprise win even for the old hands and political analysts in the USA. An election which was dominated with caustic Tweets of "Fake News" and mail leaks for the Hillary Camp which proved to be her nemesis and blew her chances of being the First Women President of the worlds largest democracy. That too for the second time since she had to withdraw from the race due to Barrack Obama's charisma 4 years back. But 1 year down the line the mood is sombre in USA what with economy not doing to well and doubts in the minds of Heads of Businesses who supported him during the run up to the election. The US President appears to be all sound and fury "All sound and No Action". Anyways lets hope thing will change for the better in the New Year 2025. On the other side of the world saw the rise of autocratic dictator

Kim Jong Un in North Korea who nearly took the world on the brink of a Nuclear escalation with his latest Inter Continental Ballistic Missile (ICBM) with nuclear war head and a boast that he can now hit USA anytime. But on a brighter side the world political map is changing with most of the Heads of States in the **average age range of 45 , with Leo Varadkar 38 (Person of Indian Origin – PIO) becoming Prime Minister of Ireland , Emmanuel Macaron 39 President of France , Justin Treudue 41 President of Canada , Sheikh Tamim bin Hamad Al Thani, 36 the Emir of Qatar , Jigme Khesar Namgyel Wangchuck, 37 the fifth king of Bhutan , Jacinda Arden 37 President of New Zealand and the youngest being Sebastian Kurz 31 the newly elected President of Austria.** Hope these young leaders take the world economy to new frontiers in the New Year giving rise to an era of peace and prosperity.

It was also a year of catastrophic events some man made some due to Climate change. A series of major storms, including **Harvey, Maria, and Irma**, caused unprecedented amounts of damage. Two major hurricanes—Harvey and Irma—blasted the U.S. coast with winds exceeding 130 miles per hour (mph), and savage Hurricane Maria rocked Puerto Rico with winds exceeding 155 mph. Totals are still being calculated, but early tabulations indicate that the U.S. suffered more than $200 billion worth of damage from 17 named storms during the season, which began June 1 and ends Thursday, November 30

Closer home floods fuelled by climate change and unplanned urbanization have wreaked havoc in India, but authorities are failing to take notice. This year has seen the highest recorded rainfall in quite some time. Rainfall records have broken in different regions of the country, and all over the world. The year has seen a spate of extreme climate events, and their toll on life and property has been devastating. India, particularly, has witnessed floods in nine states. Monsoons this year have been heavy, and the damage caused by flooding unprecedented.

India has seen massive flooding in Bihar, West Bengal, Gujarat, Assam, Arunachal Pradesh, Nagaland, Manipur, Odisha, and Jharkhand. The city of Mumbai is still under the grip of torrential rain till the end of November, and the city floods here has claimed 14 lives.

The man made tragedies also made headlines , one being the massacre at Las Vegas due to a shootout by a Lunatics spraying bullets from the hotel premises on the common people and visitors at a music show nearby. And in Mumbai there was the stampede at Elphinston Railway Station bridge , a chaos and confusion created by rain , misunderstanding and over crowding . a tragedy in which 23 lives were lost.

On the brighter side some news came in with a little surprise and brought a smile on ones lips , take the case of **Kulbhushan Jadhav** the alleged RAW agent and branded a spy imprisoned in Pakistan being allowed by the Pakistan government for a family meeting with his wife and mother in the jail. A long overdue gesture after India's leading Legal representative firmly arguing his case in the **International Court of Justice (ICJ)** against the forcing the Pakistan Government to put off his death sentence. And the silver lining being **Justice Dalbeer Singh being elected in a closely fought election in UNGA and becoming the Chief Judge of ICJ.**

On the sports front Indian Athletes shone on the International scene . **India showed its best performance ever in the Asian Athletic Championships clinching a**

total of 29 medals including 12 Golds. India finished on top of the medals tally ahead of China and Khazakstan. The championship was dominated **G Lakshmanan** winning mens 5000mts and 10000mts run and protégé's of PT Usha namely **P U Chitra** winning Gold in women's 1500mts and **Dutee Chand** winning bronze in 100 mts. A big come back by India's best known Womens pugilist **MC Mary Kom** winning a Gold at the Asian Womens Boxing. A feat unmatched by any , Having been away from the boxing ring for a long period, the 34-year-old mother of three has returned to her favored 48kg category after five years. The gutsy lady from Manipur won her 5th Asian Championships gold.

And finally 2 events that made the headlines and which were a surprise , 1 was the much talked about and trended **wedding of the year of Virat and Anushka** being branded as **#VIRUSHKA** in a fairy tale type ceremony in Tuscany , Italy. The other being icing on the cake of Manushi Chhilllar winning the Miss World crown after 17 years last being won by the Bollywood icon Priyanka Chopra.

Manushi Chhillar a medical student, was **crowned Miss World** at a glitzy event in a Chinese resort on Saturday, making India country the joint-most successful in the beauty pageant's history. Chhillar is the 6th Indian winner of the long-running contest, following in the footsteps of Bollywood actresses Priyanka Chopra and Aishwarya Rai. Aishwarya had bagged the title in 1994, followed by Diana Haydon in 1997, Yukta Mookhey in 1999 and Priyanka in 2000, the last for India. Chillar's win brings India level with Venezuela as the countries with most victories in the history of the pageant, now in its 67th edition.

So going into the new year 2018 lets hope and pray the coming year is as eventful and surprises but more positive than negative. As they say Hope and Love is what makes the World go Round. So **here's wishing more hope and more love be filled in all our hearts and let the New Year bring Happiness and Joy to all the families of my readers....**

A spin on the latest Salman Khan Bollywood trending song from **Tiger Zinda Hai - " SWAG se Karenge Sabka Swagat" , I would say SWAG se Karenge New Year ka Swagat......**

CHAPTER TWENTY-SEVEN

New Age Watering Holes for the nocturnal wild thing...

Staying and working in Mumbai can be stressful especially for the non-Mumbaikar's . It the only city that measures distance in time. Ask any one on the road for an address and the first thing that comes out from his mouth if he is a puccka Mumbaikar is ...Madam / Sir the place you are asking is at a distance of 20 minutes from here , you can take the Auto if you are lucky to get one , it will reach you in 40 minutes due the traffic else just take the good old BEST , aaram se baitho you will reach in same time but it will cost you just a Tenner. The might Time "Samay" as in the intro of the DD Epic Serial Mahabharat is entwined to the destiny of each Mumbaikar. You just can not escape it be catching the 7:04 AM local to Churchgate from Borivili or the 6:53 PM local back home. If you are taking your car to office be sure to hit the raod by 7-7:30 AM to miss the South bound rush hour traffic and commence the reverse journey either at 5PM or if you miss this not before 9 PM . Else be prepared to get stuck in Bumper-to-Bumper traffic moving at snails pace on the Western Express Highway during peak hours both in the morning and evening. I have had colleagues owning the best of wheels dumping them at home and taking an UBER / OLA or even the AC Bus , only taking out their polished cars during weekends to take out the family or go shopping with Wife.

To beat this stress some of the young and young at heart have found ways to let their heads down at least during weekends. To cater to the varying tastes of these patron Mumbai has become the Capital of new age Lounge Bars. Everyone has their own tastes and choices. And so I'm going to qualify this list by saying that these are the 3 best places that most of whom I know keep returning to, each one for different reasons -- the consistently-good grub, the engaging decor, a likeable music track, an exciting (or inexpensive) drinks list, or even just good old nostalgia

Though myself a teetotaler have friends and family acquaintances who enjoy the high spirits. So here goes a review of the 3 best watering holes in Mumbai 2 on experiences of others and 1 on personal experience.

The **Bar Stock Exchange** is among the city's most unique theme bars where, as you probably know, the **prices of the alcohol vary** according to supply and demand. Unlike the real share market however, the rates are always kept within an affordable range. While you don't need to break the bank to visit, a head for numbers does come in handy .

It's easy to understand why **The Bar Stock Exchange** is such a big hit with its patron This really is one of the most pocket-friendly pubs in town. When it opens, prices range from as low as Rs19 for a peg of Old Monk and go up to a high of Rs792 for a pour of 18-year-old Glenfiddich whisky. Even when the spot is packed to capacity at 10PM, the rum can be a thrifty Rs90, cheaper than what it's tagged at in similar establishments. Regular patrons would be very pleasantly surprised to find Gateway Brewing Co.'s White Zen beer available on tap for as low as Rs125 at the start of business. And though you don't really come to a joint like this for the cocktails you will be happy to note that they do a slightly spicy Bloody Mary, for which you shell out a mere Rs251. Perhaps the prospect of such sweet deals makes both patrons and waiters a little more patient. Alos they have introduced their own App which they insist you download using their free WiFi and order your drinks directly from the App. The most tech savy lounge bar in todays times I guess. You can spend your evening by the bar in the al fresco section , while orders come thick and fast, neither customer or bartender lose their cool even when a few folks take their time to make some mental calculations. The chain hired chef Kshama Prabhu, who has done stints at The Tasting Room cafe and The White Owl microbrewery, to oversee their menu. Her additions include the 2AM Cheese Pav , a poshed-up version on the streetside masala pav, which achieved a good balance between the cheese and spice. You can also try the poutine mushroom melt, a well-portioned and flavoured baking tray full of French fries, cheese and brown mushroom sauce.

Like the food and the simply but tastefully decorated black and glass decor, the music is agreeable if not particularly unique. They play mostly remixes just to be sure, but both the tempo and the volume of the nineties alternative rock and current pop hits playlist is at a level that enable conversation. But then who goes there for serious talk . Enjoy the night while it lasts.

Next on the list any true party animal will be the **Glocal Junction** .It is a new-age all day dining and bar concept hangout that unifies the global and local elements together. It caters to the needs of today's global local, those who are global in their appearances but local at heart. Glocal Junction is the unification of global experiences with surprise elements of local cultures, a twisted new whole which is greater than the sum of its parts.

To enhance its offerings, the restaurant starts as a soothing space as the day begins and converts into a high-energy casual night spot by sundown that potentially binds together the concepts of an all-day dining and a casual lounge seamlessly.

The food menu at Glocal Junction is an amalgamation of global cuisines with a twist of regional flavors. They have combined various ingredients and techniques to evolve different cuisines, thereby offering some of the iconic dishes in a renewed avatar - the Glocal avatar! Don't mistake it for fusion, because it is not!

The bar at Glocal Junction has a well nurtured menu keeping in mind the fact that people in today's time are well travelled, have good product knowledge, great sense of taste. But they are still local by heart and enjoy the desi/ local fun elements, even when it comes to drinking.

The layout of Glocal Junction is planned into a massive 5,000sq feet space on the ground and the first floor. The interiors have been designed with global techniques, local materials, and humble ones that too, but now distilled to a point where their inherent beauty is undeniable.

Glocal Junction, with its unimpeachable cuisine, elaborate bar menu, well-manicured interiors and exquisite ambiance is set to provide this city with a captivating drinking and dining space that allows its guests to enjoy the virtue of being local at heart.

And last but not the least is the new kid on the block " **Kaama**" in most happening of places at Kamala Mills compound . The owner **Swapneel Redkar** an old schoolmate and friend. Just 8 months old and taking its baby steps in the night life scene. Its huge with its 2500 sq ft..The Ambience is real cozy , with comfortable seating area and well lit not unlike some of the dimly lit places which seem more dingy than approachable. The space is clearly demarcated into 3 section separated by the prominent bar with trained bar tenders churning out drinks and cocktails with aplomb.

Our group of 12-16 consisting of my Wifey's cousins and other close famiy friends decided to bring in the New Year on Dec 31st here this year. We were very well taken care off by the Manager Ajay Gupat and his team of well mannered servers. Dishing our succulent and mouth watering starters like spiced potatoes (crispy potatoes marinated in India spices, Harissa and Garlic Aioli) , Char grilled Portebello Mushroom (flavoured with saffron & balck pepper served on scented Truffle Mushroom Kulcha) , Zesty Cottage Cheese (soft Paneer made into Angari Tikka and served on Mozerella Cheese Kulcha with pickled shallots) both mouth watering and with a taste that lingered on through the night. On the non veg side the Chicken Poutine with its Makhni gravy added Indian punch to the evening. Even the Chcen Seekh were well marinated with right amount of spices and done well so to melt in your mouth when bit. The other notables were crisply done Fish fingers and Tandori marinated spicy Green chutney based grilled Chicken giving it a smoky flavour.

The bar menu is well stocked with the usual brand that all drinkers would love Black Label , Chivas Ciroc and others like Absolut Jose Cuervo and Ballentine's. A special suggestion would be to try out their cocktails for their selection of cocktails, especially the ones that are tea-infused. These cocktails are made from freshly brewed tea like cardamom, basil leaves, Assam leaves and there's even an orange tea infused with hints of cinnamon. Tea lover? Mix it up with booze and enjoy. As their menu highlights the fact " Just like a secret fantasy that finds its way to the door of the shy. Kaama Tea Infusions marry desires with potency and taste with nostalgia. A serving for your every day royalty". A concoction which transports you into a different world all together and pumps up your mood and gives you a kick to beat the blues. Keeping in tune with the name of the establishment " Kaama" they have exotic drinks which go by the name of **Deep Desire , Midnight Fantasies , Mysterious Muse and Lustrous Cascade.**

The NYE 2018 event for which we had gone was kept rocking by DJ MADOC spinning musical hits and remixes both Bollywood and Classic Pop . A night to remember and a great way to bring in the New Year.

To sum it up Kaama leaves us asking for more. Food and desire go hand in hand when the flavors, fragrance and aura blend in well. Spacious, elegant and beautiful spread makes up for the ambience. Add music/dj and the dance floor with gigs and you lit up the vibe of the place.

A great place to spend an evening with family and friend and the best way to let your hair down after and tiring and stressful week and just before the start of another grueling week ahead. Head to this place for food , drinks , music and little loose the wild animal in you.

Its Saturday Night again today ,so put on you dancing shoes and head to any of your favorite watering holes with friends and have the time of your life ....**Kyun Ki .....Abhi to**

Party Shuru Hu Hai..
    Darwaje Ko Kundi Maaro
Koyi Na Bach Jaane Paaye
Dj Ko Samjha Do Music
Galti Se Bhi Ruk Na Jaaye

Daga Daga Sa Jo Feel Kare
Wo Jaake Do Red Bull Gatak Le
Aur Jisko Dance Nahi Karna
Wo Jaake Apni Bhains Charaaye
    Bas Aaj Ko Raat Hai
Kal Se Wahi Siyape Hain
Jee Bhar Ke Naach Lo
Na Ghar Wale Na Maa Pe Hain
Sab Pe Apna Raaz Hai
    Darne Ki Kya Baat Hai
Yeh Toh Bas Suruaat Hai
Yeh Toh Bas Suruaat Hai
    Are Abhi Toh Party Shuru Hui Hai..
Are Abhi Toh Party Shuru Hui Hai...
Yeh Toh Bas Suruaat Hai

Kulfio.... Kulfiwala

Since the children's Diwali vacation were still on, on a whim we decided to head to the beach or Chowpatty as called in Mumbai. We thought instead of heading north and through the messy traffic of Mumbai Suburbs towards Juhu we shuld try going to SoBo and enjoy an evening at the original Chowpatty , the Girgaum Chowpatty. So armed with some old newspapers to sit on a , Bhakti's sand castle making equipment's, Netra's Frisbee and a small beach ball we took a cab and set out on our little outing. On hindsight the decision was perfect ,we reached in about 40 minutes and landed at the entrance of Girgaum Chowpatty . As we entered the beach ,the Sun was still up but slowly making its journey across the horizon making the skyline a crimson red. We were awestruck with the clean golden sands and thought this is great but our enthusiasm was short lived as we got closer to the water we could see all the garbage strewn . The mess even more highlighted as it was a low tide evening. We put it behind us and picked up a good brightly lit spot and quickly sat in a huddle . Bhakti and Netra poured out the small shovels , bucked and the various moulds on the sand and we started building what else but a sand castle with a moat and a drawbridge et all. It was fun a little family time.

Just then I heard a familiar and loud cry from one of the sellers of most unique ice creams ---Kulfio Kulfi..... In the distant I could see a white dhoti kurta clad man carrying a wicker basket atop his head walking around the length of the beach calling out in between trying to entice the people sitting to try his cool cool kulfi's.

A family near by asked him to stop so they could choose from his kulfi's . He set down the basket .Uncovered the red cloth hiding a matka within . When asked fro type of flavours he said he had malai and kesar – badam and chikoo. The family decided to go for the malai. Then with deft hand the Kulfiwala pulled out a couple of conical moulds opened their caps and stuck a stick , pulling out what looked like the yummiest and cool kulfi. After selling them , the kulfiwala was on his way ,walking in short but confident strides and giving out the familiar cry of Kulfio Kulfiiii

Did you know these kulfi wallahs come from a small village of Wadhane 45 km from Pune. During the lean season when the farming activity is low the men from Wadhane head to Mumbai with their ancestral kulfi making skills and roam the streets of Mumbai for making some additional buck to substantiate their farm based income.These men from Wadhane come to Mumbai in groups and stay together .Its difficult to live together in a small space, take turns to cook food. Then there is the kulfi-making itself. Traditionally sold by vendors or kulfi wallahs who keep the kulfi frozen by placing the moulds inside a large earthen pot or a matka. They make kulfi by evaporating around 10 litres of sweetened and flavoured buffalo milk by slow cooking it in large containers on coal-run stoves. They have to stir it continuously, to keep the milk from sticking to the bottom of the vessel. They have to keep boiling it till its volume is reduced by a half, increasing its fat, protein and lactose density. The semi-condensed mix is then frozen in tight sealed molds or kulhars that are then submerged in ice mixed with salt to speed up the freezing process. The ice/salt mix, along with its submerged kulfi molds, is placed in a matka or an earthen pot that provides insulation from external heat. The kulfi is also sometimes garnished with pistachios, cardamom and sweetened cream. Earlier the standard flavors were pista, cardamom, mango and rose. But now people want kulfis in strawberry, chiku, sitaphal and even chocolate flavour and these kulfiwallas cater to their demands. Every villager has a designated area where he carries the matka covered with the trademark red cloth. The older, more experienced kulfi-makers get to go to posh areas such as Chowpatty, the others raom the streets near gykhana's like Bombay Gymkhana , The Oval or on the Marine Drive and Worli Seaface. You can even catch them at Shivaji Park selling their cold and milky kulfi's.

But if you are the those worried sick about hygiene , but still want to eat this yummy cold concoction there are various spots across the length and breadth of Mumbai where you can indulge your sweet tooth. Just across the Girgaum Chowpatty there's the New Kulfi Centre famous for thier lip smacking kulfi's in 25 flavors to boast. From the fresh fruity flavors of Strawberry , Chickoo , Anjir , Mango and even a tangy variety of Orange. What you will be surprised is the hot favourite of the loyal clients is their chocolate chip and orange combination. Little sweet little oragngy and loaded with choco chips . Chip away at the small square pieces fine cut by the counter staff and handed over to you on a plate.

Another place where you get the yummiest kulfi is at the Parsi Dairy Farm Parsi Dairy Farm has been packing flavours and memories in their food for over a century in Mumbai, and their kulfis are no exception.

They offer a variety of flavours including kesar, kesar pista, chocolate, strawberry, sitaphal, and more. They add absolutely no preservatives or emulsifiers and so, have some of the creamiest and freshest kulfi out there. A real melt in the mouth treat.

And closer home near King Circle just a few yard away from the famous Shanmukanand Hall is a small place going by the name of Himalaya . They offer the best ever**malai kulfi rabdi falooda** an almost a tongue-twister, a kulfitopped with generous portions of **falooda *and* rabdi**, Want more? Ask for a *malai* medium or even a *kulfi* in *badam pista* or *kesar pista* right away.In case *rabdi* is your poison of choice, you can add it as an extra to the dish, or pack it for later.

Another simple and small but yummy kulfiwala is Gupta Kulfi at Byculla. Come here for roasted almond *kulfi* . It's really delicious and a great value for money. The *malai* chikkikulfialso seems an interesting option for a day if you like to experiment a little, eat it on a plate or with a kulfi stick.

So next time after a hearty dinner you are craving a good dessert. Instead of the usual ice cream go for the traditional kulfi. And I can proudly say, nothing beats the **Indian popsicle – a cold creamy *kulfi***

CHAPTER TWENTY-NINE

The Art Of Small Talk

I am reproducing an article written and published in my **EngineeringCollege Magazine Vishwakarma** nearly 20 years ago but more relevant today more than ever...

When people find less time interacting with each other and are more on their mobiles and iPads and content at being in the Virtual World and measuring their lives with the Thumbs Up icon universal sign of Like.. So here goes a small blog..

In today's world of fast paced life no person has time for long leisurely talks with one another . Thus it has become important to know the art of small talk. The art can easily be cultivated if one knows the basic rule **"act on opportunity"**. The best issues on which small talk can be started are Politics , Sports and Films. Let us take these three subjects separately.

Politics as we know in India is a hotly debated topic. Where ever you go and at any time during the day. This topic is the most easy one to talk on .You need not be an expert in Political Science to talk about politics. All you need to know are some of the political figures both at the State level and National level and the latest hotly debated controversial topics related to our **Neta's , their Scams , the Criminal** –Politician nexus and such other issues. That's all and you have a situation where in two persons or a group of people engaging themselves in a small talk about politics. But care should be taken that under no circumstances should you go into the details about this topic otherwise it may result in arguments and spoil the fun of the small talk.

The second most favored topic for small talk is **Sports** in broader perspective and cricket or soccer in particular. If you are a resident of **Amchi Mumbai then it has to be Cricket** . But to have a small conversation on this subject you need to be aware of the current series / matches being played at the time of the conversation , which part of the world they are being played . Also it's a plus point if you know some basic Statistics such as which Bowler took how many wickets in how few balls , which batsman scored how many runs against the opponent team. What is his Strike rate and how he fares in International conditions viz-a-viz domestic flat pitches. As you know most of our Indian batsmen at Tigers on Indian brown and flat pitches and turn into meek cats when they bat on pacer friendly green tops.

But here again you need to be cautious to not delve deep into the Match history or you will be caught and bowled by a cricket crazy fan and an expert on Cricketing History who may throw Cricket statistics at you like bouncers from a West India Pacer like **Ian Bishop or Curtly Ambrose.** And you will bowled over in no time. Such an expert always relishes such situation where he can pounce on a gullible victims like a hungry Tiger on a meek Lamb.. Otherwise this is the safest topic to start a conversation even with a total stranger. Exchange a few lines and who know you will have found a new friend on the horizon.

I would have loved to tell you all on how to converse about film based topics but it has more gossip to it than any substance.

Anyways knowing these three subjects of **Politics ,
Sports and Films** one can easily start a small conversation
,any time ,any where and with any one ,even with total
strangers . Just try it the next time you are in group and
enjoy a one on one personal interaction.

Have fun. Conversing ..A real interaction than a virtual
interaction.

Chatpata Chaat.....

I'm a big-time foodie and love anything chatpata.Name one person who doesn't enjoy chaats! I don't think such a person exists. So here goes my blog a dedication to the **"Chatpata Chaat"**

Have you observed during any of your daily shopping trips to the local market or even for the weekend shopping at say Linking Road or Hill Road Bandra , the first thing that your better half would want to try during one of the breaks during the shopping spree is the mouth watering and guiltily tasty food item .. it is the Paani Puri or the Dahi Puri at the local Chaatwala . Be it a small thela or a a hole in the wall shop selling the Chaat item you will always observe a small crowd of women buzzing around the Chaatwala bhai , asking for thoda theekha , thoda medium or ek meethi wali puri. Most often each one will have a full plate of six and then still craving for more will for "Aur teen dena bhaiya" . To top it up a final –"Ek masala puri dena bhaiya" goes the order before handing over the money for the a scrumptious and lip smacking treat.

These typically spicy , mouth watering all time hit snacks are known all across India by a common name "Chaat" . Each region has their own variations and unique items that are classified as Chaat. There is the Mumbai or erstwhile Bombay Chowpatty Chat . You will find a Bombay Chat counter even in as far as Bangalore or up west in Bharuch or Surat . Not to spicy not to sweet just right for the palette of the residents living in Mumbai. Though each locality will have a Chaatwala serving his wares some have become famous as the go to places for The Chaat.

Bandra Elco's ragda to riches story can be told in plates of Paani Puri made with Bisleri mineral water that to ice cold giving it a special cool quotient. Touted to be the 'best chaat house of city', this outlet in the famous Elco Market, serving Mumbai street food for cons now stated some where in 1970's. It is known for creating a perfect balance between taste and hygiene.

It's evolved into a full-fledged twin-level eatery, a Mumbai institution of sorts for chatpati chaat like delicious Dahipuri, delectable Paani Puri, Papadi Chaat and Bhelpuri still served with that irresistible cart-on-the-curb flavour. Ragda Patties (sometimes in whimsical heart shapes; "maast"), Pao Bhaji (served with brown bread) and stuffed parathas (Paneer, Gobhi, Aloo, Cheese and Garlic) are great. Desserts here are delicious - Rasmalai, Rabadi, Gulab Jamun and Kulfi are popular. Kulfi Faluda is an Elco special. Want to throw a chaat party? Call for they do catering as well and order new items like Dahi Ragda Puri and Capsicum Baby Corn Masala. P.S. It's Bollywood's pick for chaat — Sanjay Leela Bhansali, Boney Kapoor, Govinda's wife and Preity Zinta are all regulars.

During my Engineering College days we used to frequent a Sindhi Pani Puri eatery in Chmbur going simply by the name of Sindhi Pani Puri located at Navjeevan CHS, Next to UCO Bank, Vasi Naka Road, Chembur. The USP of this joint is that the masala for Pani Puri is prepared daily. You can savour this tangy, spicy treat till your heart is content and not be afraid of contracting infection; the hygienic environment here assures that.

If its Paani puri you seek but with a little bit of a twist you should try the Phuchkas in Kolkatta. The phuchkas are arranged on a plate and filled with a mix of boiled potatoes, rock salt, tamarind water, green chili and roasted masala. Seasoned with sweet and salty curd, chopped onions, coriander, rock salt, chutney and red chili powder, these phuchkas are to die for.Another specialty is the Ghoogni chaat. This one is sure to catch your attention. Soaked, boiled and tempered yellow peas are cooked with tomatoes, onions and spices. These are then served in a small leaf bowl garnished with chutney, lime juice and onions.Piping, hot and spicy -just perfect to beat the winter blues. If you like something spicy you could try the Raj Kachori a spicy kachori bowl filled with delicious A condiments like curd, papdi, chickpeas, bhujia, boiled potato, soft pakodis, sprouts, pomegranate, sweet tamarind chutney and coriander chutney. It's crunchy on the outside and soft and spicy on the inside that makes it a delicious snack. If it's a tangy that you like you can bite into the PAPDI CHAAT Crunchy, tangy, hot and sweet flavours make it a perfect treat. The papdis are laid out on a plate and garnished with boiled potatoes, chickpeas, boondi, sprouts, chopped onions, tomato, bhujia, curd and sweet chutney. A sprinkling of rock salt, red chilli powder, cumin powder, chaat

masala, lemon juice and coriander leaves make the snack really delicious.

Another trademark of Kolkatta is the Jhal Muri a type of bhel made from puffed rice or muri (kurmura)as they are called in Bengal. Preparation involves mixing puffed rice and chanachur in a bowl, along with onion, chili, lemon and frequently shaking the bowl. Sometimes it is prepared as a soup with tomato, pudina or cucumber. Generally it is served with thonga. Sometimes it is served with bowl.The taste is a little pungent and spicy which stays on your tongue long after you have eaten it.

Going northwards there region specific chaats like the Indori Chaat from Indore in Madhya Pradesh. Head to the Sarafa Bazaar late in the evening and you can see a burstling street with chaat wallahs and their patrons. Food vendors converge on this location to set up cateries along the road every evening. The variety is superb: samosas, kachoris, pani puri, pav bhaji, chhole tikiyas, sabudana ki khichdi, maalpua and poha to name a few. There are quite a few permanent restaurants too. Joshi Restaurant is very popular for bhutte ka kees. The Bhutte Ka Kees, which made of grated corn garnished with coriander leaves and grated coconut, just melts in your mouth. These guys also sell dahi vada, bhajiyas etc. And, yes, Mr Joshi will throw in some jugglery along with the food (you

have to request for it though). The famous khopra pattis (patties) can be sampled at Vijay Chaat House. The pattis, which are made of khopra (dry coconut) with a covering of potatoes, are fried right in front of you and served with khatti-meeti chatni.You may have eaten aloo pattis elsewhere, but khobra pattis are a must when you are in Indore.Vijay Chaat House also makes aloo mattar pattis. Pattis cost Rs 5 per piece only. You can also enjoy their samosas and kachoris.

Vijay Chaat House is a standing-only place, but I guess that is the best way to enjoy chaat.

And if you are on the topic of Chaat how can you miss the all time famous and the well known Dehli Chaat. If you are in Delhi head to Chandni Chowk to the Balaji Chaat Bhandar also known as Radha Swamy Chaat Bhandar, the place is so famous that when local shop owners want to eat some Chaat they only go to Shree Balaji Chaat Bhandar as their dishes have that traditional flavour that is not found anywhere else. Their Papdi Chaat which is garnished with Kaccha Aloo Chutney & Saunth (has a very unique sweet & sour flavour) makes all the difference. Another famous eatery here in Chandani Chow is the Natraj Dahi Bhalle Corner This popular joint in the by lanes of Chandni Chowk is particularly famous for its Dahi Bhalle,but its Aloo Tikki scores equally with its consistent visitors. A plate gets you 2 aloo tikkis that are prepared using potatoes, peas and gram flour and shallow fried in oil, till the tikkis are crunchy. Served with imli-gud, coriander chutney, yogurt, ginger juliennes and boiled chickpeas; the Aloo Tikki plate is absolutely divine.

One more Chaat specialist is the Ashok Chaat Corner . This legendary place is located outside the Chawri Bazar metro station exit and is known for its snaking queues and hordes of people visiting it on a daily basis for the delicious street treats. So what's so different about them? Well their menu is quite unique in comparison to the other vendors found in the area and we highly recommend them for trying out things like Dahi Bhalle, Papdi Chaat and Kalmi Vada.

So next time you are in the mood for a little bit of indulgence on a light but lip smacking snack go for the Chaat .Not only will you mouth explode with the unique tastes and fill your belly with magical recipes it will also be very light on your wallet . And if you are the one who suggests your better half to cheat on her diet with a little bit of a Chaat expect that mischievous smile and a sparkle in her eyes and I guarantee you your evening would definitely turn into a Romantic one.

CHAPTER THIRTY-ONE

Goa ... The abode of the Gods

What do you visualize when I say GOA .. 9 out of 10 will say Beaches , Booze and Babes. The priority and ranking will be different depending upon the person you are but given a choice chances are you will want to enjoy any one or all three.

But believe me there's more to GOA, than just beaches and the now infamous rave parties. That's just superficial to attract the tourist and cater to their indulgence. Dig a little deeper and you will find the real GOA. A beautiful scenic place with lots of traditional ethos and spirituality.

Goa has had a very long and tradition of Vedic and Sanskritic learning. Goa has the ancient site of Konkan-Kashi (at Diwar Island) considered by the Puranas holier than Kashi itself. The institutions of Agrahara, Brahmapuri and Maths as eminent centres of learning which existed for Centuries . These were the three most important institutions consisting of communities of learned Brahmins whose profound scholarship attracted students from far and near. The Agraharas constituted the real universities of medieval India. Where as Brahmapuris which were the settlement of learned Brahmins in parts of towns and the third agency that played an important role in cultural life was the Math. It was a typical Indian monastery with monks, ascetics and students living within its precincts which also served as a free boarding house. The Math tradition of Goa has survived with Goa having three key Maths of Goud Saraswat Brahmin community - Kavale Math, Gokarn-Partagali Math and Kashi Math. In order to enable these institutions to carry on their work, they were richly endowed by Kings, Chieftains and philanthropic and wealthy citizens.

Historical records of the 11ᵗʰ century AD describe Govapuri "as beautiful and pleasing city, the abundant happiness of which surpassed the paradise of Indra". The prosperity continued till the arrival of the Portugese in the 16ᵗʰ century. During the Golden Age, the indigenous architect found expression not only in mansions, houses and temples but varied complexes like Agraharas, Brahmapuris and Maths"

Among the Brahmin communities of Goa, the Goud Saraswat Brahmins have always played a dominant role in religious, social, cultural and economic role of Goa. According to some sources, the first migration (700 BC) to Goa by Saraswats was directly from the Sarasvati river banks via Kutch and southwards mostly through sea routes. The three main groups who came to Goa were the Bhojas, the Chediyas and the Saraswats and maintained connections with the Kutch, Sindh and Kashmiri Saraswats. The second wave of immigrants settled at Keloshi (Quelessam) and Kushasthal (Cortallim) and were named after those villages as Keloshikars and Kushasthalikars. From here they spread to other villages. The main deities which also came along with them were Mangirish, Mahadeo, Mahalaxmi,

Kamakshi, Mahalsa, Shantadurga, Nagesh, Saptakoteshwar besides many others. Gomantak region is dotted with so many Kuladevata Temples of Saraswats which testifies to this fact

Did you know that there nearly 500 temples in this small state tucked away in each of its villages. Some operating out of old Wada's or installed in community halls with manglorean tiled roofs. With so many temples in and around Goa is also referred as the Kashi of Western India. Most of the temples are in North Goa in the areas of Ponda, Bandoda , Cortalem , etc.

A case in point is the most famous temple of Lord Shiva the Mangeushi Temple in Priole near Ponda. Shree Manguesh temple was originally located in Kushasthali (Cortalam) and was a popular centre of pilgrimage till the Portugese destroyed it and on the original site of the temple now stands a church. In 1560 AD anticipating the onslaught of thePortugese, the devotees moved Shri Manguesh Shivalinga to a safer place in the Hindu territory of Sonde kingdom across the Zuari river. The Shivalinga was kept in a scenic surroundingson a hillock covered by forest, probably in a small hutment at a place now known as Mangueshi.

In the year 1739 AD, the Peshwas donated the village of Mangueshi to the temple. Mangueshi is still a small hamlet about 1,000 families. Subsequently, a proper temple was built around 1744 AD which was supported by wooden pillars which have been preserved even today. A new temple was built in 1890 AD which was again renovated in the year 1973.

According to Manguesh Mahatmya which forms a part of the SkandaPurana, Devasharma, one of the three later Gauda Saraswat emigrants, found the Linga near the river

Agashi at Kushsthali. The discovery is a_ributed to a servant who appears to have seen Dev Sharma's cow pouring milk from her udder everyday at the same spot and this happened to be a Linga. The word Manguesh is derived from another episode according to w hich Ishwara and Parvati were playing a game and the former lost the game and left Kailasa in a huff and wandered from place to place until he reached Gomant. Parvati went in search of him till she reached Gomant. Ishwara then assumed the form of tiger to frighten Parvati. On seeing the tiger she cried out "Trahi Mam Girish" (Protect me oh lord of the mountain). Thus the word Manguesh is derived from Mangirish. Within the temple complex there are shrines to Dev Sharma, Moolkeshwar who was the caretaker of the cow belonging to Dev Sharma and Shiv Sharma who identified the Shivalinga.**The other 'Parivar' devata shrines are that of Virabhadra, Kalbhairav, Lakshminar ayana and Santeri. The annual festivals include the birthday of Sri Ram, AkshayaTritiya, Sri Anant Vritotsava, Navaratri (Dussera), Diwali, Mahashivaratri and Magha festival.**

This year I was fortunate to witness the awe inspiring Magh Jatra Utsav , beginning on Magh Saptami withVijay Rathutsav and a grand finale on Magh Purnima with the Maha Rathutsav and Samuhik Prarthana.

On the day of poornima or full moon, the main zatra at Mangueshi is celebrated. The coconut breaking ceremony in front of the the chariot is held by the swami, followed by the mahajanas and devotees. This year, the zatra of lord Manguesh commenced on January 24 and concluded on February 2.

Every year the zatra is celebrated with great pomp and gaiety. Irrespective of their religions, a large number people participate in the annual zatras. This communal harmony has been the specialty of the region for the past several centuries. Lord Manguesh is one of such deity, whose serene temple is located at Mangueshi in Ponda, who is worshipped not only across Goa but but all around the globe. In front of the temple is a lake with a music house adjacent to it. The sangodd, a procession of the idol of Lord Manguesh in the lake during the day of Zatra is delightful and pleasing to the eyes.

The annual zatra of Lord Manguesh is held in the Hindu month of magha. A number of religious ceremonies take place during the festival. The procession of the deity on **Vijayrath (chariots), Ambari (elephant) Roupyashibikotsav (silver palanquin), Rathosav are** held on the occasion. On the day of poornima or full moon, the main zatra is celebrated. The path way leading upto Mangueshi Temple is lined up with shops selling various items like bag , toys , anodized silver trinkets , decorative items made of shells and conches . You have the usual merry –go-round and Giant wheels lit with neon lights sparkling away. As you near the Temple premises there are food stalls selling Garma Garam bhajji's – Poatato and Kela and off course the Goan famous Mirchi bhajji.Eat them while they are hot and wash it dowm with Kokan Soda or the fizzy Limbu Goti Soda in those unique dark green bottles fitted with a marble for the cap. While walking towards the Temple you are awestruck with the lighting done to the entire Temple Complex. From far it looks as if the stars have descended from the sky. The Deepmala Tower with its lighting symbolizes the guiding light one yearns for in once life. A light shining so bright it takes away the darkness and with it all the ups & downs in once life. There a huge serpentine que to have the darshan of

Lord Mangesha and you move along to enter the Mangueshi Temple. There is a fore court and then main temple. Inside One can observe the statues of Nandi, the sacred bull and Grampurush, the protector, inside the temple. The devotees request the Grampurush for granting of the prasad, through the medium of a bhat, the temple priest. Once you reach the front you are mesmerized by the flowere bedecked idol of Lord Mangesha. Such beauty and serene image , unkwoningly you feet come to stand still and palms get folded in a namaskar and a thought flashes through your mind asking the lord to bestow you and your family with **Sukh Samruddhi Arogya and Ayshwarya (Happiness, Abundance , Health & Wealth).** You sit for some time inside the temple soaking in the vibrant but peaceful environment. You take the Lords blessing and move out of the Temple . Out side are again stalls selling local sweets like Khaja , Amba (Mango) vadi , Fanas (Jack fruit) poli . Some are selling the Amsul (cut and dried sweet sopur fruit) used in the Goan Xacuti and fish curries .Theres also the Tirpal and pepper which are masala's used in Goan curries.

The **Maha Rathotsav** is slated for 4.30 AM early in the morning. This year I was fortunate to be a part of this special ceremony. A special thanks to Kamat Guruji my friend , philosophe and guide who offer me to stay at his place which stones throw away from the Mangueshi Temple. I am also thankful to Datta who accompanied me to the Temple at 5 AM that early morning.

The Sun had still not risen in the sky and in the pitch dark sky you could make out the shining Temple from the approach road that we took. The Temple looked as if it was decorated with twinkling stars . In its pristine avatar the temple looked as if it was washed with milk , appearing bright white. In the Temple complex you could see nearly 5000 people queuing up for a the traditional coconut breaking ceremony.

The coconut breaking ceremony in front of the the chariot is held by the swami, followed by the mahajanas and devotees. Nearly 5000 – 6000 coconut are broken on the metal plate fixed to the Rath (Chariot) by the devotees lined up from 5AM in the morning. It is said if the coconut breaks into 2 in the first throw , your wishes will be fulfilled . Mine did , hoping Lord Mangesha blessing will make my wishes come true . The ceremony is observed by GSB ladies decked up in silk saree's and gold jewelery and other traditional fineries from the balconies of the Staying quarters / dharmashala built around the Temple. You can observe elegant old ladies seated at the balconies showering the rath with fresh flowers . Once the coconut breaking ceremony is over the heavy chariot weighing nearly a Ton and decorated with patkas and flags of red green and saffron and on which is installed the murti of Lord Mangesha is ready to be pulled by the assembled people. Yes the chariot is pulled with all the might by the devotees and taken around in a circular pradakshina around the Temple. Shouts of **Parvati Pate Har Har Mahadev** pierces the night sky and environment if filled with buzzing energy. The rath is accompanied by a brass band belting out fine bhakti music.

The Rath is made to halt an 4 specified spots where a brief puja is done and the chariot is pulled again. After two such rounds the Lord's murthi is taken down placed in a Silver Palkhi and taken inside the Sanctum Santorum of the Temple .Where it is installed and a **Samuhik Prarthana (Common Prayer)** is made by the priest's asking Lord Mangesha to bestow all those attending the ceremony and their families ,with his blessing. A Prasad of fresh cut fruit in a dried leaf dron is distributed to all in the temple complex .

By the time I came out of the temple the sun had just risen in the sky making it a tinge of crimson. **It was as if Lord himself had used some brush strokes across the sky making the occasion even more divine.**

CHAPTER THIRTY-TWO

Vanishing Icons of Mumbai...

The other day I was thumbing through the newspaper "The Times Of India" in the late evening after a day long at office. Reading some interesting articles when my eyes caught an articles which struck a nostalgic chord.. **The EROS theater** one of the last remaining single screen cinema halls screening English Hollywood movies along with the usual Bollywood blockbusters is thinking of downing its shutters. Memories came swirling of watching movies here. We travel in trains as a group land up at the iconic and buzzing station of Churchgate come out through the subway onto the pavement staring at EROS Cinema right across the road. The building architecture being Art Deco type . EROS has been one of Mumbai's most amazing movie theatres for people of all social classes and sects.

EROS theater was founded by Mr.Shiavax S.Cambata in the year 1938 at Churchgate , in the middle of Mumbai's (erstwhile Bombay) business district. Architects *Shorabji* Bhedwar designed the Streamline Moderne building, it marked the beginning of Back Bay reclamation in early 1938. The foundation of Eros Cinema was laid in 1935. The cinema opened in 1938 with a seating capacity of 1204 the largest ever for a movie theter of its kind.The construction of this building on the then newly reclaimed Backbay plot housing shops and other businesses, apart from the cinema, took about two and a half years to complete. Partially faced with red Agra sandstone, this building is painted cream. The two wings of this Art Deco building meet up in a central block. The foyer is in white and black marble with touches of gold. Marble staircases with chromium handrails lead up to the upper floor. The murals are in muted colours depicting Indian architectures.

It used to play the latest Hollywood movies from production house like Disney , New Line Cinema and Metro Golwyn Myer (MGM) The movies transported the viewers into a magical world of action , adventure and thrills. I remember watching the Hollywood Classic "The Guns of Navarone" starring the greats like Gregory Peck , David Niven and Anthony Quinn , a story revolving around World War II Battle of Leros during the Dodecanese Campaign of World War II. The movie was ibnspired by the book which tells the story of the efforts of an Allied commando unit to destroy a seemingly impregnable German fortress that threatens Allied naval ships in the Aegean Sea.A movie with twist and turns and lots of action and a grand finale in the form of a climax where when the hoist of the huge Guuns reaches a trigger set up the explosive expert, the hidden explosives set off the surrounding shells in a huge explosion destroys the guns and the entire fortress paving the way for Allied Force victory. A great experience which is still remembered even today.

But all this is lost now with the Mumbai suburban district collector Ashwini Joshi sealing the Cambata building which houses EROS theatre weeks after it filled a first information report against Cambata Aviation, and,

Bird Worldwide Flight Service for allegedly refusing to cooperate with the government offcials who were confiscating its equipment on court orders due the lobour dispute and complaint filed by their workers regarding the pending dues not being paid to them. A icon falling into oblivion and will only be remembered by loyal patrons who experienced the magical world of the movies there.

Catch a cab or Walk down to Horniman Circle and in one of the old bylane you have another icon **"The Strand Book Stall"**, Strand Book Stall began as a book kiosk in the lounge of then-glamorous Strand Cinema in Colaba in 1948. Shanbagh had come to Mumbai from a hamlet in Karnataka to study at St Xavier's College. After an of?cious salesperson made him feel unwelcome at a bookshop, he decided to set up his own where customers wouldn't be turned away for browsing and

books were affordable. The cinema manager had been so taken by Shanbagh that he had the shelves put up himself. Shanbagh got together Rs450 for his frst consignment. The earlier generations of the Tatas, Birlas and Godrejs used to come to the cinema. They started finding interesting books there and became hooked to his salesmanship and recommendations. The store kept its name when it moved in 1956, about a 10-minute drive away to its present rented address in a quiet lane in the business district of Fort. This is the bookshop that was frequented by India's famous thinkers. Scientist Vikram Sarabhai introduced India's missile man APJ Abdul Kalam to the bookstore owner TN Shanbagh saying, "Ignore his recommendations at your peril". Author Khushwant Singh once called Strand the only "personal bookshop" in India. Former Prime Minister Manmohan Singh used to drop by often during his days as the RBI Governor. Former Prime

Minister Jawaharlal Nehru was spirited inside one night after lock-up so he could browse in peace. When Shanbagh billed him the store's standard 20 per cent discount and Nehru protested, he replied, "It is my duty to serve our leaders". Shanbagh was known to offer customers who couldn't afford a either a lower price or the chance to pay later.

Vidya Virkar daughter of the legendary Mr.Shanbagh ,initiated Strand's popular annual book-sale festivals, and held book readings at the other outposts from 1995. The Strand never sold its soul. They weren't a second-hand bookshop, They also didn't want to have a restaurant or stationery to offset the loss of the bookshop. They were purists, they wanted nothing but books. Strand's many charms were the year-round discounts, the quick and able assistance, the mix of bestsellers and rarely stocked titles. But it could't fight the onslaught of the Digital World. It couldn't stand up to the increasing turn to online delivery and digital readers Earlier, they were the place that got books from the UK and US; added titles from all thier customers to make a big lot so they could keep the price low, Now only Amazon and Flipkart can import as they get enough orders to make the air freight economical.So with heavy heart on 28 February 2018, Strand Book Stall will close shop, a day after the ninth death anniversary of its beloved owner TN Shanbagh.Another icon biting the dust amongst the wind of change in this new digital age. A great loss to all the readers and the world of the written word . A place where time stood still in the form books and the atmosphere filled with soft smell of paper and ink.

From the smell of paper and ink , I remember the smell of fresh coffee and hot refreshing snacka t another icon **Café Naaz at Malabar Hill** . A restaurant literally on top of the world overlooking the Mumbai city's skyline. An unforgettable experience. From Cafe Naaz, one could see the curvaceous Marine Drive beyond the lush greens of Malabar Hill. Or maybe it was company you kept there — Mahesh Bhatt, Shobhaa De, Sanjay Dutt, Sheetal Mafatlal, theatre personalities, artistes, writers, journalists, film-makers, this was where the hip crowd gathered. Vinod and Kavita Khanna are said to have thrown a grand wedding party here. A young socialite rented the threelevel cafe for a private party, liveried waiters setting up the food before she arrived, a rather elaborate affair for a solitary guest — a textile magnate she would later marry.You who this pretty socialite was non other than Maureen Wadia .

Over 100 Bollywood movies had scenes featuring Naaz. Naaz is the stuff of urban legend, as were its chelo kababs, succulent meat on a bed of rice fragrant with Iranian saffron. Cafe Naaz was for the guy who drove up in a Cadillac as much as for the handcart-pusher who would stop for chai,says So if the Chelo kababs were priced at Rs 250 a plate, there was always a Rs 5 cup of tea to be enjoyed, the view came free. Whatever it was that drew them to this Irani cafe, it kept them returning for more.

The restaurant was started in 1944 by another generation of Iranis, when Malabar Hill was thickly forested with only a mud path leading to the top. In the late 1990s, following years of litigation, the restaurant had to fold up with the BMC ousting its tenant over an expired lease. The BMC had taken the land back ostensibly for its water works department. A few years ago, the authorities also floated the idea of an "observatory", a vantage point to look over the city, for a fee. Now, well over a decade later, part of the property is used by a municipal union as office space, the rest of the once-bustling cafe and sit-out reduced to a large litterbin and an overgrowth of weeds.

Today there's no signboard, no anticipation of a turnaround, nobody to claim the space as the city's. Cafe Naaz keeps its desolate vigil over the bay, standing over interments of memories of a different city, a city which is loosing its soul to the Glitz , Glamour and Gimmickry.

Another icon which got lost a couple of years back was the mecca of Music , a shop for all genre's – **The Rhythm House at Kala Ghoda** an important landmark in the Art disctrict of Mumbai. The store started out in the early 1940s, set up by a Curmally family friend, before Mehmood'sfather took over the business, and eventually passed it on to his brother, Amir, and Mehmood. In its early days, the shop sold imported 78rpm records. As the years went on, the family saw various mediums of recorded music come and go, as it sold jukeboxes, vinyl, then cassettes, before stocking the CDs and DVDs. They specialised more in imported western music at first and when the Indian companies came in and started manufacturing Indian records, of course they started stocking that as well. In recent years, the shop has offered a variety of styles from Indian classical music and Bollywood hits to jazz and the latest pop albums by the likes of Justin Bieber.

Bollywood music directors Kalyanji Anandji dropped in to get inspired, Shammi Kapoor and Pt Ravi Shankar were regulars. Jethro Tull, The Police, Peter Andre, Zakir Hussain and AR Rahman have all visited.

It was never "just a music shop" that sold records or cassettes . Rhythm House had a character of its own that defined it. Its USP was the knowledgeable and helpful staff and a collection wider and well curated that any other store in the city. That's what made it a winner.

But in 2016 it shut shop on 7th March , after years of standing tall against the odds of digital streaming it was put on the block for sale. Due to its ideal location in the [posh and upmarket area of Fort and flanked by Jahagir Art Gallery and Maxmuller Bhavan , it was lapped up by the then famous diamantaire –Nirav Modi who tried to convert it into a Jewellery showroom . But never got around to it.

But amonst the despair there is still some hope left .With news headlines screming loud on the Nirav Modi Banking scam of more than 12000 Crores a small story got missed out a Tweet by Industrailist Anand Mahindra putting out an idea of Crowdfunding to revive the lost icon of Rhythm House at Kala Ghoda and taking it over from the notorious Jeweller Nirav Modi and handing it to its patrons the new shareholders and owner .A great way to revive these iconic places.

As they say **Umid pe duniya kayam hai** .. So lets hope and pray that all these vanishing Icons are once again restored to their glory for the new generations to come.

CHAPTER THIRTY-THREE

Sweet Snacks... Muh meeth to karlo

What comes up in your mind when someone says snack or a healthy breakfast , if you are a North Indian its Paratha (Aaloo , Gobi or Paneer) with achar or dahi , if you are a South Indian it would be Idi , Dosa or Vadai with piping hot Sambar and Chutney , if you are a Gujrati it would be Dhokla , Khandvi or simply Fafda and if you the harried cosmopolitan living in a fast paced city where you are always short of time then it would be Bread Butter or a Cornflakes and a bowl of Milk .But can you imagine any sweet dish as a morning or tea time snack.Yes a sweet recipe for a sweet day.

The best know and all time favorite sweet snack is the **Pineapple Sheera** with its yellow hue and lots of ghee to brighten up your day early in the morning. You will get this in any Udpi joint across town . Made of semolina or rava , sugar , chopped pineapple and raisins and garnished with roasted cashew.

One of the most favourite sweet dishes for my wife and daughters is the regular Sheera. Like her mother my wifey makes the best ever Sheera as a late after noon snack which is devoured by both my daughters . Coming back from school with loads of home work and a backpack as heavy as a trekkers napsack climbing the Everest. A steaming bowl of this yummy delight surely takes away the lethargy and brings a smile on their faces .

Another sweet snack that I remember from my childhood is the **Surnali or the sweet dosa similar to the western** Pancake that my mum used to make . Surnali is a typical South India Konkani dish. Its fluffy , spongy and made of puffed rice (kurmura) or soaked poha made into a thick batter and sweetened with jaggery or sugar cane juice. Best eaten with dollops of home-made butter (makhan) or ghee or spicy Indian pickles or chutney. Normally Indians do not prefer anything sweet as their breakfast dish. We usually eat our doasa's, idli's puri's or upma etc. which are all Savory. Godu surnali is an exception in a Konkani household. A snack with lots of childhood memories when aai used to make these sweet and porous pancakes for the entire family.

Everybody loves cakes and pastries and a few years back the most trending cake was the "Red Velvette Cake " made or beetroot but have ever come across a cake made of cucumber . We ate this yummy at home all the time. Doesn't require any special culinary expertise or exotic ingredients ,. Well...this is what **Dhondas** is made of – along with jaggery and rava (sooji). And all ye veggies out there – this will gladden your heart as there is no egg involved! Dhondas is a traditional sweet made in most GSB or Konkani households from coastal regions of Maharashtra , Goa and Karnataka. It's a huge favourite with everybody from kids to grown ups., The cucumber to be used here is the large variety – which is at least a 3/4th foot long and a couple of inches in diameter. Try not to use the regular small slim ones that we use for salads etc. All this is mixed with dollops of ghee and baked or rather steamed in cooker to give it that spongy texture . In our home we had the traditional ring type baking container , the Dhondas coming out would be like a large doughnut with a hole in the middle. Cut into pieces and served to hungry kids with rumbling tummy. Bite into it as Savor its taste as it melt in your mouth. No cream , no egg or any fancy ingredient but pure magic . You absolutely MUST try this out....

Speaking of Dhondas another traditional sweet snack is the **Bonda or Mulkaa** . This is typical fried snack from coastal Goa and Karnataka . You can use over ripe banana mix it with jaggery and rawa (to make it crispy) make into a semi thick batter , made into small balls and deep fried to make these tasty fritters – bajji type sweet snack called the Kela Bonda or Mulkaa. Served hot with green chutney tastes like heaven. Sometimes these are given out in temples as Prasad . Even when cold they are yummy to taste and really filling.

One more sweet snack is the **Buns** , a popular breakfast and tea time snack in Udupi-Mangalore region. Buns are sweet, soft fluffy puris made using banana. Usually, served with a spicy coconut chutney and sambhar, but they also taste great without any accompaniment. They're amazingly flavourful & delicious.

They're super soft, super fluffy and is amazingly delicious with a hint of sweetness from bananas used. I obviously love them extra sweet.

To make them mix plain flour along with bananas, sour buttermilk, ghee, vanaspati and let them rest overnight to give us a super soft fermented dough. So that when deep fried, they give you an aerated, super soft, puffed doughnuts or what we in India call, puris.

You must have eaten the **Ukdiche Modak** during Ganesh festivals this again becomes a sweet snack but only on special occasions like Ganesh Chaturthi , Ekadashi or a Vinayaki. But there is one more similar dish famous among the Goans and Konkani's called the **Patoli or Patoleo** . The simplest version of the Goan Patoleo is prepared by smearing parboiled rice (ukadicha tandul) paste on fresh turmeric leaves (holdi pan) to which a filling of freshly grated coconut (choon) and coconut jaggery (maddacho godd) is added. Lastly, the leaves are folded, sealed and steam cooked, preferably in a traditional utensil known as chondro. These are served hot on a platter with the leaves on and eaten after peeling them off. Best eaten with a spoonful of melting ghee . Eat this ,I assure you Tum ungliyan chaat jaoge.. really a finger licking snack.

I started this blog with Sheera and I will end with a recipe of sheera but in a different Avatar. The **Sheera Poli or Sanjyachi Poli or Sanjori** as we call in my home. Sanjori is almost similar to north Indian stuffed parathas. We can find the difference only on tasting as the stuffing in this paratha is sweet sheera (roasted semolina halwa). The outer covering is usually made of maida but it can be made even more healthy buy using wheat instead of Maida. You can make these polis more flavored and nutritious by adding cinnamon powder to plain sheera or adding drynuts like chopped cashews and raisins. You can also try adding some fruits in the stuffing eg mango sheera, pineapple sheera or apple sheera. A simple but tasty sweet paratha and sure to be a hit with the kiddos.

So go ahead eat these sweet snacks either in the morning or at tea time and make your day a little bit sweeter.

CHAPTER THIRTY-FOUR

Memories of Cartoon Strips

As a regular reader of the Times of India I miss the daily dose You Said It by R.K Laxman . A political cartoon series which ran for decades sending out a small but very apt message delivered through the striking Common Man . A bespectacled figured in a chequered coat and a dhoti with an Umbrella for company going about town mutely observing the world throwing up a satirical statement each day. Through his creation of the 'Common Man', Laxman commented on chaotic day-to-day instances from the lives of thousands of Indians. An ardent believer of '*My sketch pen is not a sword, it's my friend*', gave the entire nation a silent spectator with an uncanny perception and sarcasm to explain the Indian politics through the eyes of a common man.

Rasipuram Krishnaswami Iyer Laxman or simply R.K.Laxman was an Indian cartoonist, illustrator, and humourist. He was best known for his creation *The Common Man* and for his daily cartoon strip, "*You Said It*" in *The Times of India*, which started in 1951.

Laxman started his career as a part-time cartoonist, working mostly for local newspapers and magazines. While as a college student, he illustrated his older brother R. K. Narayan's stories in *The Hindu*. His first full-time job was as a political cartoonist for *The Free Press Journal* in Mumbai. Later, he joined *The Times of India*, and became famous for *The Common Man* character.

R. K. Laxman was born in Mysore in 1921 in an Iyer family. His father was a headmaster and Laxman was the youngest of eight children: namely, six sons and two daughters. His elder brother is novelist R. K. Narayan. Laxman was known as "Pied Piper of Delhi"

Laxman was engrossed by the illustrations in magazines,the Strand, Punch, Bystander, *Wide World* and *Tit-Bits*, before he had even begun to read. Soon he was drawing on his own, on the floors, walls and doors of his house and doodling caricatures of his teachers at school; praised by a teacher for his drawing of a peepal leaf, he began to think of himself as an artist in the making. After high school, Laxman applied to the J. J. School of Art, Bombay hoping to concentrate on his lifelong interests of drawing and painting, but the dean of the school wrote to him that his drawings lacked "the kind of talent to qualify for enrolment in our institution as a student", and refused admission. He finally graduated with a Bachelor of Arts from the University of Mysore.

Laxman's earliest work was for newspapers Rohan and magazines including *Swarajya* and *Blitz*. While still at the Maharaja College of Mysore, he began to illustrate his elder brother R. K. Narayan's stories in *The Hindu*, and he drew political cartoons for the local newspapers and for the *Swatantra*. In 1951, Laxman joined *The Times of India*, Mumbai, beginning a career that spanned over fifty years.His "Common Man" character, featured in his pocket cartoons, is portrayed as a witness to the making of democracy. R. K. Laxman structured his cartoon-news through a plot about corruption and a set of characters. This news is visualized and circulated through the recurring figures of the mantri (minister), the Common Man and the trope of modernity symbolized by the airplane.

Some of his cartoons are relevant even after 25 years of their orginal publication. Like for example the cartoon doing the rounds in the wake of PNB Bank scam depicting a Bank Robber asking the Bank Manager for handing over all the money in the bank and the Manager telling the Robber " We have a Loan Scheme I assure you it is equally god . Why don't you try that instead ?

Another one from the legendary cartoonist will make you ponder **if he knew about the present state of banks back in 70s and 80s.** A Cartoon depicting the security guard of the bank telling the Common Man – " No , not a holiday , It's a full working day , Some are in Police custody , some are under suspension and some ....."

Or the one that could have predicted Padmavat's future .. A Cartoon showing a Censor board member coming out of the preview screening and telling the Producer –director of the film " Excellent full of social values , progressive ideas, fine acting . But you must get OK from Shiv Sena and BJP for public screening.

Or one that summed up the Financial jugglery the Finance Minister makes every year during the Budget season .Laxman's cartoon is uncannily relevant, when inflation has affected the Common Man the most.

And the most caustic but truly relevant about his views on Demonetization when it was carried out by then Prime Minister Morarji Desai in 1978 It is valid even today. How much more of the tiger is now in the cage?

Every morning, for over five decades, his fans like waited for the 'Common Man', who, with his signature checked jacket, dhoti, Gandhi-glasses and twin tufts of gravity-defying hair, watched life and politics in India. A really thought provoking, inspiring and a genius cartoonist.

Another Cartoonist I truly adore is Mario Miranda. Born in Goa , Mario, as he was popularly known, spent his youth shuttling between Mumbai and Goa. He worked as a cartoonist in newspapers like the now-defunct Current and later with the Illustrated Weekly of India magazine, besides Midday and later, Economic Times. The Afternoon Dispatch and Courier produced some of his best work on the city. That period also saw Mario create the endearing characters of his cartoons - the secretary Miss Fonseca, the minister Bundaldass, and Bollywood star Rajani Nimbupani. Miranda's cartoons grace the walls of one of South Mumbai's most famous hotspots, Cafe Mondegar, in Colaba. Mario Miranda's caricatures are also seen in the municipal market of Panjim, Goa.

Mumbai, seen through Mario Miranda's eyes, is at one level cosmopolitan, symbolising the good things in life, and at another level, a nightmare with its acute space crunch and sundry other civic woes. At the height of his creativity and popularity in the 1970s and 80s, Mario's work was ubiquitous - appearing in textbooks, calendars, murals and magazines. In 2005, Mr da Cunha began to work on a book on the artist, and tracked down some 13,000 drawings - just 30% of his prolific work- from myriad sources, including Mario's friends, personal collections, publications, and the Mumbai murals that had survived. Though the artists' community did not consider Mario to be one of them, it did not affect his creative urges, which found expressions in colour, pen-and-ink and charcoal. His range of styles, and command over different mediums, made him a bit of an enigma. Ironically, it was the cartoonist/illustrator's tag that stuck, limiting people's appreciation to 'just a few laughs'. Mario consciously avoided political cartooning, but his role as a social cartoonist is unmistakable

With pen & ink that were at his command to churn out lines that every nib would be jealous of, he brushed aside the old school of cartooning using the brush, and set a new norm to use the nib pen and to master it for this branch of art. Mario created characters that gave his daily audience their quota of a smile without malice. His trips around the globe produced subtle close observations of the local musings – a fitting example of how far can one stretch the parameters of this branch of neglected art.- The Art of Cartooning.

A hats off to these two cartoonists for bringing a smile to the lips of the common man, make him forget the grim and dull life brining a little sunshine at the start of the day , every day for years together....A big salute to RK Laxman and Mario Miranda.

Try some Aam (Mangoes)...

It's that time of the year again when the Sun is blazing with its full fury in the sky making you sweat profusely. Draining you of all energy bringing in lethargy and making you feel like staying at home and snooze. But work must go on whether its hot ot not. But then there is an upside even to this muggy time . Yes you guessed it right it's the season of the king of fruits the Mango or Amba or Aam as we know it in India.

The Mango or the Hapus Amba is the fruit to devour during summer's . Best had by squeezing it to bring out its Ras and sucking it or cut into pieces and lapped up during lunch /dinner or as an after dinner sweet.

The sweet taste of mangoes underlined with a subtle tang has created many fans across the globe. But, we tend to overlook how amazingly healthy mangoes also are.

Here are 4 amazing reasons to eat more mangoes this season:

1. **Lowers** cholesterol: Mangoes contain fiber, pectin and vitamin C which help in lowering the bad cholesterol. It also contains potassium which helps in controlling blood

pressure and maintaining the heart rate.

2. Remedy for skin **problems:** Mangoes are a great source of beta-carotene which helps in promoting healthy and glowing skin. Beta-carotene gets converted into Vitamin A in our body which protects the cells from damage. Vitamin A also helps in improving the eyesight Mango pulp is rich with vitamin c, which can be applied to the face to make it soft and supple.

3. Aides in digestion: Mangoes are rich in fibre which makes digestion easy. They also contain certain enzymes that help in breaking down the proteins, ease-up the assimilation of food and elimination of waste from the body. Amchoor or dry mango

powder also acts as a digestive aid.

4. Protects against heat strokes: Mangoes can protect you against heat strokes. Drinks like aam panna or mango lassi hydrate your body and eradicate the feeling of dryness. According to Ayurveda, mangoes energize the entire system and regulate blood flow.

Bung them in salads, smoothies or curries. Pickle them, make chutneys or create lovely desserts.Or you can make some special recipes from both raw mango (kairy) and ripe mango. Here are some which you make this summer.

Mango rasam -Traditionally known as mangaai rasam, this dish comes from down South. Fiery spices teamed with the tang of raw mangoes makes for a dream combination on a sunny day. In Maharashtra there is this traditional dish made from raw mango . A dish with a distinctive flavor and taste . **Ambe dal** is one such recipe. Commonly ambe dal is also referred to as 'vatli dal' or 'kairichi dal'. It is a super quick recipe to make owing to few ingredients. The grated fresh coconut gives it a sweet flavor and the grated raw mango gives it the sourness. A perfect blend of mixed tastes and good nutritive source. Amba dal is made during the Haldi-Kumkum gatherings for snack or as a side dish.

Another similar dish is the Udpi or Andhra style **pachadi**. Summers naturally bring in the craze for mangoes and mango season is incomplete without pickles and chutneys or pachadi. Whenever mango season arrives my mom makes this instant pachadi to eat with steamed rice or just like that It can also be accompanied as a chutney along with dal recipes... To make this pachadi one needs to select tangy raw green mangoes. Sweet mangoes do not work out well for this mango pachadi. Selecting tangy mangoes and chopping them into fine pieces or blending them gives us a delicious chutney and this is a kind of instant mango pachadi are in 2 variations one where no coconut is used .Or the 2nd variety in which the Raw mango chutney is made with coconut . this pachadi needs to be tempered and tempering brings out all the hidden flavors of the blended raw mango. This mango pachadi definitely is a spicy one as lots of red chili powder is added which actually gives out a yummy taste to the mangoes.

Then there is the **Maanga Pulisserry** A mango curry from Kerala which is sweet and sour in one bite. The Southern flavors of coconut, curry leaves and mustard seeds dominate the dish.

But not all Mango recipes need to be spicy and savory. The best recipes of Mango are the sweeter ones like the thick puree like Aam Ras best eaten with hot and puffy puri's .And then there is the Mango and Mint Kheer The much loved Indian dessert gets a refreshing fruity makeover! Rice kheer with mango puree, nuts, mint, saffron and cardamom.

And when you are drained of energy from the scorching heat nothing is as refreshing as the Aam Panna. Made with mango pulp, cumin, jeera and mint leaves, you'll love the freshness of this drink.

So go ahead and enjoy this hot summer with cool beverages like Aam Panna – Aam Lassi or filling recipes like Ambe Dal or a Pachadi and top it off cool Mango Popsicles or a Mango Kulfi....

Down The Memory Lane ...Mhataricha Boot and barch kahi

Just as the summer vacation of my kiddos come to an end the little one "Bhakti" suddenly burst out with request one day. She said she wanted to **visit "Mhatari Cha Boot" or the "Old Womens Shoe"** . Looking at her mischievous smile and the twinkling in her eyes I couldn't say no. So it was decided that the coming weekend we will go to Kamala Nehru Park in Malabar Hill to enjoy a fun filled family time.

The word Mhatari Cha Boot brought with it long lost memories of old school picnics as kids . Waking up early in the morning , walking to school in the early morning cold . Taking only a small bag filled with goodies , a tiffing stuffed with wafers , my favourite Britannia Coconut biscuit , some Jim jam cream biscuits a small snack of bread – butter and a water bottle . A small cap to protect from the sun . Some of the other kids who were from affluent families would bring cakes and imported chocolates. Teachers and Support staff would makes us comfortable in the class till the time the Picnic bus came. Once ready every one boarded the bus in a orderly fashion moving along in a serpentine line . Once inside the bus everyone tried to take the prized seat next to a window and the Class teacher had to shout a little to get everyone to listen.As we settled down the bus would start the journey amidst loud shouts of **"Ganpati Bappa Morya"**....To keep us entertained Teachers would sing some nursery rythms with all of us singing in chorus , shouting loudly at the top of our lungs as this was the only time besides the sports day when we could shout without getting reprimanded. As we reached the Kamala Nehru Park and entered its gate we would be greeted by the Iconic Mhatari Cha boot , a humongous Shoe in creamish yellow color with small windows and a red slanting roof. And then we enjoyed half a day in and around the garden , dancing ,playing and making merry.

Though in recent time we did revisit this Iconic landmark when my elder one Netra was small .This was the first time after the garden and the land mark was newly renovated by the Mumbai Municipal Corporation which awarded a contract to a professional private enterprise. So on cool evening on one of weekends we decided to go back to see that Iconic Old Womans Shoe. Just to enjoy the journey we boarded a BEST red bus towards Haji Ali. Sitting at the window and looking out were my daughter taking in sights and sounds of the maxim city of Mumbai. When the bus got stuck in the usual city traffic we got down and took a **Kali Peeli** the ubiquitous Mumbai City Black & Yellow Cab. The one which you can hail by waving a hand right in the middle of the road anytime during the day or night.And though over the years the typical drivers Bhaiyaas have turned a little arrogant and refusing to ply to destination that you want to go . But then due to the recent Cab aggregators flooding the city street with their newer

AC cabs which can be booked on your smart phone , the Kaali Peeeli drivers have become a little mellow and do take you in rather than flatly refusing as earlier. But you should give credit to these black and yellow cab drivers especially the older ones in White uniforms which signify them as owner drivers who have been driving since decades and seen the city change from quaint old city with British architecture to the Glass and Steel towers kissing the city sky . One thing you can trust these senior citizen drivers is their knowledge of back road gullies and smaller roads to reach your destination, taking you away from the maddening traffic and chaos and all this with out the "Google Map" and its voice assistant , without which people like you and me are totally handicapped. So our cab driver took a right turn below a flyover just after Peddar road to take us towards Altamount road and then towards Nepeansea Road past the poshest area in Mumbai. Winding up the Malabar Hill ,once a hillock and upmarket VIP residential neighbourhood in South Mumbai.. Malabar Hill is the most exclusive residential area in Mumbai,home to several business tycoons and film personalities. Notable residents include Adi Godrej, the Birla family, Shashi Ruia & family, Pallonji Mistry, Mahesh Jethmalani, the Jindal family, the Petit family, and the Lal family etc. The area dotted with old heritage buildings , luxurious bunglows and British era State guest houses and bungalows used by top ranked ministers and bureaucrats .

The cab stopped at the top of Malabar hill right at the gates of **Kamala Nehru Park**. We could see the huge shoe shaped iconic landmark looming large from within the garden. In its new avatar the Mhatari Cha Boot has been painted a bright blue with the roof and windows in brick red and fixed with led lighting strips making it more pleasing to the eye and attracting the small kids to climb it. The area near the structure is well lit and 2 – 3 junior police personnel are earmarked with duty to control the hyper active kids making them follow some discipline and climb the shoe in a orderly Que. Both Netra and Bhakti stood in the line waiting their turn while me and the Missus clicked some beautiful pictures of the renovated Mhatari Cha Boot. Up went our kids toward the viewing gallery from where they waved at us below.

Once done with selfies and some snaps, we walked toward the famous tourist viewing gallery from where you can see the entire Mumbai skyline below . The view is just breath taking . From here you can see the entire South Mumbai from the Girgaon Chowpaty to the Flood lit Wankhede Stadium to the dome atop the Ambassador Hotel to the Air India Building and towers lining Nariman Point the original business district . Take in the fresh air and get a little awestruck at the city below .

Nest we decided to explore the rest of the Garden. The park itself has been landscaped keeping in with the kiddies theme of nursery rhymes and fair tales. There are stone walls painted with lovabe characters from Rudyard Kippling's Jungle Book – Mowgli , lazy Baloo ,the smart black panther Baghira and the fearsome Tiger Sherkhan.. A little ahead are small pathways lined with abacus and little hammocks and swing for kids to play. Up ahead is another wall painted with nursery rhymes in English Hindi and even Marathi. Read them along with your kids and jog down your childhood memories. Songs like Hickory Dickory Dock , Three Blind mice and one on the Old Womans Shoe itself. In Hindi you can find the famous Machli Jal ki Raani hai and our very own Marathi Bal Geet like Mama chya gawala javuya.. Read them sing them and have total dhamaal.

Move through the park at a leisurely pace, the centre of which has a huge Clock made of bushes and stones with enormous hour and minute hands ticking away for real and letting everyone know the time. Move towards the artificial dome created near by painted with our solar system, sun and stars on the ceiling The dome so created acts like an Echo point shout loudly and your can hear your voice echo out.

Go a little further and the kid can enjoy themselves on Slides, swing , see-saws and jungle –jims . Made as per various age groups. Some ropes strung vertically to climb, some spiral slides some steeply inclined and some for tiny tots with connecting foot bridges to make the play a little adventurous. Watching the kids laughing , giggling and having fun made me realize how much mazaa it was playing in such parks . Pure and unadulterated fun no mobiles no gadets just pure play with your friends. We took a break rather a snack break with tiffin's brought along filled with mawa cake , butter chakli's and yummy Choco chip cookies.What fun. It was getting dark now with the Sun going down , we decide to move on to the next attraction the garden opposite called the **Hanging Garden** with its sculpted hedges and short shrubs in various shapes.

Here you can catch a herd of Elephants trimmed out of trees. A farmer herding a bullock cart , some wild animals like Tigers and Rhino's . The grass on the ground to trimmed to make it soft and tickly when you walk bare foot. Enjoy a game of pakda-pakdi or play catch with a beach ball or a Frisbee . Then relax on the huge garden swings installed facing the road . Enjoy the gentle movement of the swing watch the world go by or simply close your eyes and get transported to your childhood.

As it got dark and it was time to head home we decided to again take the good old BEST bus . I recommend the Bus no 103 from Kamala Nehru Park to VT or now know as CST Terminus for its sheer magic of the route it takes. Earlier it used to be the Red Double decker and you could climb to the upper deck and enjoy the joy ride through South Mumbai. Now it's a Single decker but the ride still is enjoyable. Take a seat near the window and watch the City go by. The bus takes the winding road past Varsh – the chief ministers official residence. Then towards palatial bungalow of Raj Bhavan where the Governor resides with its vast expanse and well-manicured lawns and location right atop the Malabar Hill overview the Mumbai City skyline. From the bus you can now see the Girgaon Chowpatty bathing in the flood lights and the serene glow of the Moon that has now risen in the night sky.

The bus now moves ahead crossing many a land marks, Wilson College with its Gothic architecture on the left , Marine drive with its numerous street lights making it appear as a necklace and rightly coined Queens Necklace of Mumbai. Futher ahead you can get to see Mumbai local trains whizzing past at close quarters at Charni Road Station and the famous foodie spot of Bachelor's patronized by night crawlers. The bus rolls on towards Nariman Point and take a turn at the mecca of English theatre the NCPA moving towards Colaba passing the Mantralaya the seat of power and legislation in Mumbai. At the circle near Regal Cinema you can get of other iconic buildings in the background – the Taj Hotel and the Majestic - the building hosting hostel facility for MLA's coming from far corners of Maharashtra. Up ahead the bus rolls on to the road where you can catch a glimpse of the Naval Docks and the various secured gates to them with names like Lion Gate , Cheetah

Gate , Yellow gate , moving toward the heritage building of Asiatic Library with its White façade and holding in its sanctorum millions of books of subject as wide as Philosophy , English Literature , Marathi and even books in older languages like Sanskrit and Ardha Magadhi . Enjoy the ride winding down the old Fort area with buildings like the Reserve Bank of India looming over you , then towards Fort Market with posters of Fort cha Raja one of the oldest Ganesh Mandal from last year .

Finally the bus come to a halt at the CST depot just behind the iconic CST (VT) Terminus building . A British era building and certified heritage building by UNESCO . Flood lit with hue of colours be it brilliant red or combination of Orange White and Green the colors of our National Flag or on that day in soft pink .

Looking at that building standing there right in the middle of the busy street with other heritage buildings in the vicinity especially the Municipal Corporation building in the colours same as CST building , you feel proud of the heritage and class of good old Aamchi Mumbai...

That evening I enjoyed going down my memory lane ......Hope you do too ...

CHAPTER THIRTY-SEVEN

The Sindhi's... And Sindhu food, my take...

A few months ago, read an article about an overzealous Member of Parliament stating that Government should strike off the word Sindhi from a verse in our National Anthem... as it's now part of our neighbouring country and promoter of state sponsored terrorism Pakistan... But the same was condemned by our honourable Supreme Court by stating that the sentiments of unity and cross cultural ethos stated through the verse penned by Rabindrnath Tagore should not be confined to geographical boundaries..

As matter of fact people of India should be made aware and be inspired by a community which faced uprooting, atrocities, emotional and financial loss during the worst ever event in India's history.. The Partition.

A lot has been written and documented on the vagaries and devastation faced by Muslims or the Sikhs during the partition. Even leading film maker and Sindhi Govind Nehlani brought to life the horrendous devastation on the Punjabi and Sikhs in particular in his adaptation of the Hindu novel Tamas.. A tele serial was made with stalwarts like Om Puri on the lines of todays Netflix exclusive. It was well received and even won laurels at foreign film Festival and special awards from the President of India

But if look at History the Sikhs who came over to India at least had Punjab to call their own.. But the Sindhi's, they literally became people with no motherland to call their own. Most of those who decided to flee the newly declared Islamic Republic had only one hope in their hearts, that India with its secular and accommodative culture is where they will prosper and flourish. With a prayer on their lips and hope in their hearts hordes of Sindhi crossed over and accepted the heart wrenching tag of Refugee... A large number of Sindhi's faced large scale violence and atrocities but they were resilient enough to withstand this onslaught and loss to restart and resurrect like the Mythical Phoenix that rises from its ashes... And ashes it was as the Sindhi's were mostly a trading and business community hated by the zealots in Pakistan..

If you go back in time you can understand where this resilience comes from. It comes from the inner unity among the community members and their thirst for education and love for intellect.

For several centuries in the first millennium B.C. and in the first five centuries of the first millennium A.D., western portions of Sindh, the regions on the western flank of the Indus river, were intermittently under Persian, Greek, and Kushan rule, first during the Achaemenid dynasty (500–300BC).

The original inhabitants of ancient Sindh were believed to be aboriginal tribes speaking languages of the Indus Valley

Civilisation around 3300 BC. Moen-jo-Daro was one of the largest settlements of the Indus Valley Civilisation.

The region received its name, Sindh, from the River Sindhu (Indus). The people living in the region are referred to as Sindhi. The terms Hindi and Hindu are derived from the word Sindh and Sindhu, as the ancient Persians pronounced "s" as "h" (e.g., sarasvati as harahvati). In the same way, Persians called the people of this region as Hindi people, their language as Hindi language and the region as Hind, the name which is used for this region since ancient times, and later for the whole northern part of the Indian sub-continent today. India is also known as Hindustan

Sindhi was home to both Muslims and Hindus. Muslims followed Sunni Hanafi sect. Sindhi Hindus believe in tenets of Sikhism but are predominantly Sahajdhari. As a result, this group can be regarded as concurrently following Hinduism and Sikhism

Sindhi Hindus tend to have surnames that end in '-ani' (a variant of 'anshi', derived from the Sanskrit word 'ansha', which means 'descended from'). Common surnames being Adani, Kriplani, Thadani. The first part of a Sindhi Hindu surname is usually derived from the name or location of an ancestor. In northern Sindh, surnames ending in 'ja' (meaning 'of') are also common. A person's surname would consist of the name of his or her native village, followed by 'ja', common surnames being Aneja, Taneja..

After Partition, in 1947 Hordes of prosperous people became homeless and penniless overnight. A large majority had never left Sindh before. They crossed the new border to settle in unfamiliar lands with unfamiliar food, language and customs, stepping from a zone of sparse rain into monsoon country. They quickly got used to reading left to right instead of

What made it a tremendous feat was that they simply picked up the pieces and kept moving without looking back. It wasn't just a few individuals or families who did this – it was the entire community. The Hindu Sindhis, a rather heterogeneous mass for historical reasons, and without any central binding force, behaved in this moment of trauma as one entity.

In the early days, there was searing pain, confusion, bitterness and fear – but all that was bundled up and shoved aside to focus on planning and working towards a better future. Families held together, helping each other. Those already living outside Sindh opened their doors. Besides the grit and determination one more famous aspect of any Sindhi household is their altruistic and magnanimous hospitality and offcourse their lip smacking Sindhi cuisine.

For the Sindhi's cooking provides a vital connection to their homeland. Their kitchens, with their distinct recipes and ingredients, help identify and anchor them in the palces they adopt as their new homeland.

If look closely this is the reason frugality lies at the heart of many Sindhi recipes – having to rebuild their lives from scratch led them valuing what was available to them wherever they settled.For example Sindhi's use every part of the Lotus plant be it the flower, the stem, the bud, pods and even its seeds are used in traditional dishes. What also adds to the distinct flavours of the Sindhi cuisine are three things: slow cooking, layering of garam masala and a penchant for combining sweet and savoury flavours. A love for amchoor (dry mango powder) and basar (onions that have been sautéed white instead of brown) are some of the characteristics of this robust and rustic cuisine.

Some of the Sindhi dishes have become signature dishes with its own cult following. Tak for example the Dal Pakwan a simple chat type dish but made in Sindhi house hold tastes like heaven. This simple but exquisite recipe is packed with flavours, **Dal Pakwan** is a culinary couple made in heaven. It's basically lightly spiced yellow lentils served with deliciously crisp and thick deep-fried flatbread. A perfect bite of Dal Pakwan also includes a topping finely chopped onions and fiery chilli-coriander chutney. Another breakfast favourite in Sindhi cuisine is the Seyun Patata Seyun is sweetened and ghee-soaked vermicelli with shallow-fried Patata (potato chunks) is a dish with the perfect balance of sweetness and savouriness.

Sindhis have a soft spot for **Bhee (Lotus Stem)** a high-fibre vegetable with a bland taste. However, when cooked right, Bhee is an ingredient that is sure to perk up a simple weeknight dinner. Especially when its paired with slow-cooked potatoes in a hearty tomato-based gravy –to make it into tangy yet tasty **Bhugal Bhee Alu**. Another common veg recipes in every Sindhi house hold is **The Sai Bhajji and the Sindhi Kadi**. A dish most Sindhis swear by, the healthy and wholesome Sai Bhajji is basically Dalslow cooked with spinach and vegetables. It is best complemented **with Bhuga Chawran** , which is rice cooked with caramelised onions, tomatoes and garam masala . A match made in heaven . Much Like the Dal Chawal or Waran Bhat which like the comfort food for most North Indians and Maharashtrians. For most Sindhis, a lazy Sunday afternoon is often synonymous with a bowl of hot steaming rice and fragrant Sindhi Kadhi(a besan based preparation loaded with okra, drumsticks and cluster beans). Garnished with juicy, sweet boondi and crisp alu tuk, this combination is a much-loved comfort food for the Sindhi community.

Then there is the exotic preparation like the **Tidali Dal with Juar Jo Dodo** , which basically is A soul-satiating combination of three different types of lentils – like Chana dal , Arhar / Urad and green moong – which gives a unique taste to this earthy dish that goes best withJuar jo Dodo. A Sindhi speciality, this dodo or flatbread is made with jowar and often has a spicy garlic-green chilli sprinkling mixed into it.

No Sindhi will have his meal unless there is atleast one starter in the plate if its veg it has to be the crispy and mouthwatering **Alu Tuk or even a Baigan Tuk** . Double-fried crispy appetizers, Tuk can be made from potatoes, brinjals and evenArbi (yam). What makes this humble recipe a culinary gem is a wonderfully tart flavour it gets from Amchoor (dried mango powder) that little tanginess which remains on your tongue long after you fineshed the crispy Tuk. Another famous dish is the Koki Thick wheat-flour flatbreads perked up with onions, whole seeds (of coriander, cumin and pomegranate) and a generous slathering of ghee, Sindhi Kokis are similar to Maharashtrian Thalipeeth and are made by toasting twice.

And if you thought Sindhis only eat Vegetarian fare then you are absolutely wrong, try their a little complicated baked fish preparation, **Kok Pallo**. It is basically Hilsa fish stuffed with a hand-pounded green masala (made of simple spices, green chillies, ginger, garlic and coriander) and tawa fried. Interestingly, according to traditional Sindhi technique, this stuffed fish was wrapped in a roti and roasted in a sandpit to give it a smoky taste.

Then there is the meat delicacy also play a central role in their traditional cuisine. One of the most popular ones of these recipes is **Seyal Teevam** , a delectable dish in which mutton is slow-cooked (sometimes for as long as two hours) till its moist, tender and delicately flavoured.A sure shot hit with the meat eater.

And how can the meal be complete with out the mention of their sweet dishes – **Tairi** - A must on all important Sindhi occasions,Tairi is a scrumptious dish made from aromatic rice that is sweetened to perfection, flavoured with fennel and garnished with roasted nuts. Any true-blue Sindhi will tell you that the simplicity of complex flavours in this dish literally feels like a symphony on the palate.

Then there is the **Singhar ji mithai** a mithai made from Unsalted Sev (gram flour vermicelli), Khoya and slivers of assorted nuts cooked to melting perfection is what creates Singhar ji Mithai ,a dish that may seem odd in theory but makes complete sense on the palate.

To taste these delicacies you need to be very close to some loving Sindhi family , I know I am that fortunate with my Wife's favourite Maasi Sunita (mine too) married to the effervescent , jovial and lovable Indur Uncle whose doors are always open to us.

For all the other you can try your luck at **Jhama's or VIG Refreshments in Sindhi Colony in Chembur** or **Guru Kripa in Sion** for that Authentic Sindhi food.

To my mind Sindhis were all born under different circumstances, have faced failures, succeeded through triumphs, gone through hurt, pain, showed forgiveness, showed love, and yet they are still unlocking life's mysteries by testing new destinations and goals and scaling new heights. The most amazing thing all Sindhis have in common is to be happy by putting others first, a selfless giving, by using their talents for the greater good. Being passionate, honest, giving, and most importantly being **ALIVE.**

PS – This article is dedicated to Daddy – Indur (Uncle) Jethwaney 's Father Late Shri Puransingh Jethwaney who passed away last week . An amazing octagregarian most active in the Sindhi Community and most importantly the really really ALIVE person that I have seen.

CHAPTER THIRTY-EIGHT

Exotic Leafy Greens and other veggies

Ask any kid today what veggies they like as toppings in their Pasta - Pizza , they would roll off exotic names like **Zucchini , Broccoli , Cherry Tomatoes , Mushrooms ,Bell Peppers Red & Yellow , Ice Lettuce spices like Oregano and Thyme...** Even my 5 year old Bhakti tucks into Mushrooms and Zucchini's with relish. But to me the exotics veggies are those that make me remember my childhood These veggies had their own unique taste and texure and when made into special curries would be polished off from the dinner plates. As the holy month of Shravan is about to start here's my ode to some Special and exotics Veggies some known and some uncommon to the general public.

What is the first thing that comes to your mind when you hear Leafy Green Vegetables , the obvious choice would be **Palak (Spinach) , Methi (Fenugreek) and Chauli (Amaranth)** . Either made into dry vegetables using onion as accompaniment or into curry using coconut and garam masala . These go well with garma garm Bhakri be it Rice or Jowar ones and if its made on woodfired chula the taste is heavenly with its smoky taste. But there's more to green leafy vegetables than just these **Trimutri..**

It is a universally acknowledged fact that leafy green vegetables are natures best nutrition supplements. They are packed with iron, calcium , vitamins antioxidants and are vital components of a healthy diet.

Yet apart from these usal ubiquitous suspects few people know about the rich culinary repertoire of local and seasonal edible greens that grow across India. From treating common ailments to adding variety to a simple diet, these indigenous super exotic veggies have been consumed in rural India for centuries.

So if you are looking to infuse some fresh flavors into your regular food here are some leafy greens that you might be walking past at the vegetable market without even realizing what you are missing.

Bichu buti or Sisunaak saag or Stinging Nettle is a seasonal plant which grows through out the Himalayan region of India. Once touched this unusual plant can give you an itch and a rashes that last for couple of hours. But once cooked it doesn't sting the palate. Rich in natural fibres this super nutritious plant has been used as diuretic, laxative and allergy relief remedy. It's also proven to benefit the skin , bone and urinary health.

Takla also called Cassia Tora is a wild leafy vegetable that makes its way into the local market during monsoons. It is easily available in Mumbai right from the start of the rainy season. This leafy vegetable is favorite among Konkani people. Takle is extremely beneficial for health has great medicinal value and consuming it helps to keep monsoon related ailments at arm length. One of the best recipe for Takla is its Tamboli or a green chutney type dish. Pick only the tender leaves and discard the stems. Rinse them , drain all the water and leave them to dry on a soft muslin cloth. In a frying pan heat clarified butter or ghee , add cumins (jeera) , when they crackle add pepper and green chillies. Add the Takla leaves and saute on low flame till they change colour. Cool the mix and grind into a smooth paste along with fresh coconut salt and tamarind to give it a sweet sour taste. Add more water to give it that Tamboli consistence not too thick nor too thin. A healthy and nutritious Tamboli is ready to be served. Best eated with steamed rice and fried Papad. Taste like heaven . Try it next time you are bored of the usual Kadi-Bhath or the Khichadi.

Another unusal green vegetable is the **Ambushi / Ambuti** is a local plant with its bright yellow flowers is seen growing on the roadside in rural areas during monsoons. It can be turned into a vegetable dish with minimal spices or a fresh kadhi to tackle indigestion. In Konkan local Ambushi is ground into a paste to treat severe headaches.

Then there is the **Mayalu** , a creeper which grows in wild in courtyards, pots and gardens all over Maharashtra. The thick soft leaves make a delicious vegetable that can be combined with lentils and in some coastal area even with sea food like shrimps or prawns.Known as Indian Spinach or Malabar nightshade this green veggie is supposed to have a cooling effect on the digestive system.It has a little astringent taste and is effective in tackling arthritis.

If plants could be superheroes , **Moringa** (adapted from Tamil & Malyalam word for drumstick) would definitely be one of them. Every part of this ubiquitious tree can be consumed – leaves and pods as food the seeds , bark flowers and roots as medicine. This one is also called Saijan Saag or Shevgyacha Paala . The leaves especially are highly nutritious. Can be made into dry vegetable or tasty cutlets / pattice using channa dal and jiggery . Eaten with fresh mint chutney it's a perfect evening snack during the rainy season.

Ambadi in Marathi , **Gongura in Telgu or Pulicha Keerai** in Tamil and Pundi in Karnataka is a leafy vegetable with tangy and little sour tasting leaves. This leafy vegetable is used to make tangy mutton and a zesty toor dal or a spicy pickle .

Another uncommon leafy veggie is **Kulfa / Ghol or luni saag** is highly underrated not just in taste but also in health benefits. In India, physicians have long been recommending it for everything form reducing fever to removing worms and soothing urinary infections. In fact it was a favourite of Mahatma Gandhi who wrote about in his magazine. Modern science too has made it clear why it is of such value , apart from it providing significant amounts of vitamin A, B & C and descent amounts of protein this leafy green probably contains more Omega 3 fatty acids than any other commonly available vegetable source. Interestingly most botanical studies credit India as its country of origin and Euell Gibbons the American expert on foo has even labelled it as Indias gift to the World.

Anne Soppu in Karnataka and Kalmi Saag in West Bengal or Water Spinach as it is known grows wild like a weed along river banks and in paddy fields. Its mild yet distinctly savoury tate combination of long arrow shaped leaves and crunchy hollow stems. In Bengal its stri fried with garlic , green chillie's and gram to make a lip smacking vegetable dish or in Karnataka the same leaves are made into a delicious sweet –sour-spicy chutney with urad dal to give it a binding and rough texture.

And the most famous and recognizable leafy green vegetable during the monsoon is the **Alu or Arbi ka**

patta.The potato resembling roots of **Arbi or Colocasia** is well known ingredient in most Indian households. But did you know that the jumbo heart –shaped leaves of this herbaceous plant are delicious as well. In fact, several indigenous cuisines across India especially in Bihar , Jharkhand , Bengal , Uttar Pradesh , Uttarakhand and Himachal Pradesh, have traditional dishes prepared with Arbi ka patta also called Saru Saag or Taro leaves. From Gujrati Patra or Maharashtrian Alu Wadi (a spicy besanmix is slathered over leaves which are then rolled steamed and then deep fried to make perfect crunchy side dish or starter to the thali. In south India these leaves are made into coconut milk based curry with cut leaves or leaves rolled to form Gathi or knots. The culinary variations on this vegetable are manifold thanks to its robust falvour.

Then there is the **Chakod , Chakunda or Chakramarda Saag** , the cassia tora plant grows wild like weed spreading like lush carpet during the monsoon in the forested areas of Bihar , Jharkhand and Chhattisgarh and in the coastal belt of Karnataka and Goa. It is eaten as a vada (lentil Fritters) as a vegetable mix with dried coconut and jackfruit seed (bikna) and as a simple stir fry served with finger-millet bhakri.

Some other exotic vegetables though not leafy greens are again worth their taste in gold. Like the tender bamboo shoots. Monsoon rains bring spikes of tender bamboo shoots. About 3-4 year old bamboos have a new shoot arising from the underneath root-system above the ground. Within a few weeks these bamboo shoots grow a few feet in length above the ground. Tender bamboo shoots within 2-3 feet in length are edible & are eaten as a vegetable. When a young, cone-shaped new bamboo shoot just appears above the ground surface, it is chopped off from its root attachment, generally using a spade. It is consumed as a delicacy. On its exterior, bamboo shoot has several layers of tough casing of leaves, firmly wrapped around its central cream-white heart which is the edible portion of bamboo shoot. It is crunchy in texture, and has mild yet distinctive flavor. Once boiled and cured, it however, acquires almost a neutral taste.

Fresh bamboo shoots are crunchy, even after cooking. Pickled bamboos get soft with time but still remain chewy. Young, tender shoots are a seasonal delicacy in East Asian regions, & south east Asian countries.

In Karnataka, bamboo shoots are used as a special dish during the monsoons (due to seasonal availability). It goes by the name kanile or 'kalale in Kannada. And are known as kirlu in Konkani.

Konkani cuisine includes various delicacies using fresh bamboo shoots. Tender bamboo shoots once are chopped off have a very limited shelf life. They start to go bad within 4-6 days. Hence, they are pickled/cured to be used throughout the year.

Fresh tender bamboo shoots are available only for the first few months of monsoon every year. And the only way to have ample of them throughout the year is to preserve them by curing/pickling. Season's glut is thus preserved in brine for years to come.

Fresh bamboo shoots have to be consumed only on cooking or on pickling. You can't & shouldn't eat them raw. Raw bamboo shoots contain (cyanogenic glycosides), natural toxins. Cooking, pickling destroys these toxins.

Even before you cook fresh bamboos you have to keep pieces of bamboo shoots soaked in water for two to three days, where the water is drained and replenished with fresh water each day to extricate and remove toxins.

Bamboo shoots are edible when they're young. They harden as they mature. Tender bamboo shoots are commonly sold in the local markets during the months of June to September when young bamboo shoots sprout.

Tender bamboo shoots that are collected, are defoliated, soaked in water for 2-3 days, then are boiled in water to remove its bitter taste after which it is ready for consumption, to go into a dish. The water used to cook fresh bamboo is discarded as it tastes bitter & unpleasant. These tender fresh bamboo shoots arc then used in cooking.

These fresh tender bamboo shoot pieces are then used to make various dishes like:

1. Keerla sukke/chakko (bamboo shoots in a spicy coconut masala),

2. Keerla ambade ghashi (a coconut based curry with bamboos and hog plums),

3. kirla ghashi with mugu (bamboos in a spicy coconut curry with green gram).

Konkani cuisine has it's set of tender bamboo shoot delicacies.

Pickled tender bamboo shoots are used to prepare

1. kirla bajo (bamboo fritters)

2. kirla sanna polo (spicy rice based pancakes with bamboo shoots),

3. keerla fry (shallow fried pickled bamboos),

4. keerla phodi (spicy pan fried bamboos),

5. suyee ghashi (coconut based curry) from the pickled bamboo shoots.

Some people who taste fresh, cooked bamboo shoots for the first time may feel an unpleasant taste/smell. But proper cooking removes the unpleasant taste & smell.

So next time you go to your local vegetable market , during the monsoon season pick up these seasonal vegetable till the rains last. If you manage to get them do not skip trying these truly exotic Indian vegetables as they are not only good for health but even great to taste...

Wheeler the world of books....

For a person like me who is constantly travelling the lengths and breadths of India and sometimes abroad due to my Software Sales profession my constant companion is my travel bag and my Kindle or the Kindle app on my Mobile. It's the only support in case of delayed flights at the Airport lounges or during the yawning waits at Railway station waiting rooms. It's the best use of time to catch up on reading through all the chaos swirling around. Instead of getting agitated and all stressed out on the delays. I always keep a book handy in my hand baggage or the Laptop bag-pack as means to de-stress.

Thumbing through the pages of the latest paperback take my mind away from the urge of constantly being connected over **Whatsapp, Facebook or Instagram** . And the best thing is you don't have to feel frustrated over the slow speed of WiFi or mobile data and the constant scare of your mobile battery getting discharged to zero. All you need is well light and a good cozy spot in the lounge or the waiting room and a clear view of the Flight Status display or the Train arrival rolling display to take the right decision to move to the departure area / correct platform to catch the next flight or train to your next destination. The in between time is spent in a mystical word of words enjoying a fast paced action Thriller like **"Inferno"** or a detective novel like **"Murder on the Orient Express"** or the action packed mythological thriller like Oath of the **Vayuputras or Sita the Warrior Princess.** Each one bring joy and containment as you read along. When I am out of stock for the books that I carry or have forgotten to pack a novel the one thing that comes to my rescue are those **A.H Wheeler book stalls on the ubiquitous Indian Railway platforms.** These small but well stocked stalls are present on almost all the railway platforms across India . You will find them even in the remotes station in India. Manned by a single person dishing out everything from News paper to magazines to year books, Cook books, latest English paperbacks to self help books and books in Hindi and other local regional languages. You will find a **Wings of Fire by the late APJ Abdul Kalam sharing space with a Amish Tripathi's ":Immortals of Meluha" and jostling for space with a racy Hindi horror book like "Khooni Aatma" or even a coffe table book on the Tastes and Flavours of India.**

But did you know how these unique book stalls mushroomed on these lazy Indian Railway platforms. **A. H. Wheeler** or simply **Wheeler**, is an entirely <u>Indian</u> owned company. It owns a bookstore chain that was co-founded by Emile Moreau, a French businessman, T. K. Banerjee, an Indian businessman and others in Allahabad in 1877, operating from railway stations

A. H. Wheeler borrowed its name from the then-successful London bookstore and its owner, "Arthur Henry Wheelers", who was also a friend of Emile Moreau and helped him financially.

At a time when booksellers everywhere appear to be threatened lot, the life of Emile Edouard Moreau who set up A H Wheeler & Co, the chain of railway bookstalls that endure to this day ,appears as a fascinating example of a man with interests that spanned continents , and yet about whom there remains much that is mysterious.

In 1877 , when he was a young man of around 20, Moreau set up what would be the 1ˢᵗ of the A H Wheeler bookstalls at the Allahabad Railway Station. The East Indian Railways, which had commenced operations from Calcutta northward in 1854, was then expanding its operations from Allahabad to north India. The line from Allahabad to Jabalpur had already been constructed in 1867 and so far the first time Calcutta & Bombay were connected by rail via these two cities.

Moreau was at that time a young employee of the managing agency Bird & Company in Allahabad. Moreau's familiarity with the railway station at Allahabad , where he lived , meant that he soon noticed the demand for reading material , especially from the first class passengers. As the story goes when a friend of his , AH Wheeler concluded that he had way too much books in his home library, Moreau decided to sell them from a wooden Almirah at the station.

Encouraged by the response he got , he set up a few others the A H Wheeler & Co (named after his friend) , in Allahabad. In late 1880's A H Wheeler & Co found fame and controversy in equal measures. Moreau developed bigger plans and decided to become a publishing house. The Railways had expanded and Wheeler's bookstalls a familiar feature at Railway Stations across the United Province (the erstwhile combined state of Uttar Pradesh & Uttarakhand which included the princely states of Agra and

Awadh) , the North Western Provinces and beyond in the first decade of its existence.

In 1888 still in Allahabad, Moreau made a business proposal to Rudyard Kipling (author of Jungle Book) who was a writer for The Pioneer and also the Civil & Military Gazette or CMG (newspapers published out of the city). Kipling's 1st novel a collections of his short stories called The Plain Tales from The Hills, had already been published by the Calcutta –based Thacker and Sprint & co. It was Moreau who offered to publish his stories in book form.

Over next few years several of Kipling's early novels formed part of Wheeler's Indian Railways Library Series. The other books beginning with Soldiers Three were "Wee Willie Winkie" , "Under the Deodars", "The Story of the Gadsby", In Black & White , The Phantom Rickshaw and the other Eerie Tales , which has the famous story , The Man who would be King. These were sold for a princely sum of One Rupee.

When Rudyard Kipling reached London he found more fame than he had bargained for. Moreau had sent copies of the Indian Railway Library Series publications to the British firm Sampson Low, whose editor Andre Lang saw huge potential in these stories.

Soon the agreement between Wheler's and Kipling was to be reworked all publication rights Wheeler's had on Kipling's work outside India were sold back to him , Wheeler's continued to retain the Indian rights. In his memoirs, Kipling apparently mentioned his early encounter with Moreau, describing him as someone who **"came of an imaginative race , used to taking chances"**

Once World War I began , Moreau found himself greatly in demand by the British Government , especially by the Ministry of Mutinies under which the Propaganda department functioned. Britain's war propaganda department was set up only after realization of the efficacy of the German Propaganda department .Moreau's knowledge & experience of the East made him indispensable and it was Edward E Long the Chief of Eastern Propaganda who collaborated with Wheeler's to disseminate information during War time.

By June of 1915 the department had distributed 2.5 million books in at least 17 languages. In particular the Bryce Report written around this time relating to German atrocities on Belgian citizens in late 1914 was translated into 30 languages.

Towards the end of World War I in 1917 A H Wheeler split into 2 distinct branches with Arthur H Wheeler & Co operating in London and A H Wheeler & Co in India. Moreau however had numerous other interest. He travelled widely and servered as Director of Companies with interests in Rubber in Java and oil in Malay States.

Little is known of his family life but he remained devoted to his institute Framlingham College till his death in 1937. He was a generous individual benefactor – instrumental in setting up sports facilities for its students and instituting scholarships that carry his name and are provided to this day.

These A H Wheeler book stalls on India Railway platforms, a legacy inherited from the British Raj but one which keeps the written word alive and kicking in today's day age of the Digital revolution...

So next time if your train is late and you find yourself waiting in the AC Waiting Rooms leave those power hungry Smart phones. Instead of checking your Facebook, head down the platform to the nearest Wheeler and pick up a paperback and emerse yourself in the mesmerizing world of words.

Happy Reading...

CHAPTER FORTY

Melody Memories

Is it just me or do you also feel that Bollywood song & dance department has been taken over by in your face Punjabi lyric and want to be musicians doubling up as song writers peppering the songs with Punjabi words just to make the songs hit on the dance floor. Does anyone really know what the lyrics mean or is it the intoxicating beats that accompany the song that makes them groove to the music. Call me old fashioned I still think the lyrics of yore in pure Hindi or even peppered with chaste Urdu were much melodious than the current lot. Take the case of hit songs of the **original Bollywood Triniti – Raj Kapoor –Dilip Kumar – Dev Anand** .

They were pure melody , pure hindi lyrics composed by heavy weight like Shailendra ,Sahir Ludhyanvi , Majrooh Sultanpuri to lilting tunes by stalwarts like Salil Chowdhary ,Shankar Jaikeshen , S.D Burman and sung by great singers Kishore Kumar , Mohd Rafi , Lata Mangeshkar and Asha Bhosale . The songs are still remembered word for word. Your brain can jog down memory lane whenever you hear the first sound bar of these compositions on the radio .

A song like Dil Tadap Tadap ke keh raha Aa bhi jaa .. Tu Humse Ankh na chura ...Tujhe Kasam hai aa bhi jaa.. from Madhumati sung by Mukesh and Lata didi picturised on Dilip Kumar –Vyajanthi Mala can be picked up easily from its opening bars. Or take for instance the song **Suhana Safar Aur ye mausam haseen .. Hume dar hai ke hum kho na jaye kahi** from this same film ...a litrally haunting melody again recognized by its unique composition and simple lyrics. *Suhana Safar Aur Yeh Mausam Haseen* **carried the composer's trademark brand of haunting vibe** about it, and brilliant lines from Shailendra that were simple yet profound. The unassuming charm in Mukesh's voice also lent beautifully to the composition. Salilda's arrangement made brilliant incorporation of Western harmonies et al over a folk base – particularly noteworthy was the employment of flutes like birdcalls, to go with Dilip Kumar's nature walk onscreen.

On a related note: Among the folk elements Salil Chowdhury brought into Madhumati's soundtrack, one had its sources in Europe. One of the album's big hits, **Dil Tadap Tadap Ke**, was based on the **Szla dzieweczka do gajeczka**, a Polish folk song. This movies play list included other hits like Aaja Re Pardesi , Chad Gayo Papi Bhichooaa , Ghadi Ghadi Mera Dil Dhadke ,Julmi Sang Aankh Ladi and even the funny song Jungle Me Mor Nacha Kissi ne nahi Dekha ... Ham jo thodi si pi ke zara Jhume haay re sab ne dekha picturized on the legendary comedian Johnny Walker and exceptionally sung by Rafi is stuck In your head once you hear it.

If songs from Dilip Saab's movies were melodious and lilting , songs from Dev Anand movies were more peppy and effervescent like Pal Bhar Ke Liya Koi Hume Pyar Karle ..Joota hi sahi ... or Chudi Nahi hai mera dil hai dekho dekho tute naa.. or the nok jhon wala song between Dev Saab and the ethereal beauty Madhubala

Acha ji mai hari chalo man jao noa .. Dekhi sab ki yari mera dil jalaon na .. Chhote Se Kusur Pe Aise Ho Khafaa Ruthhe To Hujur The, Meri Kyaa Khataa
Dekho, Dil Naa Todo Chhodo, Haath Chhodo
Dekho, Dil Naa Todo Are Chhodo, Haath Chhodo
Chhod Diyaa To Haath Maloge, Samajhe ....Aji Samjhe

And then there were the songs from the original **Showman Raj Kapoor** , songs that were simple in its lyrics but carried great essence .. Sajan Re Jhoot mat bolo khuda ke paas jana hai na haathi hai na ghoda hai wahan pe paidal hi jana hai .. Others made you laugh **Echak Dana Bichak Danan, cry Jina yahan Marna Yahan Eis ke siva jana kahan** and sing along with ..Dum Dum Diga Diga or Pyar Hua Ikrar Hua...These songs are evergreen classics .

Talking of Classics the era of late 50's . 60 and 70's was the golden age of Bollywood in terms of movies being made and the songs that were created. On the one hand you had Music composers like **Madan Mohan** who dominated the Bollywood industry from the 1950s to the 1970s. He was known for the Ghazals he composed, mainly using the voice of Lata Mangeshkar, Talat Mahmood and Mohammed Rafi. Lata Mangeshkar christened him the "**Ghazal ka Shehzadaa**" (the Prince of Ghazals). Lata, in a live concert in the late 1990s, said that she found Madan Mohan's compositions difficult to master. Songs like Aap Ki Nazron ne Samjha from Anpadh , Lag Ja Gale form Woh Kaun Thi ,Jhumka Gira Re from Mera Saaya ,Teri Ankho Ke Siva from Chirag and Tum Se Kahoon Ek Baat from Dastak are some of his gems .The tunes have become immortal and remembered even today.

Most of the top film actors of those days had fallen into a groove with their preferred composers. For instance, **Raj Kapoor had Shankar Jaikishan, Dev Anand had the**

Burmans, Dilip Kumar had Naushad.

As these Troika peaked another start slowly roze on the horizon . For long Shammi had tried unsuccessfully to fit into the conventions set by the reigning troika of **Dilip Kumar (the eternal tragedy-king), Raj Kapoor (the Chaplin-esque vagabond) and Dev Anand (the perpetual chocolate hero).** Now he would set his own rules and make his own norms. So out went the old Shammi, the soft, sophisticated, sentimental lover sporting longish hair and in came the new Shammi, the raw, robust romantic aggressor, showing off a duck-tailed hairstyle a la Elvis Presley and James Dean. He became a hero who fully embodied the wacky *Junglee-Jaanwar-Badatmeez-Pagla Kahin Ka* spirit.

This new Shammi did what no other hero had done earlier. He swayed, sashayed and sizzled while singing songs on screen. He became the first dancing star of Bollywood. And yes, he also made 'Yahoo...' a war-cry for macho lovers! The way he smiled, the way he pouted and the way he looked into heroine's eyes, everything was infectious; simply because it was fresh, fun and flamboyant. Even his famed dances were never choreographed; on the dance-floor, he just needed a catchy melody and a zingy beat and then he rock 'n' rolled his way into countless hearts.

In the realms of classic Bollywood music, Shammi Kapoor-songs have become a genre by itself. Racy, robust, rhythmic and romantic numbers composed by the master composers like O.P. Nayyar, Shankar- Jaikishan, Ravi, Usha Khanna and R.D. Burman added their own magic to this rebel star's screen persona.

Some of my Favorite Shammi Kapoor songs are **Yun to humne laakh haseen dekhe hain** fromTumsa Nahi Dekha composed by O.P. Nayyar *Yahoo...Chaahe koi mujhe junglee kahe* from **Junglee** composed Shankr Jaikishan *Baar baar dekho* – **China Town** – Ravi *Dil deke dekho dil deke dekho dil deke dekho ji*- **Dil Deke Dekho** – Usha Khanna *Yeh chaand saa roshan chehra* – **Kashmir Ki Kali** – O.P. Nayyar *Asman se aaya farishta*- **An Evening In Paris**-Shankar Jaikishan *Aaja aaja main hoon pyaar tera*- **Teesri Manzil** -R.D. Burman *Aawaz deke hamein tum bulaao*-**Professor**-Shankar Jaikishan *Dil ke jharoke mein tujhko bithakar*- **Brahmchari**- Shankar Jaikishan *Re Mama Re Mama Re* – **Andaz** – Shankar Jaikishan

Shammi Kapoor, Mohd. Rafi and their songs have become inseparable, from each other and from the swinging 60s that they represented.

By the 70's the scene changed with one Superstar looming large on the Indian Silver Screen .Say Rajesh Khanna and all you can think of is his trade mark smile , the tilt of his head , dialogue delivery and his silver screen romances. Essential to making him a superstar and the ultimate romantic hero are some evergreen tunes that resurrect during Valentine's Day.

Rajesh Khanna's Romantic songs ruled the roost . Be it Mere **Sapno Ki Rani from Aaradhana** , the **sensous Roop Tera Mastana , Kora Kagaz Tha ye dil mera a declaration of love againfrom Aaradhana , O mere Dil ke chain from Mere Jeevan Saathi** . And in romance sometimes there is the feeling of heart brake . While Khanna made ladies swoon , he also excelled at expressing the pain of love in a song like **Yeh Jo Mohabat Hai from Kati Patang.** But in the same movie there was another song which was more uplifting **Yeh Sham Mastani.** A peppy and foot tapping song from Rajesh Khanna's movie Aap Ki Kasam was **Jai Jai Shiv Shankar** . But two of his songs become anthem for Celebration of Life or a sort of Salutation to life one being **Zindagi Ek Safar Suhana and the other from his landmark film Anand – Jindagi Kaisi Hai Paheli** . A Film in which Khanna diagnosed as person with Cancer Limpho Circoma of the intestine to be exact ,spends his last moments with his doctor played by Amitabh Bacchan and changes the perspective of life for the people around him . Making them believe Life is to cherished even if it is shortlived. A dialogues is still etched in my mind **" Jindagi Badi Honi Chahiye Babumoshay Lambi Nahi"**

With this film another star was born and become the face of the Angry young man of the 80's the legend Amitabh Bachann. Even though most of his films were filled with resentment and aggression against the socio –political scene of the 80's , they too had memmerising songs be it O Saathi Re from Mukadar ka Sikandar , Choo kar mere man ko from Yarana or that zesty song Khai ke Pan Banaraswala sung by the vivascious Kishore Kumar. Legend has it to get exact feeling Kishore da had a special Banarasi Paan made for him and actually chewed the same before singing this hit song. Then there were the softer numbers like **Tere Mere Milan Ki ye Raina form Abhiman with unforgettable lines like "tujhe thaame kayi haathon se miloonga madbhari raaton se" and the other gem Inteha Ho gayi Intezar Ki again with memorable lines which go 'baat jo hai usmein, baat wo yahaan kahin nahi kisi mein, wo hai meri bas hai meri, shor hai yehi gali gali mei.'**

In late 70's and early 80's you had films from Basu Chaterjee and Hrishikesh Mukherjee with the common man's hero Amol Palekar in the lead and unforgettable songs like Janeman Janeman Tere Tere do Nayan , Uthe Sab ke Kadam Dekho Ram Pam Pam ,Gori Tera Gaon Bada

Pyara , Suniye Kahiye Kahiye , Na Bole Tum Na Maine Kuchh Kaha and Aanewala Pal . All these songs as affable as Amol Palekar himself.

Those were the days of pure melody , with songs touching your heart with lyrics so simple and hummable that every time you heard these songs you wanted to sing along. To end I would like to rededicate one of my favorite songs and one which I used to woo my then fiancé and now my sweetheart wifey Kashmira ..

Bade Acche lagte hai
Kyaa????
Yeh Dharti, yeh nadiyaa, yeh rainaa aur?
Aur tum
Bade Acchee lagte hai
Yeh Dharti, yeh nadiyaa, yeh rainaa aur?
Aur tum mm mmmm
Hum tum kitane paas hai
kitane duur hain chaand sitaare
Sach poochho to maan ko jhoothe lagate hain yeh saare
Magar saccche lagate hai
Yeh Dharti yeh nadiyaa, yeh rainaa aur?
Aur tum mm mmmmmm
Tum in sab ko chood ke kaise kal subah jaaogi
Mere saath inhe bhi to tum yaad bahut aaogi
Tum in sab ko chood ke kaise kal subah jaaogi
Mere saath inhe bhi to tum yaad bahut aaogi

Bade Acche lagte hai
Yeh Dharti, yeh nadiyaa, yeh rainaa aur?
Aur tum mm mmmmm

Bade Acche lagte hai
hmmmm hmmmm hmmm hmmmm hmm

hmm hmm hmmm

A Little more of Kandil & Diya ...A Little less of Crackers & Baksheesh..

The Great Indian Festival is ON not on the online e-comm portals of Amazon or Flipkart but in our homes in the real world ....**Its Diwali Time folks** . The real deal the biggest and brightest festival celebrated across India. The festival for which you can shout out Lights (Diyas , Kandils & Twinkling Rice bulb streamers) Sound (sounds of crackers) Action (little kids in the family scampering around the house with energy)..Yes the festival that creeps up on us all to bring in lots of positive energy and family bonding..

But the anticipation starts building nearly a fortnight in advance with plans being made for shopping and list been drawn for gifts and sundries to be purchased. On top of the list is shopping for ethnic wares for the kids and the Missus. Be it deals on dresses at the neighborhood shops or the latest designs at the Malls. But the best places to shop for Salwars , Kurtis or the latest one –piece dress for the women folk are the nooks and corners of the old markets like the shops in **Hind Mata Market or the Gandhi Market in King circle** or even the cloth market in MJ Market or the Mangaldas Market in South Mumbai . If you're after cloth by the meter or un-stitched dress material to make Indian outfits, **Mangaldas Market and Mulji Jetha Market (also called M.J. Market)** are where you should head.

Located close to each other, these sprawling wholesale markets are among the largest textile markets in Asia. Rows and rows of stalls are filled to the brim with a diverse assortment of fabrics, from bling to block prints. Mangaldas Market, traditionally home to traders from Gujarat, is a mini-town, complete with lanes of fabrics. Even if you're not the type to have your clothes tailored, drop by DD Dupattawala for pretty scarves and dupatta's and the latest in thing Lehriya dupatta's at great bargain prices .

These fabric or the semi stitched dresses can then be tailored at your neighborhood and faithful family tailor .Special instructions are given on cut and design taking inspiration from the loyal Google or that one special go person in your family who is an expert in Fashion.

With clothes out of the way the next on the shopping list is the **Faral the sweet and namkeen savories** to be gorged during Diwali. Traditionally this is a community activity in which the ladies of the house gather together and make all the yummy delicacies like Besan Ladoo , Rava Ladoo , some age old specialties like Chirote similar to a Karanji but more flatter and crispy or Balushahi also known as Sathe a mini doughnut shaped sweet covered with sugar layer on both sides. The faral making sessions make for a great get together in the families with aunts , sisters , mother and mother-in-law and Aaji all coming together and enjoying several afternoons making the delicacies and sharing some much wanted gossips.

But times have changed with most of the ladies of the house being working all these faral items are bought from well known Maharashtrain shops like Panshikar's and Godbole's in Dadar or a Aswad in Shivaji Park some smaller gems like Ashok Masale at City Light where you get the tastiest Bhajani chi Chakli .

Once the sweets and the Namkeen are bought next on the list is the favourite item for the bacha company ---The Crackers. Depending on the age and the desire crackers are bought for the colourful lights they emit or the sound thye make. The usual favourites being the flower pot and zameen chakri emanating beautiful colors make the evening bright . during my childhood you could hear the ear shattering sounds of a sulti bomb or a square bomb going off every now and then and the king of crackers the 1000 or 10000 chi Laddi which would go on for 15-20 minutes . But better conscience coupled with positive campaign of lowering the decibel have made people choose light over sound during Diwali.

But Diwali cannot be said to be complete without the decoration of lights . To buy the best Kandil's go to the Kandil Galli in Mahim . Here you can catch sight of beautiful kandils (lanterns) in all shapes, sizes, colours, and patterns. Shops stretching from Citylight cinema all the way up to Hinduja Hospital situated next to Bombay Scottish School are flooded with kandils and in the evenings the entire place is lit up giving the feeling as if we are inside a lantern festival. Mahim's Kandil Galli, located at LJ Road, is known as the lantern market of Mumbai, and during Diwali, people from all over the city come to buy lanterns from shops in this locality, which have been operating for decades.

Another Diwali ritual or more like the Colonial hangover is the Baksheesh. The scores of community helpers suddenly lining up you door asking for "Sir ji Diwali". The usual postman , the security guy , BMC cleaners , the telephone lineman and till some time back the mostly invisible Telegraph man (Taar wala) –the bearer of extreme good news or the urgent bad news . Every one of them expecting some extra cash . But this has now dwindled over last few years to the very basic people who serve us and you don't mind giving them a little "Diwali"

And finally you have to shop for the earthen diyas from **Kumbharwada's in Sion - Mahim.** Be it the small star shaped or heart shaped diya the size of your thumbs or the bigger palm sized diyas in shapes of leaf's , conch or the Paisley motifs. Some brightly colored and some bedecked with shining stones . Light them in the evening and sit back and enjoy the wick burning bright and emanating a serene glow as if Goddess Laxmi herself showering you with her blessings....

Happy Diwali to all my readers.....

CHAPTER FORTY-TWO

Mawa Cakes and Mutton Puffs

The Brit's gave us a habit of high tea with evening snacks. Further nurtured by our very own gora's the Parsis.It could be a light snack of Cheese Sandwiches or those light and succulent and fluffy Chicken or Mutton puffs. But sometimes they also used to have a sweet muffin or a brownie. A muffin is an individual-sized, baked product. It can refer to two distinct items, a part-raised flatbread and a cupcake-like quick bread. The flatbread is of British or European derivation, and dates from at least the early 18th century, while the quick bread originated in North America during the 19th century. Both are common worldwide today.

Quickbread muffins (known in Britain as American muffin or simply as "muffins") originated in the United States in the mid-19th century. The use of the term to describe what are essentially cup cakes or buns did not become common usage in Britain until the last decades of the 20th century on the back of the spread of coffee shops such as Starbucks. (There is lingering resistance in the UK to the term as being inapplicable to cakes.) They are similar to cupcakes in size and cooking methods, the main difference being that cupcakes tend to be sweet desserts using cake batter and which are often topped with sugar icing (American frosting). Muffins are available in both savoury varieties, such as corn meal and cheese muffins, or sweet varieties such as blueberry, chocolate chip, lemon or banana flavours. They are often eaten as a breakfast food, often accompanied by coffee or tea. Fresh baked muffins are sold by bakeries, donut shops and some fast-food restaurants and coffeehouses.

In India especially in Mumbai where there is our very own version of this sweet piece of snack...the Mawa cake . Those perfectly round brown cupcakes sitting in big glass jars or glass top cake display units at the famous Irani Cafes like Jimmy Boy , Café Britannia , Café Mondegar in SoBo district or local Irani café's in old Mumbai areas of Dadar – Matunga like the famous Koolar's at King Circle or Café Colony in Hindu Colony . Order a cup of chai and peel of the butter paper around these delicious savouries and gobble them up. And if you have sweet tooth you wont stop at one.

The mawacake is maybe not the most aesthetic looking creation of the cake world, although SodaBottleOpenerWala does seem to have prettified it with icing and such. Everywhere else though, it's just a plain dense cake, made with mawa. Sometimes it is prepared as a slab, and thick slices are lopped off and served. And sometimes, it is served in dainty cupcake form with a little frill of a paper wrapper around it that requires careful unwrapping. The mawa in the cake makes it dense and rich, and adds a caramelised flavour. The richness is laced with a hint of cardamom and sometimes nutmeg. Traditionally, it comes with cashew nuts and sometimes almonds, crowning the top. It is the sort of cake you would order with a cup of hot tea, after a long, miserable day that has dulled your spirit.

Nobody can really say how the cake came about: the birth of the mawacake is a mystery that has been lost in the shroud of history. Certainly, B Merwan claims to have invented it but then so does Pune's Royal Bakery. Perhaps it was the fortuitous result of twiddling and tweaking the boring old sponge cake, or an upgrade of the traditional **kumas**(a sort of semolina cake). It may well have been a way to preserve milk from spoiling in the days when there were no refrigerators (after all, *mawa* is the milk product you get after boiling milk for a long time, until it turns into a blob of dough-like milk solids). There's only one thing for sure - there was certainly no *mawa* cake before the wave of immigrants that took over all the corner spaces in the city and opened their Irani cafes.

If you want to try the best Mawa Cakes then you should visit the old Irani / Parsi bakeries which double up as Café's . Like the Kayani Bakery and Café just opposite Metro Cinema at Dobhi Talao. Perhaps the oldest Irani café of them all, it's located in the most central area of Dhobi Talao, with Metro cinema, and St. Xaviers college serving as its important landmarks. As such, one can safely say that the ever-constant popularity of Kyani makes sure it doesn't need any. Standing out as a proud structure of heritage amidst the bustle of South Mumbai, a peek into the café will always be greeted with crowded tables, and friendly staff.

Located at a stone's throw away from Kyani, the century-old Sassanian is the one-stop place for anyone craving a serving of great bun maska, puddings, cakes and khari, a flour biscuit one eats with tea.

Another favourite snack with that hot pipping cup of chai are the special Chicken / Mutton Puffs or pattice as they are colloquially called .These triangular multi-layered fluffy pattice are to die for satisfying those late afternoon hunger pangs and giving you the much needed extra energy to take you through the evening time. If you ask me where do you get the best Mutton puffs only 2 places come to my mind. Sunshine Snack Corner, about ten minutes away from the bustle of Causeway, is one such place, selling the most delicious puffs, cutlets, and sandwiches, and at budget friendly prices. The first thing that drew you into Sunshine Snack Counter is the Pink Panther mural on its walls.

The second thing—and this one's the keeper—is the counter stacked with mutton puffs, cutlets, and samosas. This no-frills eating joint takes up a small corner near Colaba Post Office and is made up of a counter and a couple of tables presided over by the aforementioned cartoon mural. As citizens of Mumbai, I've eaten my share of mutton puffs, so when I say these were some of the best I've had, I do hope you take me seriously. The pastry outside is light and perfectly crisp and flaky, while the filling—to quote our favourite picky eater—is just right. Not too spicy or bland, not too dry or too soggy, it was just the right amount of piquant with a welcome dash of freshness from the chunks of tomato and onion that hadn't been cooked down into an unrecognizable paste. The cutlet is similarly tasty, with a rawa-fried batter and a filling typical of most Parsi-style mutton cutlets – erring on the spicy side but tempered with bits of potato. This is a real gem to have your Mutton puff / pattice.

Another famous place is in Bandra goes by the name of Hearsch Bakery. The J Hearsch Bakery that flanks the Holy Family Hospital is a Bandra Landmark that even townies are known to make the pilgrimage to for a hearty meal of burgers , puffs and freshly made lemonade.What no one knows is that this friendly neighbourhood bakery wouldn't have been around had Britain not declared war on Germany in 1914 and gentleman named Hearsch had not met a Colaba lady. Hearsch bakery is a remnant of a time when Bandra's hub of street couture, Hill Road, was renowned merely for its hospitals. Nearly a hundred years ago, a young and enterprising Goan girl ventured onto the very same street. Having just pulled the curtains down on her most recent venture -- Connaught Bakery on Colaba Causeway -- Sophia Liberata Fernandes was disillusioned about the future. It was here that she first heard of a German baker, who wished to lease out his bakery. Rather urgently as well, from the sound of things

In the wake of the First World War, relations between Germany and Britain had witnessed a significant decay. Britain's colonies, including India, were no longer safe for Germans. It was in the 1920s, under such trying circumstances that a bread man, J Hearsch, reluctantly decided to give up his labour of love, a small bakery, and head for the safer shores of Germany. Quite by chance, he met Sophia, who was keen to start a bakery in Bandra, after shutting down her shop in Colaba. Hearsch entrusted the passionate Sophia with his life's work, and fled to Germany, and obscurity.

Hearsch bakery is located on the busy Hill Road, and knowledge of its closest landmark, Mocha Mojo, won't do you much good. However, ask the most lethargic local for directions and he will guide you with alacrity, and some pride even. Located within the idyllic premise of a forbiddingly-gated British era bungalow, the bakery is a hidden gem of sorts. Top a juicy burger (Rs 50) off with some velvety mousse (Rs 30) and wash it down with lemonade (made fresh, on the spot and for Rs 20 only), and you are still light by only a hundred rupees.

By 7 AM, the bakery is abuzz with cooks and bakers working on preparations that have made Hearsch famous. A good mixture of youngsters and veterans work round the clock in the kitchen, kneading, baking, frying and decorating all that food which graces the counters of the store. The puffs and sandwiches are the fastest moving items, with about a hundred of each prepared in a single batch.

The special mayonnaise, Hearsch's best-kept secret, is the trickiest concoction. Vary but a little from the original recipe, and the D'Sa brothers -- Melvin and Steven, who mind the counter at different times of the day -- have to suffer much criticism from patrons

The prices are the least of Hearsch's links to a time long forgotten. The idyllic positioning of the bakery makes it a perfect romancing spot. Construction rocks next to the bakery are inadvertently positioned underneath an ageing tree and are enclosed by furry emerald patches of grass. While the area does not technically fall under the property of the bakery, Mr.D'Sa the current manager admits to witnessing a wealth of romances blossom here over the years.

Most patrons sit on the well-laid out stones that also serve as table tops for their glasses of shake. The neighbourhood cats keep a keen eye on their paper plates too, but being well-mannered, they wait patiently for patrons to throw them in the waste bins. They then proceed to rummage the bins, fighting only with the crows, who tend to get there first.

This suburban bakery, barely a stone's throw from actor Salman Khan's house, is visited by celebrities too

So next time you are a little bit hungry and want that much needed cup of chai , try these awesome places for a little bit of mawa cakes or mutton puffs to go with your piping hot cuppa.

CHAPTER FORTY-THREE

Sakhar Chapati and other memorable childhood snacks...

The other day read an article in The Times Of India about the Marathi Actor **Amey Wagh** who played **Banesh (Faster) Fene** in last years one of the top Marathi grosser "Faster Fene" talking about his favorite childhood tiffin snack of **Tup Sakhar Poli** made by his mother and given in his school dabba. Most of us too have had this snack while growing up as kids. The taste of freshly made chapatti smeared with healthy amount os Tup or homemade ghee and then sprinkled with sparkling crystals of sugar and slightly heated on the Tawa to make it a little crispy.Bitting into this yummy snack would leave a mouth-watering after taste which would linger on for hours together. A similar version can be made with the mixed fruit jam smeared on the same chapatti and rolled to make jam roll , but its nowhere near the **Tup Sakhar Chapati (Poli)**

Another favorite tiffin snack was the **Thikhat Meethachya Purya** , those fluffy puris made with whole wheat as basic ingredient and only salt and red chilly powder mixed in the right proportion to make them a little salty and a little spicy. These could be eaten all by themselves or with the ever faithful Tomato Ketchup. A lip-smacking snack which could be had anytime either at lunch time during tiffin break or as a energy recharger in the evening just before going down to play. A sweet version of these also was a hit with us kids . The puris made with mixing ripe bananas into the atta and then frying them golden brown. But these needed to be had right out of the kadai , hot and sweet and if you had a mint and dhania chutney to go with it toh kya Baat. Yummy and delicious. A special version of this sweet snack was the **Banana Mulka or Banana Appam** made with ripened banana and jaggery mixed to form a batter then wheat flour added to this mixture as a binder , salt to taste , Elaichi powder to give is a flavour and sometimes a little semolina or Rava as we call to give these fritter that crispiness. Deep fried to dark brown and served hot these small round bhajji type mulka are heavenly to taste also filling for the energetic young kids.

We did not have the concept of breakfast during school days as the school itself was from 10AM to 5PM with 2 lunch breaks . So most days breakfast was a mugful of milk with Parle G or Prasad Toast. But sometimes if we were bored we had desi cum continental breakfast. Yes desi-continental in terms of Rice flakes our Maharashtrian Patal pohe dunked in a bowl of Milk and sugar. A healthy and wholesome snack. The same snack could be made into a salty one by using yogurt instead of milk and pinch of salt instead of the sugar. And if you could get Mom to use her magic by giving it a tadka of finely chopped green chilies , some roasted peanuts , crackling mustard seeds and few curry leaves the snack could be turned into a mini meal by itself. To be savored by all in the family. A close replica of the Curd –Rice or Tahir Sadam from down south.

Another favorite tiffin snack and the most simple to make was the chutney sandwich with its sweet –salty green chutney spread over 2 slices of bread mostly a **Wibs or a Modern bread.** And yes a white bread there was no option of Brown bread or the mutli grain that you get today. But this little snack would be shared during tiffin time and gobbled up to the last crumb. The chutney sandwich was also a favorite at birthday parties and was most popular next only to the humble Samosa-Wafer combination.Makes my mouth water up just thinking about these nick-knacks.

Most times the tiffin was filled with the chapatti bahji which was made at home to save on cooking time.

But at times when this got boring a request would go out to Mom for a Frankie type veg roll or a paratha to make lunch time in school a little bit interesting. Now a days instead of the veggies my Wifey makes an indulging Cheese roll for my kids which get devoured by them during tiffin time without even a small morsel coming back. Though what comes back are compliments from fellow students in their class eagerly shared with their Mom at the end of the day.

On certain days of the week like a Wednesday or Friday we were allowed to take non-veg items to school. Nothing fancy but a small variation like the **Anda Paratha** with Chapati as the base and whisked egg omelette on top , roasted to perfect union and then rolled up to make a lip smacking snack was a to die for snack as also much awaited break from the regular bhaji chapatti

.The other spicy option was **Bhurji Chapati** made with tomatoes , sauteed onion, a pinch salt of some chopped green chilies and a pinch of red chilly powder added to the scrambled eggs to make a perfect dish to go with the drab chapatti.A tasty and filling tiffin time option.

I still remember those school lunch break . A time to pool in the variety of snacks among our regular group. Sharing the food and some lively banter. Joking ,Laughing and sometimes pulling each others and generally having a great time.A well deserved break from the stern teachers and days long studies.

Here's wishing all my readers year full of Gastronomic adventure and a fabulous New Year 2019. Enjoy the food , Stay healthy and Happy Reading.....

CHAPTER FORTY-FOUR

New Year ...New Calendars.

The latest joke going around on the social media is **" Utarli Kaa ???........Bhinti Varchi Calendar's....ha ha ha...**

As the New Year starts, it's the start of a new yearly journey and new beginning for every one of us with the start date set at January 1st and end date set at December 31st . The 365 days in between for us to live our life to the fullest and make some of our dreams come true. Some milestones to achieve, so important events to attend ,have some great time with our families and overall make some memories.

Every one knows that the English Calendar or The Gregorian calendar is the most widely used civil calendar in the world. In 1582, when Pope Gregory XIII introduced his Gregorian calendar, Europe adhered to the Julian calendar, first implemented by Julius Caesar in 46 B.C. Since the Roman emperor's system miscalculated the length of the solar year by 11 minutes, the calendar had since fallen out of sync with the seasons. This concerned Gregory because it meant that Easter, traditionally observed on March 21, fell further away from the spring equinox with each passing year.

The Julian calendar included an extra day in February every four years. But Aloysus Lilius, the Italian scientist who developed the system Pope Gregory would unveil in 1582, realized that the addition of so many days made the calendar slightly too long. He devised a variation that adds leap days in years divisible by four, unless the year is also divisible by 100. If the year is also divisible by 400, a leap day is added regardless. While this formula may sound confusing, it did resolve the lag created by Caesar's earlier scheme—almost.

Though Pope Gregory's papal bull reforming the calendar had no power beyond the Catholic Church, Catholic countries—including Spain, Portugal and Italy—swiftly adopted the new system for their civil affairs. European Protestants, however, largely rejected the change because of its ties to the papacy, fearing it was an attempt to silence their movement. It wasn't until 1700 that Protestant Germany switched over, and England held out until 1752. Orthodox countries clung to the Julian calendar until even later, and their national churches have never embraced Gregory's reforms.

According to some accounts, English citizens did not react kindly after an act of Parliament advanced the calendar overnight from September 2 to September 14, 1752. Rioters supposedly took to the streets, demanding that the government "give us our 11 days." However, most historians now believe that these protests never occurred or were greatly exaggerated. On the other side of the Atlantic, meanwhile, Benjamin Franklin welcomed the change, writing, "It is pleasant for an old man to be able to go to bed on September 2, and not have to get up until September 14."

Julius Caesar's calendar reform of 46 B.C. instituted January 1 as the first of the year. During the Middle Ages, however, European countries replaced it with days that carried greater religious significance, such as December 25 (the anniversary of Jesus' birth) and March 25 (the Feast of the Annunciation). The latter, known as Lady Day because it celebrates the Virgin Mary, marked the beginning of the year in Britain until January 1, 1752.

New year doesn't begin on January 1 for everyone.It can vary in different religions and cultures.Among the variations, there is Chinese New Year which takes place sometime between January 21 and February 21 each year and includes celebrations in China and among Chinese communities across the globe.This year 2019 is said to be the Year of the Pig.Which will be celebrated with gusto and pomp . With Dragon parades and two of the most famous Chinese food items as part of their traditional lunch the Jiaozi or the dumplings and Tang Yuan or the glutinous rice balls.

There's also Islamic New Year, which also has a variable date.In 2019, it will start on September 10 - the first day of the month of Muharram and the start of Islamic year 1441.The Islamic calendar is based on the moon and this means dates move back by 10 or 11 days each year within the longer, sun-based, January-to-December Gregorian calendar used by most of the Western world.This can make it difficult even for Muslims themselves to keep track of the dates.

The Islamic calendar or Hijri calendar follows the cycle of the moon.Hijrah is an Arabic word meaning migration - it refers to the migration of the prophet Muhammad from Mecca to Medina in 622 AD, an event that marks the start of the Islamic calendar.

In 17 AH (638 AD/CE), Abu Musa Ashaari, one of the officials of the Caliph Umar in Basrah, complained about the absence of any years on the correspondence he received from Umar, making it difficult for him to determine which instructions were most recent. This report convinced Umar of the need to introduce an era for Muslims. After debating the issue with his counsellors, he decided that the first year should include the date of Muhammad's arrival at Medina (known as Yathrib, before Muhammad's arrival). Uthman ibn Affan then suggested that the months begin with Muharram, in line with the established custom of the Arabs at that time. The years of the Islamic calendar thus began with the month of Muharram in the year of Muhammad's arrival at the city of Medina, even though the actual emigration took place in Safar and Rabi' I. Because of the Hijra, the calendar was named the Hijri calendar.

The first day of the first month of the Islamic calendar (1 Muharram 1 AH) was set to the first new moon after the day the Prophet moved from Quba' to Medina (originally 26 Rabi' I on the pre-Islamic calendar) i.e., Friday, 16 July 622 AD/CE, the equivalent civil tabular date (same daylight period) in the Julian calendar. The Islamic day began at the preceding sunset on the evening of 15 July. This Julian date (16 July) was determined by medieval Muslim astronomers by projecting back in time their own tabular Islamic calendar, which had alternating 30- and 29-day months in each lunar year plus eleven leap days every 30 years. For example, al-Biruni mentioned this Julian date in the year 1000 AD/CE. Although not used by either medieval Muslim astronomers or modern scholars to determine the Islamic epoch, the thin crescent moon would have also first become visible (assuming clouds did not obscure it) shortly after the preceding sunset on the evening of 15 July, 1.5 days after the associated dark moon (astronomical new moon) on the morning of 14 July.

Four of the twelve Hijri months are considered sacred: Rajab (7), and the three consecutive months of Dhū al-Qa'dah (11), Dhu al-Hijjah (12) and Muḥarram (1). As the lunar calendar lags behind the solar calendar by about ten days every Gregorian year, months of the Islamic calendar fall in different parts of the Gregorian calendar each year. The cycle repeats every 33 lunar years. Each month of the Islamic calendar commences on the birth of the new lunar cycle. Traditionally this is based on actual observation of the crescent (*hilal*) marking the end of the previous lunar cycle and hence the previous month, thereby beginning the new month. Consequently, each month can have 29 or 30 days depending on the visibility of the moon, astronomical positioning of the earth and weather conditions. However, certain sects and groups, most notably Bohras Muslims namely Alavis, Dawoodis and Sulaymanis and Shia Ismaili Muslims, use a tabular Islamic calendar in which odd-numbered months have thirty days (and also the twelfth month in a leap year) and even months have 29.

The important dates like Shab e Barat (or Lailat al Bara'a) , Ramadan (Ramzan) Eid , Eid Ul Fitr , Moharram and Milad al Nabi (Prophet Mohammed's birthday) are based mostly on astronomical charts and are adopted by some Muslims, particularly governments that must plan forward for civic and public occasions.However for a lot of others, a sighting of the primary crescent of the brand new moon is required to find out when a month or occasion ought to truly begin so among the dates may change barely nearer the time.

The boisterous and jovial Sikh's also have their own Calendar, "The Nanakshahi calendar" . It was created to establish fixed dates for observing important Sikh commemorative events related to the history of the Sikh gurus which took place in ancient Punjab. It includes Birth (Prakash – The manifestation of Light), Inauguration as Guru (Guru Gadee – Enthronement) and Martyrdom or Death (Jyoti Jot – the merging of manifest light into Divine Light)

Sikhs have traditionally recognized two eras and luni-solar calendars: thc Nanakshahi and Khalsa. Traditionally, both these calendars closely followed the Bikrami calendar with the Nanakshahi year beginning on Katak Pooranmashi (full moon) and the Khalsa year commencing with Vaisakhi. The methods for calculating the beginning of the Khalsa era were based on the Bikrami calendar. The year length was also the same as the Bikrami solar year .The calendar has twelve lunar months that are determined by the lunar phase, but thirteen months in leap years which occur every 2–3 years in the Bikrami calendar to sync the lunar calendar with its solar counterpart.References to the Nanakshahi Era have been made in historic documents .Banda Singh Bahadur adopted the Nanakshahi calendar in 1710 C.E. after his victory in Sirhind (12 May 1710 C.E.) according to which the year 1710 C.E. became Nanakshahi 241. However, according to Dilagira (1997), he "continued adopting the months and thc days of thc months according to the Bikrami calendar".Banda Singh Bahadur also minted new coins also called Nanakshahi.

The revised Nanakshahi calendar was designed by Pal Singh Purewal to replace the Bikrami calendar. The epoch of this calendar is the birth of the first Sikh Guru, Nanak Devin 1469 and the Nanakshahi year commences on 1

Chet. New Year's Day falls annually on what is March 14 in the Gregorian Western calendar. The start of each month is fixed. The solar accuracy of the Nanakshahi calendar is linked to the Gregorian civil calendar. This is because the Nanaskhahi calendar uses the tropical year instead of using the sidereal year which is used in the Bikrami calendar or the old Nanakshahi and Khalsa calendars.

The amended Nanakshahi calendar was adopted in 1998but implemented in 2003 by the Shiromani Gurdwara Prabhandak Committee the governing office of Sikhism located in the Punjab to determine the dates for important Sikh events and mandating its use The events and dates of The Nanakshahi calendar entries given may differ by months, or even years, from original historical records such as the *Vikram Samvat (SV), or Bikram Sambat (BK)*, calendar based on lunar cycle dating. Some of the names of the Nanakshahi months are like those of the Hindu Calendar. Like for example Vaishakh , Jeth , Savan (Shravan) , Bhadho (Bhadrapad), Magh and Pahgan (Phalgun).

Talking about Hindu Calendars the most famous one is the Kalnirnay Calmanac. the iconic calendar was born in 1972, originally in Marathi.Jayant Salgaokar creator and the publisher ,envisioned it as more than a calendar. Published in nine languages, it performs a multi-pronged role. It serves most crucially as a panchang, an astrological diary that informs you about the position of planets and hence, is consulted before selecting appropriate and auspicious times for important occasions. It lists festivals, carries a horoscope, recipes, medical advice, and articles written by experts in their fields, by stalwarts like Durga Bhagwat and PL Deshpande. It also serves as a reminder for the woman of the house. It even allows you to jot notes on the number of clothes given to the dhobi or items that have to be procured for the kitchen. So, essentially, everyone in the home would use it.

As Kalnirnay enters its 45th year, the thrust is on conquering the digital space. They were the first in Mumbai to have an online retail website, much like Amazon is doing today. This was way back in 1995. They shut it down eventually when competition arrived. They launched an app in 2010, when apps were a new thing. So they have always been ahead of the times, Right now, they are using the Facebook and Twitter platforms to figure what their customers want. This is in a testing phase. Though their core business will always be the printed almanac, they want to widen their social media imprint to reach their existing customer more effectively while attracting a new audience. Kalnirnay currently prints 20 million copies of the calendar and the app has 5 million subscribers.

In a new advertisement released on their YouTube channel, the almanac is no longer the gift given to a daughter when she is married. Now, it goes with her to Harvard. Kalnirnay is a tradition that's passed down over generations. But now, they don't just rely on the institution of marriage. People from all over the world order it every year. Patel Stores in New York displays it proudly when it gets there at the start of the year, Shakti Salgaonkar Yezdani grand daughter of late Jayant Salgaonkar and her young social media team ensure that it's not just the almanac that reaches out to their audience but even the writings of literary greats.They go through back issues and pick interesting archival reads for the new reader. It's about giving them everything the almanac offers and more.

Recently, the office of the Prime Minister called Jayraj Salgaonkar son of Jayant Salgaonkar and the current

Managing Director of Kalnirnay and asked, Does Kalnirnay have a Gujarati version?' He said, yes. 'Is it available on iPad?' He said, no. 'Do you know Mr Modi reads on the iPad? He won't be happy if he can't read it in Gujarati on his iPad'. He promptly called his contact in Silicon Valley and got the app designed in Gujarati. That's what you call Changing with the Times . As in the famous Bob Dylan song **"The Times, They Are A Changing"**.

So this New Year Ring out the Old and Ring In the New, in your life both metaphorically and in action.

Wishing all my readers a very Happy New Year 2019 and Happy Reading.....

CHAPTER FORTY-FIVE

Eggcellent Eggilicious Sunday's

One day in the week everyone looks forward to after the daily grind and other family responsibilities taken care off is the SUNDAY. A day spent catching up on lost sleep, relaxing and generally lazing around at a pace much slower than the rushed up week days. Sunday's is also for those late breakfasts in between many cups of tea and the customary reading of The Sunday Times to catch up on the weekly news , views and all that in between on Arts Culture and Sports . A perfect start to the morning or late afternoon depending upon when you get up.

But the one thing I look forward to is the Eggiliscious breakfast on such lazy Sunday. I am passionate about eggs. For a person who doesn't quite enjoy toiling in the kitchen, an egg is like a wonder ingredient. From plain, simple and sumptuously satisfying omelettes to the more exquisite preparations including the worlds of the Benedict, Scotch eggs and much more - it is an item that can go along with its master - whether a beginner or a sophisticated chef. I don't care much about my breakfast till it is energy dense, full of nutrients sans any junk. Perfectly done eggs along with a glass of juice or our kadak chai, a couple of slices of whole grain bread or the soft ladi pav and I am set. Though I am the kind of person who doesn't get bored of classics easily, having a profession which involves a lot of travel, a chance to eat a variety of egg preparations for breakfast is something I would call my personal bliss.

Moreover, there is just so much that one can do with eggs. You don't need elaborate prepping to cooks eggs. While omelets, half fries and the classic hard-boiled would seem passe to most food enthusiasts, the poached, scrambled, baked or for that matter deviled versions are a certain hit with foodies. Lets admit, eggs and breakfast go hand in hand for most of us. It is as ubiquitous a combination as that of a needle and thread. But for those who loathe monotony and detest routine in their days there are recipes that are yummy and also fills the tummy. Some mouthwatering some pleasing to the eye and some just spicy to make your taste buds dance with ecstasy.

Parathas are undoubtedly a staple Indian food that can be eaten with almost anything. **Mughlai Paratha or the Baida Roti** as famously known in Bengali household is one such variety that has a huge fan following. Parathas or Rotisstuffed with eggs and fried to perfection, **Baida Roti** is popular Bengali street food that is relished right from Kolkotta to Mumbai.

Staying in Matunga and surrounded by Irani / Parsi Café's like **Koolar's , Café Gulshan and Café Colony** one of the special egg recipe is the **Akuri.** Akuri is the perfectly scrambled eggs for the Indian palate – tad spicy, creamy, hint of coriander. It forms a perfect breakfast dish or a snack sitting neatly on top of a crisp toast.Also can be had with laddi pav or the crunchy Brun or Kadak pav as it is known in Mumbai.

Another favorite egg dish while sitting at any Irani Café is the Masala Omelette. A spicy combination eggs whisked with flavorful spices, onions and tomatoes. Masala omelette is the classic Indian breakfast recipe that is quick, easy to prepare and full of flavour. Another specialty at **Koolar's Café is The Wrestlers Omelette.** The aptly named Wrestler Omelette packs in five eggs, and is vouched for by some of the city's best body builders including fitness expert Kaizaad Kapadia. This five-egg omelette may constitute a typical breakfast for a wrestler, but for those of us not in the muscle flexing business, it's a breakfast challenge. The omelette takes about 20 minutes to prepare, but is well worth the wait. The eggs are whisked with chopped onions, green chilies and some coriander, and seasoned with just the right amount of salt. Two people can easily split the dish, or if you're feeling particularly indulgent, take it on by yourself.

A complex egg recipe is the Eggs Benedict . Bread topped with blanched spinach, smoked salmon, a delicately poached egg and Hollandaise sauce with a pinch of paprika. Let your taste buds go on a roller coaster of flavors with this classic egg dish.

One more difficult egg recipe is the stuffed egg. A little bit of effort and this recipe helps you tap your culinary potential. Hard-boiled eggs loaded with masalas, nuts, cheese and tamarind paste, dipped in a smooth batter and fried golden. One of my favorite recipes and made lovingly by my wifey's maternal aunt Sunita Maushi. Yummy to taste and finger licking recipe, when you eat this you can't stop at one.

One egg recipe which I found was unique and unusual was the Omelette Curry introduced to me Jagdish dada , again my Wifey's cousin from Goa. As you know Omelettes are simple, filling and never boring. This recipe offers a fresh depart from the usual, a tomato based curry with omelette chunks dipped deep in. A twist to the usual omelette that we have in breakfast, turn it around and relish it for lunch too

And how can you write about egg recipes and not write about the childhood favorite Egg and Cheese French Toast. The mouthwatering breakfast option is made up of slices of bread coated in a batter of egg and spices along with a generous helping of cheese.

I can not but skip a very unique eggitarian dish I recently had during one of my sales visits in Ahmedabad. An otherwise pure vegetarian city but there is this place called the Ahmedabad Food Truck an open area / ground near Karnawati Club where you will find 10-12 food trucks parked duiring the day and night. During evening time this area comes alive with lights and action . With smeels of delicious non-veg food wafting from each Truck. It's a non-vegetarians paradise. Here your get Tandoory chicken , Chicken tikka's and kabab's. Wraps of multiple kinds , some spicy some cheesy but all of them mouth watering. Some specialize in Chicken and Mutton dishes and 2 in egg dishes. At one of these trucks called the **Egg's World you get Old and famous John Ki Roti** a really scrumptious egg wrap made in a very unique way.It has and hot dog bun filled with sauteed tomato onion and cheese mixture blended with garam masala to give it a spicy taste. This subway type sandwiches is coated with a batter of whisked eggs and fan fried to perfection .Cut into bite size pieces and Served with mint chutney. The first bite itself will explode in your mouth with flavours you have never tasted before. A truly mouth watering and heavy dish. One **John Ki Roti** and your tummy is full.

Besides these they serve lots of other egg recipes be it the simple boiled egg salad sprinkled with chaat masala to make finger licking. Omelette curry masala with bread slices and many other delicious dishes to choose from.

And finally for those midnight hunger pangs and food craving what best than the classic Mumbai roadside Masala Egg Bhurji. Scrambled eggs made the **Mumbaiya Ishtyle**. Eggs, lots of chopped onions and tomatoes a little bit of masala and butter all coming together to make this much loved street food. This recipe of Egg bhurji is a personal favorite among all the eggetarians since these scrambled eggs are easy and quick to make. Great with toast or pav and is sure to satisfy any palate.

Eggs are versatile to make just about anything.So go ahead try an egg next itme when you are hungry . A meal my itself and rich in protiens. So what are you waiting for **Sunday Ho Ya Monday Roj Khao Ande....**

CHAPTER FORTY-SIX

Trams Tam-Tams & Pilots ...Unconventional modes to commute

Ask any young guy or girl or Millennials as they are known, how they commute in the city and pat comes the reply " Take out the mobile open the **Uber / Ola app** put the destination check the wait time for the cab and book it . Simple" And if you ask who pays for it answers is simple " Dad's Credit card is already configured" .What about when these aggregator cabs were off the raod during the several strikes few months back. And the answer would Oh then "Kaali Peeli hain Uncle" . Wow that's great I say. Ask them if they ever travelled in the BEST bus or the local train few of them laugh at you for such a sinful suggestion. They will say **"Kaun jayega us bheed mein" or "Uncle AC kahan hai usme"**.I laugh at my own advice and shake my head in despair. We as parents are to be blamed for not making our kids bold enough to take the public transport. The transport we as kids used to travel across the length and breadth of our Mumbai city.

So the following weekend which was the Republic Day long weekend when we had decided to head to Alibaug for a short RnR vacation I decided to try out our public transport and teach my elder daughter Netra how to use the fastest means of travel to reach a place in Mumbai. Since she had school on Jan 25th as also oral exams scheduled we could not allow her to bunk school. So rest of the family members my wife my little one Bhakti along with extended family members went ahead in the afternoon taking the Gateway to Mandwa jetty launch (boat) service. Me and Netra had to reach Gateway once she came home from school around 6:45PM well in time to take the last launch at 8PM. Once she was ready I said lets take the train to CSMT (good old VT station) rather than a Kali Peeli or Uber so we can reach early.

And I was correct it took us exactly 20 minutes to reach CSMT station. Then from just outside the station we took the cities landmark Red bus from BEST to reach Chatrapati Shivaji Maharaj Museum near Regal Cinema and onward we marched to Gateway on foot to reach at exactly 7.35 well before the last launch would depart at 8PM. Being a long weekend there a huge line of at least 50-60 people already waiting there. We joined the serpentine line and Netra took a food break of sandwich and Frooti back in her backpack. We spent some time enjoying the great view of the floodlit Gateway standing tall against the rough sea in the background and the chilly wind swirling around.

After waiting for sometime and with the que not moving we got uneasy, and then the Police van came announcing the unfortunate news . The launches which had gone to

Alibaug in the evening had not returned due to the rough sea. As a result the further services stand cancelled. Both of us were crest fallen. All this rushing for nothing. We decided to give it one last shot to try to reach Alibaug. I said lets try to get to Mumbai Central Bus depot and take the MSRTC Shivashahi AC bus or in worst case the Lal Dabba. Again we rushed outside to where we could take the Share Cab to Churchgate so as to take the train to Mumbai Central the best possible way to reach in the fastest possible time.

Once we reached Churchgate I said let grab some Burgers from Burger King right across the station as did not know how long and when we could eat on the way to Alibaug in a bus if go ahead with the travel.Taking the next train to Mumbai Central , we reached the Bus depot in 15 minutes.

Once there I checked if a bus was available for Alibaug , a bus was present but filled to capacity with not even a space to stand . I then checked with the Bus Stand administrator when was the next bus he said it will be at 12 AM . With 5 hour journey to take that bus would have taken us the wee hours of the next day to reach our destination. Dejected I decided that it was better we call it off for the night and catch the 1st launch the next morning at 6AM. I could see the dis-appointment in Netra's eyes but she understood that it was a good decision. On the way home I asked her how was her experience of travelling by these mode of transports and she was enthused to travel more . We took a cab back home reaching home for a late dinner of Whopper Burgers and Fries and retired for the night with hope in our minds of making it early the next morning.

Next day we got up real early and reached Gateway of India again , this time the line was short and it moved swiftly . We took the upper deck of the **Ajanta Launch** . When it left the jetty we could see the Mumbai skyline light up in yellow glow of the street lamps. The launch moved at an even pace and we enjoyed the gentle breeze on the deck , it was still little before Dawn with Sun still below the horizon and the darkness engulfing the sea ahead. In just a few minutes though the entire scene chaged with the Sun rising and the sky turning the shade of red and then slowly the sky getting bright. A gagglc of Scagulls hovcring closc to the launch and the few passengers on the deck giving them bread crumbs or wafers to get them to come closer for some selfie moments. We reached Mandwa in an hour and 10 minutes that was around 7.15 AM. Next we had to reach the Hotel at Chondi as we walked down the road outside we found a odd looking yellow coloured rickshaws locally called Tam-Tams. A 7 seater with 2 parallel bench behind the driver to seat 6 and one could sit next to the driver on the front extended seat. I have seen these Tam-tams all across Maharashtra be it in Raigad , Pune or even in the western Maharashtra belt while travelling for work. Most often than not the driver takes 8-10 passengers during a shared ride to make the most of the trip in monetary terms.

We reached the Hotel in time for a hearty breakfast of Poha and garam chai and some sugar dripping jalebi's and some rava cake courtesy my Wifey and my Brother-in law Naazim. It was a great experience using some of the unconventional modes of vehicles to reach our destination.

But if you travel across the vast country as India you are bound to come across much more of such unconventional means. Take for example the city of Mathura , when I was stationed there for a Software project for IOCL refinery we were put up in a 2 storied Kothi near the city center and the only means to travel to the refinery were the **Phat-Paht's** used by the locals as share-a-ride option. The most iconic bikes of the Second World War era became a mode of public transport in the North of India. Imagine a Harley Davidson bike accommodating 10 people. Well, that's what a little "Indian Jugaad" (innovation) can do. Popularly called as Phat-Phat because of the bike's loud exhaust sound. Phat-Phat is modelled from Harley Davidson's WLA motorcycles, which were manufactured during the Second World War. In the years leading to the War, Harley Davidson Motorcycle Company was unionized and received a contract to manufacture a variant of the civilian bike for the United States Army. During the Second World War, the WLA motorcycle symbolized reliability and was used in massive numbers. However, with the advancement of communication technology post Second World War, these bikes became redundant for military use.

In the US and Europe, most of them were sold as surplus. Sold cheaply, these bikes led to the rise of the 'chopper' and 'biker' culture, where they were modified. In India, the Harley-Davidson WLA got a fancy new avatar and a new lease of life. It was transformed into a public transport vehicle rambling on crowded Delhi streets, ferrying daily passengers across the city.

The motorcycles front part and the engine was attached to a bright rear passenger-carrier covered with an umbrella, often painted in some bright hues.

Somewhere along the journey, **the Phat-Phat was redesigned to seat six to eight passengers. In reality though, these were seen ferrying at least ten passengers.** If circumstances and size permitted, the enterprising drivers would have two more passengers sharing their own seat.

Across the river from **Mathura is the Temple town of Vrindavan** a sleepy little place with small bylanes for streets but a sacred place for Hindus due its importance as the town where Lord Krishna grew up and many a temples built to honour the great lord of pure love . On one of the off days I and my colleague ventured out to see the **beautiful temple of Banke Bihari** right in the heart of Vridavan. To reach there we took the Phat Phat from Mathura upto the main chowk of Vrindavan and then asked some locals for direction to reach the old heritage temple. We were told the best option would be to take **the cycle rickshaw**

.So we hopped on to one and asked the rickshaw puller to takes to the temple. And rightly so the bylanes were so narrow that it could accommodate these cycle rickshaws and may be a person walking besides them. On reaching the temple we soaked in the sights and sounds of the centuries old wooden pillared temple with the most beautiful and innocent looking Banke Bihari Krishna. As we entered the temple premise we could see the pillars and roof smeared with bright pink Gulal . When we asked about the same we were told that the temple plays host to the Colourful Holi festivities for 5 days when the locals and tourist alike enjoy playing with Abhir and Gulal like the Lord himself did with his fellow friends , gopikas and his devotees . We had reached during the evening Aarti time and so stayed back to experience the once in a life time spiritual experience. As the Aarti ended loud shouts of Hathi Ghoda Palki Jai Kanhaiya Lal ki and Banke Bihari Lal ki Jai went up in the air .

When I travelled further east to Kolkatta I could see even more options of travel. Besides the State transport buses there were the big fat & completely yellow old Ambassador cars turned into taxis. Travelling in them brough back memories of childhood when I used to travel in my maternal Uncles pristine white Ambassador Mark IV with its spacious rear seat which was more like a sofa seat . Even the front seat was a sofa seat as the gear being part of the Steering wheel giving enough space for the co-passengers sitting next to the driver.

You can also travel the city streets on Cycle rickshaws and till a few years back you had the Human rickshaw pullers who would pull and run taking the heavy load of their Bhadralok's.

These hand pulled rickshaws are banned by the honorable Supreme Court and by law as it took into consideration the plight of rickshaw pullers and their inhuman conditions of their bleeding feet on tar / concrete roads and most pullers suffering from an eventual TB related death due to poverty and malnutrition on the meager wages they earned from their trade.

Moving around in Kolkotta is cheap though as you can still hop on to a running tram chugging gently on the roads taking the passengers from point to another. These relics of the past are very environment friendly as they run on electric cable which runs like a spiders web all across the older parts of the city. Trams are known to be fun to ride with its mild speed and old world charm.

Did you know even Mumbai had a network of tram lines and station well into the late 1960's. the idea of mass transport system in Mumbai was originally proposed by an American company in the 1860's. Envisioning a horse drawn tramway system , the American company proposed a system that would connect Pydhoni (Central Mumbai) with Colaba (the southern tip of the city). At the time during the American Civil War, Mumbai had advanced as a global exporter of raw cotton to the United States. Unfortunately after the Civil War ended in 1865 Mumbai's cotton production declined and the entire country fell into an economic depression. Due to the depression the proposed American tramway system was never implemented.

But in 1873 with the permission on the **Bombay Municipal Corporation (BMC) , Bombay Tramway Company Ltd (BCLT) the earlier avatar of BEST** was licensed to begin perating the horse drawn trams throughout the city. Nearly one year after its establishment the company started operating 2 routes from Pydhoni (Dot #11) to Colaba / Sassoon Dock (Dot #1) and from Bori Bunder (Dot #5) to Pydhoni (Dot #11) . Despite revolutionizing transportation within the city, the initial horse drawn trams were not popular with the residents in Mumbai because they were perceived as expensive and slow. Due to lack or ridership the company closed down the horse drawn tram system in 1905.

Shortly afterwards in 1907 the **Bombay Electric Supply and Tramways Company (BEST) purchased Bombay Tramway company Ltd (BTCL)** and began operating the city's 1st electric tram system. The electric tram system was incredibly popular with the local Bombay residents because of the price and the comfort of the system. Soon the company added additional routes to the tram network introduced Double Decker trams and even began the Red bus service inspired from the London bus service. The tram and bus network covered the entire city .

In 1964 because of low ridership operating losses and inefficient technology BEST company shut down the nearly 100 year old tram system. The company still continued operations of the city's bus network which to this day represents an integral part of Mumbai's transportation system.

"Kahin Building, Kahin Traame, Kahin Motor, Kahin Mill..." - the vanished trams that the '60s Bollywood hit had immortalized may soon make a comeback, not in their old trundling form, but in a modern avatar.

Recently , while speaking on the coastal road project in Mumbai, Union Minister for Environment Prakash Javadekar announced that trams may be part of the multi-modal corridor planned between Nariman Point and Kandivali.

The draft notification, he said, "mentioned that the metro, buses and trams could be included... The electric tram runs fast. If anything of that sort is incorporated, it will help the people."

May be these old-world transportation will add to the charm of the maxim city making traveler and tourist friendly.

Another unique mode of transportation that Uber and Ola are trying to start is the Bike cabs . Since the traffics situation in most metro and big cities getting bad to worse with long traffic jams the latest trend is that people are shifting from cars to bikes . Much easier to zip past and manoeuvre in the traffic . They have been doing pilots in cities like Pune and Ahmedabad where the response has been great. But there is one state where Bike taxis have been part of the road-scape since last 30 years is Goa. There they are known as Pilot . Painted black and yellow like auto-rickshaws or taxis, these two-wheeler motorcycle pilots are found waiting for passengers in almost all towns, cities and even villages, along 1200 km of major and minor arteries of Goa. The unique system of motorcycle pilots started during the Portuguese rule in Goa. It was later recognized by the Indian government and the Motor Vehicle Act in 1979.

Today, it's a well-regulated business carried out under the watchful eye of the State as well as a code of conduct willingly formulated by the Pilot's Association.

Struggling with a handful of papers and files or carrying luggage? Need to rush to work or have an urgent appointment in court, a government office or an interview? Late for school or college? **Motorcycle pilots *swoop in to rescue you from distress.***

They ferry the day's newspapers to the remotest village before you wake up. Take you to visit relatives untraceable on Google maps. Hired to drop tiny kids to kindergarten, young girls and married women rely on them to reach their destinations safely. You would not come across any eve-teasers, street fighters, hirelings or drunkards among pilots as they go strictly either by self-discipline or their own code of conduct. They even censure or reprimand each other for any misbehaviour.

A motorcycle pilot is also considered 'a trusted neighbour, guide, helper in good times or bad and a trustworthy friend'. Staying far away from all forms of rash riding even if their clients coax them to. There are a negligible amount of rash riding incidents involving motorcycle pilots in Goa.

So if you are an avid traveller or even the regular commuter do go beyond the app based aggregator cabs and experience the charm on any city / place you visit by travelling in the local mode of transport. You will experience the thrill and adventure associated with the place and also be able to catch the sights and sounds which you are sure to miss in the AC enclosed environment of the Uber / Ola cab..

Have fun, travel wide , stay safe and experience the thrill.. Happy journeys and make some happy memories.

CHAPTER FORTY-SEVEN

Puran poli ,Gujia , Thandai and the festival of colors

Holi re Holi Purnachi Poli.. up goes the shouts as the Holika Dahan flames touch the sky. You stand near the bon fire soaking in the heat feeling warm and happy inside, praying to the Lord Almighty to burn away the sorrows , despair , poverty and all things negative and bless us with health , wealth, happiness and prosperity.

Its that time of the year when winter is ending and Summer is about to start , that's when our ancestors created a festival to usher in the Summer . Holi comes at a time of the year when people have a tendency to feel sleepy and lazy. This is natural for the body to experiences some tardiness due to the change from the cold to the heat in the atmosphere. To counteract this tardiness of the body, people sing loudly or even speak loudly. Their movements are brisk and their music is loud. All of this helps to rejuvenate the system of the human body.

Besides, the colours when sprayed on the body have a great impact on it. Biologists believe the liquid dye or Abeer penetrates the body and enters into the pores. It has the effect of strengthening the ions in the body and adds health and beauty to it.

There is yet another scientific reason for celebrating the Holi, this however pertains to the tradition of Holika Dahan. The mutation period of winter and spring, induces the growth of bacteria in the atmosphere as well as in the body. When Holika is burnt, temperature rises to about 145 degrees Fahrenhiet. Following the tradition when people perform Parikrima (circumlocution or going around) around the fire, the heat from the fire kills the bacteria in the body thus, cleansing it.

The way Holi is celebrated in south, the festival also promotes good health. For, the day after the burning of Holika people put ash (Vibhuti) on their forehead and they would mix Chandan (sandal paste) with the young leaves and flowers of the Mango tree and consume it to promote good health.

Some also believe that play with colours help to promote good health as colours are said to have great impact on our body and our health. Western-Physicians and doctors believe that for a healthy body, colours too have an important place besides the other vital elements. Deficiency of a particular colour in our body causes ailment, which can be cured only after supplementing the body with that particular colour.

All this is great but the best part of celebrating **Holi and Duleti (Dhulivandan)** is sweets and other nick nack you can savor and hogg on. Leading the way is **Puran Poli a Maharashtrian delicacy** without which you can not imagine Holi being complete. A soft and flaky roti made of Maida (kanik) stuffed with Puran made of chana dal and jaggery spiked with cardamom(velchi / elaichi) and nutmeg (jaifal) to give it that extra flavor. Eat it hot and pipping smeared with a generous trikle of pure desi ghee . Or try it like I do by dipping its pieces in milk and then finally smack your lips and give a hearty burp to acknowledge the host / puran poli maker of the pure joy and satisfaction you had enjoying the sweet meal . Every year all of us gather at my mom-in-laws place on Holi and after celebrating the Holi Dahan in the society compound devour the scrumptious and best ever Puran Poli made by **my mom-in-law Namrata Desai – Mummy** ,made with her secret recipe which includes a dash of extra special ingredient of love and care.

Another favourite Holi recipe is the **Gujiya** a classic North Indian sweet among **Holi special** dishes. In the festive season of holi eating gujiya is a **tradition.**It is made in most part of India and has different names like Karanji and Ghugre. The filling of **gujiya** is a mixture of roasted **dry coconut, nuts, mawa, cardamom powder and powdered sugar**. It can be glazed with sugar syrup. To coat or not to coat gujiya in sugar syrup is an option. Bite into this sweet snack and let it melt in your mouth.

For Goans / Karwari like me Holi is very special and a unique sweet associated with Holi is the **Mangane** .A sweet dish made from Chana dal cooked with jaggery and coconut milk ,added with Ole (Wet) Kaju and Kismis (Raisin) to produce this famous wholesome dessert.It can be had with hot and fluffly puri's or simply devoured like a kheer.

Still remember this sweet dish made by my mother in a special round bottom utensil slowly cooked on a low flame and kept on a simmer for a long time to get the perfect taste which still lingers on my tongue..

But if you are not the sweet eater types you can always enjoy the good old bhajia or crispy pakora made from onion or potato . Or the all time favourite namkeen the **Samosa** . And where else can you satisfy your taste-buds but the famous A1 Samosa of Gurukripa's at Sion .

Fried to perfection of golden brown with its special potato mix stuffing not too spicy not too salty but just right that even the kids and adults love its taste and if its served with chole or mint chutney toh kya kehne..

And how can you forget the **Thandai** to quench ones thirst after eating all these oily and fried namkeens and sweets. This Holi's official drink is mainly found in Rajasthan and the north of India. But now a days also available in pre-mix bottles. The most famous being Guruji'd Thandai.Thandai is a very popular drink made with almonds, saffron, milk, sugar and a variety of herbs. It's also possible to find a version made with bhaang for the extra effect. But mind you it can get you into a tipsy situation which not even the hardest of liquor can match. People drinking this concoction of Cannabis (bhang) combined with milk, refined butter, mango and spices are know to get into a state of psychotropic liberation that makes them emotional and express themselves in loud manner. So I would suggest caution if you are thinking or getting a kick this Holi.

And finally after eating all these sweets I hope it will definitely make you a happy person if not a sweeter person.

So let me pray to God that **this Holi bless us all with Happiness and joy and make us a better person for years to come. Happy Holi to all my readers....**

Lets enjoy this Holi and Dhulivandan with that famous song from **the Blockbuster movie "Sholay"** which goes like this ....

Holi ke din dil khil jaate hain
rangon mein rang mil jaate hain
holi ke din dil khil jaate hain
rangon mein rang mil jaate hain
gile shikwe bhool ke doston
dushman bhi gale mil jaate hain
    Holi Hai.......

Amba pikato ras galato kokan cha raja jhimma khelato...

Yes it mango time once again. The best yummiliscious fruit one can have on a balmy summer morning or noon or night or for that matter anytime is Amba time during mango season.

Just as you enter into March this small fruit deep yellow on outside and fiery orange on the inside peeps out of wooden crates or cardboard boxes. Pick it up slice it or dice it and eat this king of fruits or just squeeze it and suck on the sweet pulp.

Aam or hapus as you know can be eaten in many forms besides eating it as a cut fruit.

You can have it as Amba Poli which has hapus pulp mixed with sugar and sun-dried on flat steel plates. The dried pulp forms stiff layers which are stacked on top of each other. The stacks are then cut into large squares before packaging.

The same pulp is mixed with sugar and nuts, then cooked along with boiled white rice. Once the pulp is reduced and evenly coats the rice grains, the Ambebath is ready to be consumed.

A special sweet dish combination is Amba Sheera in this the pulp is mixed with sugar and nuts, then cooked along with semolina in water or milk. Once cooked, the mixture looks like an amber-coloured paste and is ready to be consumed.

One of the finest of ripe mango curries is the Konkani ambya umman / humman. Since time immemorial, huge mango trees have been growing all over the plains, foothills and plateaus of India. In summer, these trees produce luscious mangoes in great abundance, shedding the ripe fruit every day on the ground. The birds, squirrels and bats feed to their hearts content but they are able to polish off only a portion of the bounty, leaving the rest for humans to enjoy.

These wild mangoes (called goyante ambo in Konkani) unlike the hybrid commercial cultivars, are generally smaller in size, have fibrous pulp and pack a punch in terms of flavour. It is these wild mangoes that the Konkani people love to turn into delicious, lip smacking ambya humman.

Some of the smallest varieties are just a trifle bigger than a lime, have thinner skin, are lemon yellow inside and have sweet sour flavour making the best mouthwatering Umman.

But just as the summer arrives traditional Maharashtrian also stock up on the best recipes of summer coolers to douse the heat and fatigue from the mugginess of the Mumbai weather.Take the case of Aam Panha made from the boiled pulp of raw mango mixed with the right quantity of cardamom and sugar and in some case a dash of cinnamon to give it the extra flavor. Once cooled and stored in the form of a concentrate it can be used any time to make a fresh drink when mixed with ice cold water or now a days to give it a fizz with soda . Drink this once you come home from the blazing sun outside and re-energize yourself.

Some other favorite raw mango or Kairi as it is called in Marathi and one that gives the tangy taste when you pronounce the word Kairi itself. The tangyness of raw mangoes pairs really well with the sweetness of tomatoes and the pungent flavour of ginger to make the Raw Mango Rasam The bright flavours will make everyone happy. Pachadi is a popular South Indian side dish similar to Raita. It is usually made with yogurt, chillies and coconut. This one blends in the additional vibrant flavour of raw mangoes.

A similar Maharastrian recipe is Aamba daal . This is one of those quick-n-simple recipes that make you wonder how such a simple recipe can taste so heavenly. Raw mango being an essential element of Aamba Daal (sometimes also referred to as 'Vatli Daal or 'Kairichi Dal'), it is a dish associated with summer.

In fact, during haldi-kunku gatherings – a popular social tradition in Maharashtra – in the month of Chaitra as per the Hindu Calendar, Aamba Daal & Kairi Panha is the standard menu.

One my favorites preparation which goes well with hot steam rice is the Aam Ras ki Kadhi Quick, easy and tangy, Aamras ki Kadhi is a delicious blend of raw mango puree, buttermik and besan along with a host of other spices and chillies. Make the most of the mango season with this delicious curry where the focus is the fresh flavour of the fruit.

But no lunch / dinner in the summer season is complete without the thick sweet and mouthwatering Aam Ras. The word "aamras" is derived from the Sanskrit words amra (Sanskrit: for *mango*) and *rasa* (Sanskrit: for *juice*), so the literal meaning is "mango juice". Made from the pulp of the mango fruit. The pulp of a ripe mango is extracted, usually by hand, and is consumed together with pooris or chapati. Sometimes ghee and milk are added to the pulp to enhance its flavour. Sugar is also added to adjust the sweetness.A regional version of aamras is a popular dessert in Rajasthani cuisine and Marwari, Marathi, and Gujarati homes.

If you are in Matunga try the best Aam ras from **"Sheetal Dugdhalaya "** near Loharwadi in a small bylane in the Matunga Market. Its fresh and lip smacking. **"Sheetal Dugdhalaya "** has been the foremost manufacturer and supplier of Mango Milk shake (Aamras) and milk products in Mumbai since 1979.They are pioneer is Aam ras and their ras goes to 80% of the caterers across Mumbai. **"Sheetal Fresh"** is a leading manufacturer and supplier of premium quality Mango Milkshake (Aamras) and Shrikand, Basundi, Curd in the city of Mumbai. Established in the year 1979 in Malad-Kandivali area by the name "Sheetal Dugdhalaya" by its founder Mr. Bharat S. Mehta. He played the key role in the successful running of the company, creating "GOODWILL" and escalated it to the level where it stands today. "Sheetal Dugdhalaya" is also known as **"KING OF MANGO MILKSHAKE"** since 1992, when it was first launched by Mr. Bharat S. Mehta in Mumbai Metropolitan Region and since then the brand is famous for its Shrikand , Basundi and Mango Milkshake, more particularly in Gujarati Community.\

The Aam ras is available in Hapus , Pairi or mix in ½ kg an 1 kg foil sealed packs. Refrigerate it and serve it cold with you hot piping puri's of just eat it as a dessert.

Take my word you won't stop at one bowl ...So go ahead enjoy the king of fruits Ambaa to the hilt this summer.

CHAPTER FORTY-NINE

Ye re ye re pausa....

Just yesterday I was having a conversation with little Bhakti . I was in Ahmedabad for my office work for last 4 days .The conversation went something like this – Bhakti – Hi Papa where are you ..Me – In the office , working. Bhakti – Are you in an AC cabin . Me—Yes its too hot here in Ahmedabad . I will get scorched if I go out ... Bhakti – But its raining heavily in Mumbai right now...Me – Wow that's great ..Bhakti – Papa why don't you sing **"Ye re ye re pausaa "**, then the rain in Mumbai will come to Ahmedabad and the Sun will come to Mumbai . How is the idea ... Me – Ha ha ha that's really good idea. And then we sing the song " Ye re ye re pausa " together and laugh out loudly ...

But seriously these Marathi nursery rhymes or Bal Geet as they were called were so much more fun . You must have read the funny Whatsapp post going around – Do you know why we are facing Rain deficit ...All our tiny tots in English medium school are singing " Rain Rain go away , Little Johnny wants to play , Rain Rain go to Spain" instead of " Ye re ye pavsaa." And God always listens to the kids when the ask with a pure heart ....Ha ha ha..

I still feel that our traditional Bal Geet's in Marathi are more positive and with beautifully crafted lyrics than the Englishnursery rhymes. Take the case of **"Jhuk Jhuk Aagin**

Gaadi , Dhuranchya Regha Havet Kadi , Palti Jhade Pahuya ...**Mamachya Gavala Jauyaa**...Mamach Gaon Motha , Sonnya Chandicha Petha , Shobha Pahun Gheuya ..Mamachya Gavala Jauyaa...Mamach Baiko Gorti , Mhanel Khuthli Porti , Bhachyanchi nave sanguyaa.. Mamachya Gavala Jauyaa....Such creative lyrics and so much fun while singing..

Then there is the ever famous Bal geet penned By Marathi Poet Mangesh Padgaonkar ... which goes like this " **Sang Sang Bholanath Paus Padel kay ?,** Shale Bahvti Tale Sachun Sutti Melel Kay ?...Sang Sang Bholanath Paus Padel Kay ? ..Bolanath Dupari Aai Jhopel Kay ? Ladoo Hulch Ghetana Awaz Hoil Kay ? ..Bholanath Bolanath.... Bhola nath Bholanath khar sang ekdaa, athwdya tun Ravivar yetil ka re teenda ? , Bholanath udya ahe ganitacha paper , Potat majhya kal yeun dukhel kare dhopar ? Bhonath Bholanath ...Sang Sang Bholnath Paus padel kay ?... Such a michievious song with every kids truest wishes ..

One more memorable song that I rember hearing from an old Vinyl record played in my childhood on a HMV gramophone was the sweetest song ever . Yes you guessed it right " **Assava Sunder Chocolate Cha Bangla , Chanderi Soneri Chamchamta changala** , Chocolate chya banglya la Toffee che Daar , Shepti chy jhupkya na jahdun jaeel khar, Gol Gol lemon chya khidkya Don , Hello Hello karay la Chotasa Phon...Biscuitan chya Gachhi var Mor Chandaar , Peper mint chya Anganat Phoole Lal lal, Chandi chy ajhada mage chandoba rahto , Motya chya Phoolan tun lapa chappi khel to, Unch Unch Jhoka Khel Rangala..Mayne cha pinjara var tangla... Kiti Kiti Sundar Chocolate cha bangala ..Chanderi Soneri Chamchamta Changla....Such beautiful lyrics bringing together a wishful thinking of a small kid .. What if there was a Bangalow made of chocolate with doors made of Toffee and windows of lemon drops . So sweet nothing as terrifying as the similar Bungalow made of sweet candies in the Tale of Hansel and Gretel where the evil witch lures small kids with these lovely goodies only to imprison them and later try to eat them up...Though unsuccessful in her en-devours and ultimate the kids out fox her and kill her .. The thought of being alone in the woods and being trapped by the sweet looking Bungalow itself is scary .

For that matter of fact the English nursery rhymes that most of us have learned all through our childhood and even our kid now get to learn in their pre-schools , are quite dark in nature and have a sinister back stories

Take the case of the simple **"Jack and Jill went up the hill**, To fetch a pail of water.Jack fell down, And broke his crown; And Jill came tumbling after". Did you know the roots of this poem are so dark that they should not be allowed anywhere near children. Jack and Jill are actually France's Louis XVI and his wife, Marie Antoinette, who were convicted of treason during the French Revolution, otherwise known as the Reign of Terror, and beheaded. Jack or Louis XVI, lost his "crown," i.e. his throne and his head. And Jill, or Marie Antoinette's head soon came tumbling after.

Then there is **"Ring around the rosie ,A pocketful of posies**, Ashes, ashes .We all fall down! "The origin for this rhyme is by far the most infamous. The rhyme refers to the Great Plague of London in 1665. The "Rosie" from the rhyme is the rash that covered the ones who contracted the disease, the smell of which they tried to cover up with "a pocket full of posies." The "ashes" were the cremated remains of the deceased, and well, they all did fall down.

Or the innocent sounding **"Baa baa black sheep, Have you any wool?** Yes sir, yes sir, Three bags full. One for the Master, One for the Dame, And one for the little boy Who lives down the lane.... While this rhyme sounds innocent enough, it actually dates back to feudal England, and is not so innocent. There was an extremely harsh wool tax imposed on the farmers back then by King Edward I in the 13th century. One-third of the wool was taken for the king or the Master, one-third for the Church or the Dame, and one-third for the farmers. Some older versions of this rhyme ended with "But none for the little boy / Who cries down the lane," showing us just how little was left for the people who cultivated the wool.

So is the nursery rhyme **"Goosey, goosey, gander**, Whither dost thou wander? Upstairs and downstairs And in my lady's chamber. There I met an old man Who wouldn't say his prayers; I took him by the left leg, And threw him down the stairs.. The lyrics actual meaning is in its back story .After England turned Protestant following King Henry VIII's creation of the Anglican Church, there were plenty of Catholic priests who refused to follow the Protestant faith. So, to avoid punishment, they set up small rooms in their homes, called priest's holes, to pray in. If they were found praying in Latin, as the Catholics do, they would be "thrown down the stairs," or put to death.

Plagues, prostitution, burning at the stake—none of these are topics you would talk to a toddler about. However, so many of the nursery rhymes we all grew up singing have such dark origins that you'd be shocked to find you were taught these in school, and kids are still being taught these rhymes.

I would anytime go for the traditional childrens songs by our Indian poets especially the Marathi ones like Mangesh

Padgaonkar , GaDiMa or G D Madgulkar or the sweet Shanta Shelke..Try these one for their best ever lyrics ... **Bubble Gum by Mangesh Padgaonkar** .. Which goes something like this " **Aadhi Baba detat Dum , Mag antat Bubble gum** , Aadhi Baba detat Chaddi mag chocolatechi melte vadi ...Aai ghete vachun dhada mag dete Batavada...

So much fun ...And a short one by Shanta Shelke goes something like this " **Sakhrech Kahu Tai Roj Khate , Tarich ti itki god god gaate ... Aai mala roj ghalte na jeu ? Mhanunach ticha maar sudhha mau mau"**

And the most famous rain song ever to be written and melodiously sung goes like this

" **Nach re mora ambyachya vanat , nach re mora** ...Dhaganshi vara jhunjala re, Kala kala kapus pinjala re , Aata tujhi pali re Vij dete taali .. Phulav pisara nach ...Nach re mora nach.........

.... Pavsa chi rim jhim thambali re Tujhi majhi Jodi jamli re , Abhalat Chan Chan Saat rangi Kaman .. Kamani khali tya nach ... nach re mor nach....

So next time my kids asks me to sing along any of these Marathi Balgeets I would enjoy singing them ,have some fun and create our own memories ....memories that will be cherished all thorough our lives....kudos to our Marathi Literature and Marathi Kavi's for penning such memorable songs.

CHAPTER FIFTY

Punjabi Dhaba in the Midst of Mumbai....

A small news appeared on the inside page of the Times of India today. **Kulwant Singh Kohli the owner of Pritam Da Dhaba and creator of the World famous "Butter Chicken"** passed away at a ripe old age of 85.A legend in his turf of culinary and hospitality industry. A soft spoken person with a golden heart a person who introduced Mumbai to the authentic taste of traditional Punjabi cuisine.

It all began in 1942 when a Rawalpindi entrepreneur Prahlad Singh Kohli - the father of Kulwant - came to the erstwhile Bombay to start a small Punjabi eatery, 'Pritam Hotel' in Kalbadevi, but it failed miserably and he was left virtually penniless. He then decided to move to the 'labor class' populated Dadar with the hope of cashing in on the upcoming movie studios in And his gamble paid off. Kohli was known to go out of his way towards the struggling actors who patronized his joint. A meal then would cost Rs 19 and Rs 38 for two. With many studios in south Mumbai and the still infantile suburbs cradling the success of the film industry, the **Pritam Hotel** also thrived, with the menu lovingly supervised by his wife, Harkaur.

In 1953, the young Kulwant, then barely 11, reluctantly joined his father in the business in Mumbai. His pleasing manners and helpful nature he soon became popular with the film industry folks and even leading politicians of the era.Most of the leading star of Bollywood at that time were from Lahore from erst while Punjab in Pakistan and would crave their original north Indian cuisine in alien Mumbai. They now had a place in the heart of the city where they but could relish and relive the flavors of Punjab.

Actors like Dilip Kumar, Manoj Kumar, Sanjeev Kumar, Raj Kapoor, Raaj Kumar, Sunil Dutt, Dharmendra Deol, Rajendra Kumar, Dev Anand, Jagjit Singh, Anand Bakshi, Shanker-Jaikishen, Chetan Anand, Kamal Amrohi, BR Chopra, Yash Chopra and many more became friends with Kulwant Kohli bonding over food and drinks.

As a sharp businessman and restaurateur the Kohli's expanded the place by buying out neighbourhood properties to offer a restaurant, a typical Punjabi-style 'dhaba', fine-dining, a full-fledged four-star residential Hotel MidTown Pritam, etc.

As the hotel's name spread far and wide ,it was now patronized by all foodies who had a taste for asli Punjabi cuisine. Bollywood's original Showman Raj Kapoor came to inaugurate the renovated and centrally-air conditioned Pritam Hotel in 1975, kicking off the trend of fully air conditioned eateries which picked up in a big way and is common today.

It was the only restaurant till then which didn't have a formal menu, but served all time popular mouthwatering Punjabi cuisines like butter chicken, chicken masala, tandoori chicken, mutton kheema, fish fry, parathas, biryanis, etc. Till date these are the best dishes when you land a seat during the weekend rush. Kohli prided himself on introducing authentic 'butter chicken' to the the Mumbaikar's in the 1950-1960's, which was a raging hit and now a 'must-item' on all city restaurant menus.

Around 1985, his sons introduced the 'dhaba' concept to the city with an open-air extension to the existing restaurant, 'khatiyas', charpoys, an open kitchen and friendly service, which went down well with the Mumbaikar's

Kohli also ventured into the film industry with Sangeeta Films Corporation, which acquired the world distribution rig for the films "Paakeeza" and "The Burning Train. Story has it that even Sunil Dutt and Dharmendra when they were stragglers couldn't afford a decent meal would land up at Pritam's and have their fill . Their relationship with Kulwant was such that , they would eat to their hearts content and pay when they were flush with funds.

The legacy is being taken forward by Kulwant Kohli's grandson Abhayraj Kohli . The junior Kohli, who has a Masters in Hospitality Management and is the brain behind the parent company's launches, Grandmama's Café (Dadar and Lower Parel) and MRP (My Regular Place).

By end of the year in 2016, Stashes of photos frames of senior Kohli bonding with yesteryear icons like Sanjeev Kumar, Manoj Kumar and Rajendra Kumar graced the walls of Pritam Restaurant & Bar . The idea was to re-brand the company and allow guests to walk down memory lane Pritam Da Dhaba, the dhaba section will also see changes. They will offer dishes inspired from the famous Highway Dhabas across India and also , give them credit. Instead of eating dhaba food elsewhere , the patrons will experience the culture right there . The walls now tell a new story but the food won't. It will always be wholesome North Indian Hardcore Punjabi food. No diet food but a meal for the masses with familiar smell taste and flovors.

While no one in the clan has been christened as Pritam, Kulwant Kohli's father wanted a name that meant beloved in as many Indian languages as possible and hence, chose **"Pritam"**.

An apt name for a truly Punjabi restaurant. A true tribute to this restaurateur would be to order a Butter Chicken and Crisply done Tandori Roti , gorge on the lip smacking dish ,clean out the plate and burp loudly to your hearts content as a salute to **Kulwant Kohli the Butter Chicken Man..**

Bole Sau Nihaal Sat Sri Akal ...Wahe Guru Da Khalsa Wahe Guru Di Fateh....

CHAPTER FIFTY-ONE

Gaon Tithe ST ... Hath Dakhwa Bus Thambwa...(Where Theres a Village there's an ST .... To Stop Bus Just Wave)

With the Ganesh Chaturthi fast approaching the natives from Konkan called **"Chakar mane"** or the Blue collared workers earlier working in Mumbai Textile Mills and now in Service sectors of Couirer, Transport (Drivers) and Food Service (Swiggy , Zomato , Uber Eats) will get ready to go back to their villages in the Mangaon ,Dapoli, Khed , Furoos ,Chiplun and upto Ratnagiri some even going till Sawantwadi / Shiroda to celebrate the Ganesh festival for 10 days . Before the Konkan Railway was established on the West Coast and even today all these people along with there families and extended family members would make dash to Mumbai Central ST Bus depot to catch the red coloured ST bus . These ST buses are called "Lal Dabba" in the local slang and literally they are like boxes made of steel painted the trademark Red and with the yellow MSRTC log on the sides. The insides of these have around 45-54 uncomfortable barely cushioned bench type seats with typical dark green regzine covers and with windows which mostly don't open due wrong design or non-maintenance. The bus when it leaves during this festive season is filled to full capacity with additional people standing in the gangway. The luggage's of the travellers are loaded on top of bus fixed with strong ropes.

But these ST buses are the only mode of transport for villagers residing in very remote places to reach their home. Theres a common saying in Maharashtra **Gaon Thithe ST , which literally means "Where there is a village there a ST buses which services it"**. Another common phrase is **Haath Dakhwa Bus Thambwa which means just wave your hand at any given notified ST Bus stand or even at large signals at prominent junctions and the driver of the ST bus will oblige you with a pick up** so you can reach your village safe and sound.

Going back in history The Maharashtra State Road Transport Corporation was established by the State Government of Maharashtra as per the provision in Section 3 of RTC Act 1950. But the first bus was flagged off from Pune to Ahmednagar in 1948.

Tracing the history that saw this development, we go back to the 1920s; when various entrepreneurs started operations in the public transport sector. Till the Motor Vehicle Act came into being in 1939, there were no regulations monitoring their activities which resulted in arbitrary competition and unregulated fares. The implementation of the Act rectified matters to some extent. The individual operators were asked to form a union on defined routes in a particular area. This also proved to be beneficial for travelers as some sort of schedule set in; with a time table, designated pick-up points, conductors, and fixed ticket prices. This was the state of affairs till 1948, when the then Bombay State Government, with the late Morarji Desai as the home minister, started its own state road transport service, called State Transport Bombay. And, with this, the first blue and silver-topped bus took off from Pune to Ahmednagar

There were 10 makes of buses in use then – Chevrolet , Ford , Bedford, Seddon, Studebaker, Morris Commercial , Albion , Leyland , Commer and Fiat. In the early 1950's two luxury buses were introduced based on Morris Commercial Chasis. These were called **"Neelkamal" and "Giriyarohini"** and used to ferry passengers on the Pune-Mahabaleshwar route. They had 2-2 seats, curtains, interior decoration , a clock and green tinted windows. A little upscale as compared t the **"Lal Dabba".**

The interior was little spacious with good leg room and seats where sofa cushioned. Some buses had seats with a stick at the side to make the seat recline a bit. Also the concept of hand rest were introduced to divide the passenger seating area so that passengers avoid fighting in slang Marathi **"Are tujya baapachi seat aahe kay. Ticket gehtle manje purna bus vikat ghetli ki kay "...over seat space.** A classic case of over demand and under supply.

The condition of the ST Personnel especially the drivers is not good. Just imagine how stressful is the condition of these drivers who have to ply over 70 million passengers every day in the 1,50,000 buses operated under the MSRTC Road Transport Undertaking. From the well laid to those replete with potholes, from the ever bumpy, undulating, and broken to just a dirt track, is what makes up the massive 55 lakh km-long road network of the state.And a safe long-distance journey under most of these circumstances needs expert manoeuvring skills and an undisturbed mind for thousands of drivers that traverse these roadways.

Providing efficient, economic, safe and reliable public transport in urban, hilly and rural areas is by no means an easy task. It becomes all the more challenging when you see most staff still clamoring for adequate compensation, benefits, good working conditions and even some respect. After all, they are responsible for helping millions of passengers reach their destinations safely despite battling a hostile terrain in many parts, undertaken under harsh working conditions.

Moreover, many drivers in the ST who are not on the governments' payrolls or are out of the regulatory net earn one-tenth of what their counterparts working in the Private Road transport units earn.

The complaints from drivers who are not getting sufficient benefits are intensifying as even State transport corporations are increasingly opting to put their bus services on contract. Officials in the corporations admit in private that there are also cases of buses that operate under State carriage permits where the drivers are not paid as per the mandated rules. Besides inadequate and disparate payments, drivers often face difficult working hours and a tough working environment. This can lead to fatigue and accidents. There were 37,487 bus accidents that resulted in 12,088 deaths and 50,686 injuries in 2016, according to Road Ministry data.

Leading transport experts say Drivers should be given resting places every 400 km, so that they can sleep, freshen up and have nutritious meals at reasonable rates. There should be medical benefits, with at least ₹20 lakh compensation on accidental death.

Lawmakers, it seems, have taken note of this issue. Stressing the need to improve drivers' working conditions, a recent Parliamentary Committee deliberating on amending the Motor Vehicle Act has recommended that action be taken to alleviate drivers' stress arising due to climatic factors and long working hours. Responding to the suggestion, the Ministry of Road Transport and Highways informed the Committee that setting up of stop-over points along highways for the drivers is being considered. While these steps from the Government will require time and resources, for the passengers to give a little respect to the 'captain of the bus' can come free and with immediate effect.

Drivers often crave that respect from their passengers. "In Sweden, bus drivers are called 'Ambassadors'. Why can't we do the same in India? If flights can have pilots, ships can have captains, don't the bus drivers require some recognition and respect?

So next time you are ridiculing the ST service and bad mouthing the arrogant attitude of their drivers, please stop , think of all those times when you used the ST and reached your destination in the remotes part of Maharashtra safely and was able to enjoy the festive season with your extended family and had a gala time for a few days of your otherwise stressful life and then compare it with the plight of these ST drivers. Give due respect to them and patronize the ST Service whenever possible so that this great service does not disappear from the face of the earth.

www.ingramcontent.com/pod-product-compliance
Lightning Source LLC
Chambersburg PA
CBHW041304120726
48005CB00014B/1858